D0773406

Tax
Havens

Tax Havens

How to Bank, Invest, and Do Business— Offshore and Tax Free

Hoyt L. Barber

McGraw-Hill, Inc.

New York St. Louis San Francisco Auckland Bogotá
Caracas Lisbon London Madrid Mexico Milan
Montreal New Delhi Paris San Juan São Paulo
Singapore Sydney Tokyo Toronto

Library of Congress Cataloging-in-Publication Data

Barber, Hoyt L.
    Tax havens : how to bank, invest, and do business—offshore and
tax free / Hoyt L. Barber.
        p.   cm.
    Includes index.
    ISBN 0-07-003659-4 :
    1. Tax havens. I. Title.
K4464.5.B37   1992
343.04—dc20
[342.34]   93-13291
                                                                CIP

    2 3 4 5 6 7 8 9 0   DOC/DOC   9 8 7 6 5 4 3

ISBN 0-07-003659-4

*The sponsoring editor for this book was David Conti, the editing supervisor
was Jane Palmieri, and the production supervisor was Donald Schmidt. It was
set in Baskerville by Carol Woolverton, Lexington, Massachusetts, in cooperation
with Warren Publishing Services.*

Printed and bound by R. R. Donnelley & Sons Company.

Regulations, prices, and fees quoted in this book may change occasionally without notice by the various government bodies and private companies mentioned in this book.

This publication is designed to provide accurate and authoritative information in regard to the subject matter covered. It is sold with the
understanding that the publisher is not engaged in rendering legal, accounting, or other professional service. If legal advice or other expert assistance is required, the services of a competent professional person
should be sought.
            *—from a declaration of principles jointly adopted by a committee
            of the American Bar Association and a committee of publishers*

To my parents, two individualists who generously gave years of inspiration, guidance, and support to their children.

In fond memory of my loving mother, Peggy Barber, physically gone but never forgotten. And, to my father, Harry Barber, friend and confidant.

Thanks for the many interesting times. The memories will give me years of great recollections.

About the Author

Hoyt L. Barber, a leading expert on offshore tax havens and international business, has a diverse business background. He has worked extensively offshore as an entrepreneur, investor, financier, and consultant and has conducted business from Europe, Canada, Hong Kong, Central America, Mexico, and the Caribbean.

Mr. Barber is the author of numerous books, including *How to Incorporate Your Business in Any State; Copyrights, Patents, and Trademarks: Protect Your Rights Worldwide;* and *Tax Freedom,* and continues his writing pursuits while acting as a consultant to international clients on the use of tax havens.

Contents

Part 2. Profiles of Tax Havens

Part 3. Contacts and Resources

Preface

Tax Havens is the first and most comprehensive book for the nonprofessional newcomer to offshore business. Although intended for business executives, financial planners, institutional and private investors, and the financially well healed, professionals will find it a valuable reference guide to hard-to-find information and professional contacts worldwide.

The world of offshore business is introduced and covered in an easy-to-understand fashion. In Part 1, the reader discovers why tax havens today are important and viable options that are available to overburdened taxpayers everywhere. They learn how these novel jurisdictions can be used to their benefit and how they are illegally exploited. Find out how to do business from an offshore base, create the preferred legal entity, invest using an offshore conduit, gain complete financial privacy, reduce personal and business tax liabilities, and much more.

Tax Havens is informative and insightful, but where a more thorough understanding of an area is advisable than can be adequately treated in this one book, the author has made appropriate references to other works. With the guidance of this book, readers can learn everything they need to know about tax havens and how to use them.

Every significant tax haven of the world is profiled in Part 2. Thirty-two major offshore centers are spotlighted and divided into two sections: country profile and business profile. Another baker's dozen of marginal and incidental havens are briefly described.

The country profile elaborates on the features of the tax haven and covers government, legal system, economy, and communications. This information assists the reader when judging the validity of a country from a nonbusiness perspective. Each of these areas can be important considerations in the selection process.

The business profile gives more relevant information for picking a given offshore center. Profiled are banking, money, and foreign exchange; legal entities; taxation; financial and investment incentives; tax treaties; and business contacts.

For instance, legal entities explains the types of legal forms that are recognized and that can be chartered. This may include several types of corporations, insurance companies, and categories of banks. Legal entities also covers issues such as who may be a shareholder, how ownership may be held, restrictions on ownership or transfer of shares, number of directors required, incorporation requirements, capitalization requirements and structure, corporate documents, initial incorporation costs, annual corporation fees, and other pertinent information that will be valuable to the reader when comparing tax haven entities and for ultimately establishing one.

Every effort has been made to provide the most timely and accurate material available, but unfortunately it is bound to change. More important, this book is intended to give a thorough understanding of tax havens, enlightening and inspiring readers to greater triumphs through increased awareness. The options and alternatives presented here should give every reader a decisive business advantage.

Acknowledgments

Special thanks to my lovely wife for her generous assistance on the preparation of the manuscript that sped completion of this book. But, particular gratitude goes to her tolerance of its author.

Dozens of individuals from Antigua to Western Samoa were helpful with providing valuable and timely material that aided my seemingly endless research efforts. These persons work in accounting and law firms, government offices, banks and trust companies, management firms, publishing offices, chambers of commerce, and tourist offices.

Hoyt L. Barber

PART 1

The World of Offshore Business

1
Why
Tax Havens

Tax havens have gained increased popularity worldwide over the past 30 years. The most obvious purpose of a tax haven is to lower tax liability. But there are other, equally important reasons for going offshore.

An American who uses a tax haven to reduce taxes has the same motivation as an American who hires an accountant for advice on using the U.S. tax laws to save tax dollars. Both patriots are engaging in tax avoidance, which is perfectly legal.

The U.S. government should not be surprised by Americans who desire to use tax havens to reduce taxes, considering the fact that the nation's forefathers left England in order to avoid overly oppressive taxation. Until 1913, there was no income tax in the United States. Today the federal government taxes individuals up to 33 percent on worldwide income. With state and local levies, personal income tax hovers around 40 percent. U.S. corporations pay approximately 40 percent.

Fortunately, there are still ways to tread the sea of taxation and regulation. And taxpayers are obligated to themselves to survive. Years ago Supreme Court Justice George Sutherland eloquently declared, "The legal right of a taxpayer to decrease the amount of what otherwise would be his taxes, or altogether avoid them, by means which the law permits, cannot be doubted." Americans still have the right to avoid taxes!

Types of Tax Havens

Tax havens are the nucleus of the offshore world. The IRS study conducted by Richard Gordon entitled *Tax Havens and Their Use by United*

States Taxpayers—An Overview (1981) defines a tax haven as "any country having a low or zero rate of tax on all or certain categories of income, and offering a certain amount of banking or commercial secrecy." The IRS defines 29 countries as official tax havens, but depending on the circumstances any country could feasibly be a tax haven. Although a high-tax jurisdiction, to many foreigners, the United States is a tax haven.

Basically, tax havens fall into three categories. There are no-tax havens that have absolutely no taxes—on personal or corporate income, capital transfers, estate and inheritance monies, the list goes on. Residents and nonresidents are treated alike.

Then there are low-tax havens that tax local income but no foreign source income or profits. In this same group are low-tax havens that have double-taxation treaties with the United States, the United Kingdom, and other countries, alleviating the obligation to be doubly taxed. A citizen would pay the foreign tax and reduced U.S. taxes. These treaties usually allow for exchange of information on tax matters. In tax havens that have no treaty, there is less threat of information disclosure.

Finally, countries like Liechtenstein grant special privileges to certain types of companies. Holding companies in Liechtenstein qualify for low tax rates.

Tax Haven Incentives

Many tax haven countries offer financial and investment incentives. An example is encouraging onshore investments to beef up a local industry or launch an altogether new one. Grants, loans, guarantees, and tax holidays are common enticements.

Tax havens are conducive to business in many ways. They are international by nature, providing top-notch banking and state-of-the-art communications. Foreign banks offer services that Americans can't always get in the states. They can assist or lend money in cases where an American counterpart might be restricted by federal or state laws. Common-law countries automatically practice confidentiality in banking transactions. In certain tax havens strict secrecy laws are enforced, ensuring an account holder maximum privacy. Finally, minimal government regulation designed to stimulate business and banking is highly appealing to citizens of heavily regulated countries.

Unique or modern corporation laws can provide advantages and open new opportunities. Some tax havens allow a corporation to act as director of another corporation. Some permit bearer shares rather than registered shares. Bearer shares are transferred simply by handing the next stockholder the stock certificate. Telephonic board meetings can be held to eliminate the expense and trouble of meeting in person. There are a multitude of novel features in offshore entities that are not found in U.S. corporations.

Banking laws are more lenient than in many countries. Certain tax havens welcome first-time bankers who wish to start their own offshore bank. These banks usually have low or no reserve requirements, liberal lending capabilities, and low capitalization requirements. The same applies to insurance and trust companies. Offshore bank ownership has distinct advantages for Americans over the use of a tax haven corporation. (See Chapter 6, "International Tax Planning.")

There are many totally legal reasons to use a tax haven. Their uses are limited only by your knowledge of the law and by your own imagination. An individual or company can protect against unwarranted lawsuits and asset seizures by placing assets in a tax haven corporation. Perfectly legal!

Trading companies—those in the business of importing and exporting goods to and from other countries—can reduce taxes through reinvoicing and accumulating funds offshore. Reshipments can be accomplished offshore to save time and money. Transfer of ownership of goods can be facilitated with a minimum of red tape, and documentation can be executed efficiently offshore.

Individuals and companies with patents, trademarks, and copyrights will find advantages to holding these intellectual property rights in a tax haven corporation: Avoid unnecessary lawsuits; conduct simple ownership transfers; accumulate royalties, dividends, and interest; and initiate agreements offshore.

An offshore holding company is perfect for owning stocks and bonds, effectively centralizing control of business interests and assets.

These strategies and untold others are practiced every day by shrewd businesspeople and investors on every continent. They have learned how to play the offshore game to elevate their financial posture. The tools are available.

As the world moves closer to a global economy, visionary investors will internationalize their financial affairs and gain the fluidity necessary to ride out unforeseen future political and economic developments that can threaten their financial well-being.

Reasons for Going Offshore

Here are 10 tangible reasons for going offshore that speak to genuine concerns faced by Americans:

1. *Failure of U.S. financial institutions.* Many U.S. banks, S&Ls, and insurance companies are teetering on the brink of collapse.

2. *Failure of U.S. government guarantee agencies.* The FDIC, FSLIC, and other agencies continue to face their own potential insolvency.
3. *The U.S. national debt.* The horrendous figure now exceeds $4 trillion.
4. *Erosion of U.S. liberties.* Every citizen's liberties under the Constitution and Bill of Rights are threatened by a growing "deprivatization" of information.
5. *Invasion of privacy.* Financial privacy, in particular, is not respected in America.
6. *Increased U.S. taxes.* Big increases can be expected, the fuel necessary to support expanding government.
7. *Vulnerable personal and business assets.* Americans are sue-happy. Assets are always subject to potential lawsuits. The IRS can grab assets first, ask questions later.
8. *Poor investment performance.* The average return in the stock market since 1922 has been 10 percent per annum. Today U.S. banks pay less than 6 percent interest. Both types of investments are substantially eaten away by taxes and inflation.
9. *Lack of financial security.* When taxes continue to increase, financial institutions continue to fail, and assets are exposed to litigation and/or seizure, security is difficult to attain.
10. *Cost of death.* Even in death Americans are subject to taxes. Estate taxes and probate cost upwards of 90 percent.

These are just a few of the major problems that U.S. citizens must personally resolve if they hope to preserve their present fiscal standing, brighten their future prospects, and retain the same quality of life for their families and themselves. Today's headlines shouldn't be accepted casually.

Doing business, banking, and investing from offshore is a major step that can quickly enhance U.S. taxpayers' financial security. Offshore opportunities promise greater returns on investment, while allowing taxpayers to structure their affairs in a way that will reduce their annual U.S. tax liability.

Americans, overly accustomed to a strong and stable nation, have been clinging to a sense of security for years. Faith in an infallible government and institutions has led us to discount the notion that there are other avenues for improving our personal lives.

The Global Economy

Regardless of whether we accept change, it's coming. Our nation will become more and more internationalized by the simple fact that U.S. economic and financial systems will be merged into the developing global economy. Emphasis will no longer be placed on a nation's financial strength but on the financial strength of an international market. Ponder these thoughts:

- Americans are commonly concerned that foreign financial institutions are unstable. To the contrary, many foreign institutions are older than the United States and have liquidity ratios greater than 100 percent, assuring depositors and investors against loss in the unlikely event of bank or institutional failures.

- Certain foreign investments are not allowed to be advertised in the United States. Why? Because returns are often so much greater than U.S. investments, Americans might take their money elsewhere.

Consider these investment opportunities worldwide: Danish bonds paying 22 percent annually, tax-free. One Channel Island checking account pays 10.5 percent and more annually depending on the average balance. There are 5-year CDs that yield over 36 percent per year after monthly compounding (that's at least 29 percent better than the best returns in the United States). Investment funds and trusts of all types return 15 to 60 percent and up per year. In Mexico, where there are no bank failures and where banks have been nationalized (backed by the government), one bank pays 10 percent every 4 weeks, or 130 percent annually!

Surprised? Returns in the United States are paltry compared with the returns illustrated here. Worse, there is growing concern about whether investors will get their principal back if a U.S. financial institution fails. When you compare U.S. returns with opportunities abroad, the expression "the world is your oyster" takes on new meaning.

2
Selecting the Right Tax Haven for Your Purpose

There is no such thing as a perfect tax haven. Every tax haven has advantages and disadvantages depending on what you hope to achieve. Of the 45 tax havens covered in this book, several should stand out as likely candidates.

Tax havens like the Bahamas and Cayman Islands instantly pop to mind, since they have received much publicity and are generally well regarded. This knowledge alone, however, is insufficient for making a proper evaluation according to your own circumstances. There are dozens of reasons that can influence your selection.

Indicators for Judging Tax Havens

The 13 indicators identified here for judging a tax haven's potential will help you gauge how each potential tax haven stacks up against your goals. The object, of course, is to find a tax haven with the maximum number of advantages that satisfy your requirements.

1. Tax structure
2. Political and economic stability
3. Exchange controls
4. Tax treaties

5. Government attitude

6. Modern corporation laws

7. Simple incorporation procedures and competitive fees

8. Communications and transportation

9. Banking and professional services

10. English common law

11. Secrecy and confidentiality

12. Investment incentives and opportunities

13. Location

14. potential for above factor's to change

Part 2 profiles these indicators by tax haven, simplifying the selection process. Once the most attractive havens are sorted out, you can make a more thorough investigation by engaging in further reading and making personal contact with professionals working in the tax haven.

Let's take a closer look at each of these significant indicators.

Tax Structure

Tax structure is probably the single most important reason for using a tax haven. The fact that tax havens usually have no or low taxes makes them attractive for conducting business offshore and for accumulating funds. Tax havens commonly have a two-tax system: one tax for residents and resident corporations and another for nonresident entities.

Political and Economic Stability

Stability is another leading factor when choosing a tax haven. Both political and economic stability best ensure an investment and the steady continuance of a favorable business climate.

Panama is an example of a tax haven that is economically stable but, until a short time ago, politically unstable because of the military ouster of Manuel Noriega. Typically, investors and businesspeople reacted by moving their money out of Panamanian banks and redomiciling their businesses to other jurisdictions. Fortunately, because of its economic stability, Panama was able to ride out the storm. A smaller, less prosperous tax haven may not have recovered.

Exchange Controls

One form of control that governments frequently exercise is exchange control, restricting the free flow of currency between countries. An example is the Russian ruble. In order for the former Russian states to enter international trade and have a truly free market, they will inevitably have to allow the flow of rubles in and out of their independent states and permit rubles to be exchanged for other currencies.

"Flight" capital typically occurs when a government restricts its citizens from freely moving their money out of the country and when its citizens are fearful of future prospects. Hong Kong is a perfect example.

Most tax havens have no exchange controls or very minimal requirements. This is important to the offshore investor who will be transferring funds in and out of the tax haven on a moment's notice. No exchange controls are the best situation.

Tax Treaties

Tax treaties are discussed in greater length later in this book. They are worth understanding when planning taxes. An offshore corporation organized in a tax haven that has a double-taxation agreement with the United States will avoid paying taxes twice. Unfortunately, these treaties also frequently incorporate a tax information exchange agreement (TIEA) so that both governments will assist each other with exchanging information for a tax investigation. All these issues are moot, of course, in no-tax jurisdictions.

Government Attitude

Many tax havens openly welcome offshore business while others only tolerate it. It's best to do business with the former. Sometimes a political party in office supports the tax haven industry, but opposing political forces would abolish it if they ever gained power. If you are aware of the political ideologies that exist, you can anticipate change with reasonable comfort. But if a tax haven has no election process to speak of, it may be that on any given day a new political faction will overthrow the existing party.

Modern Corporation Laws

The tax haven business is competitive, like any other business. Over the years tax havens have modified their corporation laws to accommodate offshore business. Tax haven corporation laws often have features that are not found in U.S. law. This in itself offers advantages not available in the states. Some tax havens, such as Panama, have patterned their laws after Delaware to make the legal structure more familiar to Americans while still providing certain unique characteristics.

In addition to existing resident and exempt corporation laws, a tax haven may have passed progressive legislation for the establishment of an IBC, or international business corporation. IBCs are designed specifically for offshore use by nonresidents and are usually exempt from taxes.

Simple Incorporation Procedures and Competitive Fees

Modern corporation laws should provide for simple incorporation procedures and fees that are competitive with other tax havens. Incorporation delays and exorbitant fees discourage offshore business. It's not uncommon for an offshore investor or businessperson to have numerous corporations. If incorporation and maintenance procedures and fees are unreasonable, investors will simply go elsewhere. The cost to maintain numerous offshore corporations adds up quickly. Lack of a simplified incorporation procedure is a sign that the tax haven is not actually attending to the needs of offshore business.

Communications and Transportation

Excellent communication is vital to an active offshore corporation or investor. If, however, funds lie dormant offshore or there is nominal business activity, communication is less important. Normally a tax haven trying to attract business understands the need for state-of-the-art communications. And when business must be done quickly, this often underestimated asset can be paramount to success. Fax capabilities allow international business to be fluid.

Transportation facilities will be a factor if there is a need for frequent travel to the tax haven or if your business warrants shipping. Courier service is very handy when needed. Fortunately, most business can be handled by telephone and fax.

Banking and Professional Services

Banking offshore is sophisticated. Most major international banks located in a tax haven cater to international companies and offshore investors. They can provide valuable banking services between branches and correspondents. Local banks can provide more personalized service and are guided solely by their own jurisdiction's laws, eliminating undue influence from outside sources.

Offshore corporations can establish an account with a bank in the jurisdiction where they are chartered, but quite often they prefer to conduct banking transactions in another country. If a tax haven does not have adequate services, corporations can easily bank elsewhere to suit their needs. For instance, although Nevis is an attractive tax haven in the Caribbean with modern corporation laws, it is not a banking center. A Nevis corporation most likely would bank elsewhere, possibly in the Bahamas, the Cayman Islands, or Switzerland.

Owners of an offshore corporation in a tax haven that has some form of exchange controls may find it beneficial to do their banking in another tax haven that offers very favorable banking services and no exchange controls.

Owners should have ready access to professionals who know the laws of their tax haven. Accountants, lawyers, and management companies provide valuable support services, including communications, to offshore business. The lack of support services can be a problem.

English Common Law

Half of all tax havens are based on English common law. Most of these are former British colonies whose external affairs are still handled and protected by England.

English common law has a long tradition and case law history to draw upon. It is definitely the preferred choice of legal systems. Confidentiality in financial transactions is customary practice and required under common law. Americans will find this attitude refreshing.

Secrecy and Confidentiality

Tax havens on the whole, whether common-law countries or not, practice confidentiality in business dealings. Some countries have specific bank secrecy laws protecting account holders from financial information disclosure. A few countries have very tight secrecy laws that bear strong penalties if breached. Liechtenstein, the Cayman Islands, and Vanuatu are examples. If secrecy is mandatory, know the laws that safeguard your interests. Don't assume that "confidentiality" automatically provides secrecy. (See Chapter 4, "How to Use a Tax Haven.")

Investment Incentives and Opportunities

Aside from the attractive financial and service benefits that tax havens offer, some governments also encourage onshore investment to develop industries that will create new jobs. The incentives vary by tax haven. A few have very extensive programs, including tax holidays, grants, and loans, to stimulate investment. For the right investor, these capital and investment incentives can translate into exciting new opportunities. Incentives are a good sign that a country is progressive and that business is welcome.

Location

Location is important to investors. They feel closer to their money when their tax haven is only a few hundred rather than several thousand miles away.

To illustrate: Australians commonly take their tax haven business to Vanuatu and the Cook Islands; Asians use Nauru and Vanuatu; Europeans go to the Channel Islands; Americans use tax havens in the Caribbean; Africans prefer Madeira or the Seychelles. Preference for location also narrows down the selection process.

Although Europeans seem to shun Caribbean tax havens and Americans think the South Pacific is too far and Asians prefer the Central Pacific over the Caribbean, the fact is that location really has nothing more than psychological significance.

The individual attributes of a given tax haven should dictate your preference. With advanced communications and banking, offshore business can be conducted anywhere. You may prefer to have your offshore corporation in the Bahamas because it's only 50 miles from Florida and a nice place to visit. However, there may well be a better choice of tax haven for your business and financial purposes.

Time zone differences between you and your tax haven are probably the most significant drawback to distance. However, they may also offer advantages.

International entrepreneurs and investors do business around the clock. As an American offshore investor, you will want to call the Channel Islands late at night or early in the morning, phone Asia well into the evening, or call the Central Pacific in the late afternoon. You may want to fax a letter to Europe before you go to bed, knowing it's morning there, with the anticipation that by the time you awake you'll have a reply. A California investor doing business from the Bahamas is actually operating on Eastern Standard Time. It's just a matter of adjusting your thinking to other time zones.

To a lesser extent, the following other factors in the host country come into play when selecting a tax haven:

Wages and per capita income

Gross national product

Historical rate of inflation, currency devaluation, and interest rates

Unemployment rate

Size of foreign debt and trade balance

Form of government and national history

Diplomatic relations

Size of foreign investment

Language can sometimes be a drawback, but most tax haven professionals and international bankers speak English.

3

How Tax Havens Are Illegally Exploited

The offshore financial world is truly unmeasurable. Enormous sums of money and assets flow through dozens of tax havens around the world. Trillions come and go and even more trillions quietly rest undisturbed for short and long periods, safely out of anyone's reach.

There are many reasons why the offshore world exists and has grown to such proportions. In a sense, it's a small world where all types of people with every imaginable purpose intertwine to create a powerful sanctuary for depositing their gains.

Most major corporations in America today maintain some kind of offshore unit(s) for a variety of financial reasons, including reinvoicing, import-export, insurance, banking, in-house financing, tax reduction, investment, and foreign sales. Major foreign companies do the same.

These corporations have the financial resources at their disposal to create the corporate and financial mechanisms necessary to achieve their goals, capture new markets, increase sales, acquire new assets, beat the competition, and gain more power—usually with the intent to show a healthy bottom line to shareholders, creditors, bankers, and others.

Large corporations must continually meet substantial commitments of all kinds in order to progress and remain financially healthy. They are motivated to seek out every conceivable method to reach their goals. Although talented lawyers, accountants, and other professionals do not come cheap, they have the knowledge, ideas, and contacts to help companies creatively circumvent the barriers that most smaller investors are forced to accept. There are two reasons: (1) most Americans

14

are unaware of the myriad of opportunities around them, and (2) few individual investors have the financial resources to warrant attempting the same strategies as the big companies.

Entering the Gray Zone

Offshore has grown as the world has grown, but in today's information age it's spreading faster. The exclusivity of the offshore world is no longer limited to major corporations and rich individuals. It's becoming more crowded as the pressures of taxation and regulation are increasingly imposed by governments, and this consensus generally applies everywhere in the world. The more developed a country becomes, the more taxes and regulations are stepped up. The forerunner in this game is the United States. As a nation, we have a hungry stomach, but although the refrigerator is bare, the bureaucratic animal still has to eat. The U.S. Senate, in its 1985 investigation on crime and secrecy, was surprised to learn of the widespread use of offshore banks and companies by Middle Americans, people like your next-door neighbor.

Legitimate corporations, following their capitalistic instincts, and illegal businesses, seeking a safe hideout for their ill-gotten gains, both have a desire to go offshore. The significant difference is that illegitimate business originally acquired its money and assets from illegal activities (defined by whose laws were broken), as opposed to legal enterprise.

Consider for a moment the offshore world as a shopping mall where all sorts of products and services may be acquired. In this offshore mall, the items for sale are financial services, secrecy, corporate and financial vehicles, professional services, and most importantly trust. And for every product and service, there is supply and demand. Cost and price are determined according to these free economic forces. As any shopper knows, there is something for everyone.

The offshore world is a "gray zone" where the lines of sovereignty, power, law, and money meet and commingle. Here illegally acquired money mixes with legitimate funds. Offshore, under the guise of anonymously owned corporate vehicles and banks, all money appears to look the same. The funds flow in, mix, are reinvested, and flow out. There are numerous combinations of money flows, depending on the outcome required.

The Secrecy Shield

Regardless of why legitimate and illegitimate businesses go offshore, the common denominator is that both want secrecy, discretion, and confidentiality. Ingo Walter conducted a study on secrecy and the flow of offshore funds in his thoroughly researched *Secret Money* (Lexington, MA: Lexington Books, 1985).

Illegal money needs to be laundered so that it can be reinvested as clean, legitimate cash. An intricate series of steps is followed to lose its trail of origin. Along the way, secrecy is desired as a shield so that enforcement and investigatory people cannot follow. Of course, as each phase is accomplished, the scent grows weaker, eluding the bloodhounds.

Legitimate money wants secrecy for similar reasons. Corporations want to channel and reinvest their money into new avenues as they choose. As their money flows, they are engaging in sophisticated tax reduction strategies orchestrated by professional advisers. This money may ultimately go back to the corporation in one form or another, but it may take an alternative route and be secretly reinvested into new enterprises anywhere in the world. By the time it reaches its final destination, it is no longer associated with its origins. However, the corporation that originally made the profits still controls the money and its uses.

New companies spring up from apparently nowhere with enormous unknown resources but with definite ambitions, run by managers who have no idea who pulls the strings. Each year new fortunes are made, often tax-free.

It is impossible to trace most offshore connections. The people and companies who are engaged offshore certainly don't want anyone to know. Much of the world's wealth is submerged there. Its secrecy gives it unmeasurable power and security to the people who control those funds and assets through layers of corporations, trusts, and banks.

Chapter 4 ("How to Use a Tax Haven") details how to get offshore, establish the preferred vehicles, and utilize offshore banks and other strategies while keeping secrecy in mind. Chapter 5 ("Banking and Investing Abroad") examines offshore banking and investments and how to establish appropriate accounts with the desired privacy.

Government Countermeasures

In their continuing effort to collect more taxes to pay for expanding government services, developed nations impose burdensome regulations and restrictions on taxpayers. In order to gain more tax dollars, governments often redefine how and who they can control and under what circumstances. Since the avoidance crowd tries to stay a step ahead of government's tightening grasp by exploiting offshore angles, government feels compelled to follow, reaching into other jurisdictions with an arsenal of means: exchange-of-information agreements and tax treaties; tax code revisions; high-tech eavesdropping; infiltrating confidentiality by engaging unscrupulous professionals and officials; and muscling other countries in an overt effort to erode privacy and discourage tax havens.

Some of these tactics appear innocent; others fall below the belt. Whatever the methods employed by government, their purpose is easy to understand: greater control.

The gray zone is conducive to those who wish to protect their interests. Here complexity arises out of opposing country laws and their interpretation and application. Skilled operators use several corporations, each thoughtfully incorporated in a different tax haven, to confound the flow of money and block the best efforts to obtain information.

Laws of justice and procedure also cause a problem. If an investigation commences in the United States and records of a foreign bank account are needed from a tax haven, with certain exceptions many jurisdictions will consider such a request a "fishing expedition" and refuse to cooperate. In the tax haven an indictment would first be appropriate before any such disclosure could be made. However, in the United States, such demands are made of institutions here and abroad all the time. And the information garnered is used as evidence to get an indictment.

A tax haven that thrives on offshore business because of its strict bank secrecy laws, its corporate laws allowing complete autonomy, and its golden reputation cannot allow itself to be tarnished or destroyed. Trust is an all-important factor offshore. If a tax haven is perceived as being too lenient with foreign regulators and information snoops, or if a client gets burned by a host country's negligence, the adverse effects will ripple through the offshore world. It takes years for a tax haven to shake off a tarnished image while attempting to rebuild a once-lucrative offshore trade.

There are sufficient loopholes and discrepancies in the tax laws around the world to keep lawyers, accountants, and tax havens going for a long time. Some of these openings would have adverse effects on individuals and corporations if closed; others are inadvertently created when new laws are enacted. Some powerful people can exert enough influence to keep a loophole open or to invent a new one, often for the purpose of stimulating investment in certain areas. These loopholes create gray areas in the law, open to interpretation.

The U.S. government itself has found it difficult to thwart the swelling tide of offshore funds and to continue investigating and collecting offshore taxes. Assistant Attorney General (Tax Division) Ferguson's own statement to the Ways and Means Committee in 1985 made this clear:

> As you might expect, evasion of United States taxes through sham business transactions involving foreign entities is difficult to detect, hard to recognize when found, and, where foreign witnesses and

documents are crucial, sometimes impossible to prove in court. Even the most transparent transactions are likely to have sufficient documentation to satisfy a surface inquiry by an auditor and enough complexity to discourage a deeper look. Furthermore, being dependent on form and multiplicity of steps, such transactions will utilize entities in tax haven jurisdictions offering business and banking secrecy to conceal their lack of substance.

Organized Crime Offshore

"Good news travels fast, bad news travels faster." So goes the saying. In recent years there has been a wave of adverse publicity about criminal use of offshore havens. Media coverage of criminal activities linked to a particular tax haven often creates the impression that crime results directly from tax haven activity. To some extent, this is a distortion of the facts.

A tax haven is only a vehicle. To knowledgeable people who understand them and know how to use them, tax havens are highly regarded and viable tools. That is why so much legitimate money rests offshore; that's why tax havens do have credibility.

The illegal activities that go offshore are generally highly organized and constitute a small percentage of the sum of offshore business. The folks who hijack truckloads of cigarettes on the order of higher-ups are unlikely to be sophisticated enough or have the financial resources to be offshore; however, the organization behind their bosses might very well be. Crime is everywhere and in abundance, but its presence is usually a fraction of total commerce.

Eric Ambler weaves an interesting tale of the abuses of international law and financial intrigue in his 1979 novel *The Siege of the Villa Lipp.* As the plot unfolds, a tax haven "consultancy" group is uncovered as a vehicle to induce unsuspecting investors and businesspeople into the shadowy web of extortion. The "able" criminal is revealed—mastermind of the offshore jungle, predator extraordinaire. The book is a primer of the secret activities of an invisible breed. In reality, those activities do not stop with extortion. And the fictional characters in Ambler's novel have real-life counterparts.

The underground economy flourishes offshore because it's difficult to detect. Ill-gotten gains are usually kept in the form of secret money vehicles, such as U.S. dollars, foreign currencies, gold, silver, coins, stamps, cashier's checks, money orders, jewelry, and bearer bonds. All are typical ploys to avoid using the national banking system, in which unusual activities are much easier to detect. Secret money vehicles are conducive to bartering, and the one in possession of the goods is generally considered the owner. Ownership change is hard to trace. These assets are often difficult to move around, especially in volume or in larger sums. The owner is susceptible to theft.

Moving large assets outside one's own country is difficult, since any attempt may readily be detected. This is why going offshore is inviting to sizable underground businesses, which are able to undertake the necessary preparations and expense to divert their incomes offshore. Assets are also transferred to offshore entities, alleviating the cumbersome task of physically smuggling them out of the country.

Underground business prospers from risky ventures that capitalize on the supply and demand of illegal goods and services. These enterprises involve evasion of government regulations and taxes. The list of criminal activities is long, but common operations include extortion, bribery, murder, drug trafficking, gun running, smuggling, theft, prostitution, robbery, racketeering, fraud, securities violations, and money laundering.

Just because they are illegal doesn't mean these operations are unsophisticated. Bumbling may be evident on the lower rungs of these organizations, but upper management employs the same devices as major corporations and retains the same educated professionals to keep financial activities tidy.

Offshore, money comes in several colors. Americans are most familiar with greenbacks, but there are two other distinct colors: black and gray.

Black money is derived from the above-mentioned criminal activities. In the drug trade, black money is called "narco dollars."

Gray money comes from laundering funds from soft crimes such as skirting around currency control laws, avoiding tax and economic sanctions, and engaging in graft and covert government activities. According to *Time* magazine, gray money is a $1-trillion-a-year racket.

The International Laundromat

At the root of major international criminal enterprise is money laundering. In order for the organization behind dubious activities to prosper, it is vital that black and gray money be "washed" in a cycle that produces "clean" currency whose origins are untraceable. Only in this fashion can ill-gotten funds safely be reinvested in the world markets. The United States is a preferred haven for investment of these funds.

The "wash cycle" is a complex series of transactions that spans the globe and entails laying groundwork and relying on various participants to conclude each phase successfully. In 1986 Congress passed the Money Laundering Act to thwart activities associated with laundering and curb the cleansing process. *Time* magazine's cover story "A Torrent of Dirty Dollars" (December 18, 1989) gives a fine illustration of money laundering and how the wash cycle actually works.

The single best example of illegal exploitation of tax havens is the nefarious Bank of Credit and Commerce International (BCCI). This rogue bank has brought a lot of dirty linen out of the closet—more than we'll probably ever hear about. How dirty? The U.S. Justice Department has been accused of hindering investigations into the matter in an effort to conceal damning information and evidence.

The "Bank of Crooks and Criminals," as it has been dubbed by government insiders, caught a wide range of people in its net. The offshore world makes strange bedfellows. Accused of being an enormous money-laundering machine, among other things, this global $20-billion bank unraveled the murky financial dealings of a parade of characters: sheiks, drug lords, dictators, smugglers, arms dealers, launderers, swindlers, organized crime bosses, politicians, and the CIA, to mention only some of the big fish. The revelations accompanying its demise have far-reaching implications.

BCCI employed every means of enforcement known to organized crime: extortion, kidnapping, bribery, murder, and high-tech spying. This colorful banking enterprise coddled politicians and influence peddlers in a diabolical attempt to win favors and turn heads. Considering the magnitude of BCCI's activities, and the length of its continued operation, the whole affair smacks of political corruption at the highest levels. It will be many years before this story rests.

Flight Capital

Flight capital frequently occurs when a country's economy and government become unstable, causing its citizens to lose confidence. In an effort to protect their financial resources and ultimately their personal safety, citizens move their assets offshore—against local laws—just prior to their own physical relocation. Of course, all this depends on their financial ability to escape.

Today billions of dollars in flight capital are held outside Latin America, Hong Kong, and communist countries. Expatriates of these countries seek financial freedom and safety from declining or transitionary governments with faltering economies or signs of growing oppression. The scenario has been repeated throughout this century's history: Germany in the 1940s, Iran in the 1970s, Mexico in the 1980s, Hong Kong in the 1990s.

Morgan Guaranty Trust Company has compiled some statistics estimating the amount of flight capital held by expatriates of Latin American countries: Mexico, $84 billion; Venezuela, $58 billion; Argentina, $46 billion; Brazil, $31 billion. Most of these assets will never return to their homeland.

The nature of offshore business and tax havens attracts all types of people and their money. It's not surprising that the system harbors corruption, but the percentage is probably no greater than that in any major city. The sums are just larger.

There are untold angles to the offshore game. For a better understanding of illegal uses that players should avoid, read Richard H. Blum's *Offshore Haven Banks, Trusts, and Companies: The Business of Crime in the Euromarket* (New York: Praeger Scientific Publications, 1984).

4
How to Use
a Tax Haven

To benefit from tax havens, you need to know how to use them. This knowledge can be very simple or very complex depending upon your own circumstances, desires, and goals.

Two avenues, or a combination of both, can be implemented to carry out business offshore. The first involves opening an offshore bank and/or securities account. The second requires establishing a legal person, better known as a corporation or trust, in the chosen jurisdiction.

An offshore account can be established by either an individual or a corporation to facilitate offshore banking and investing. By using a corporate conduit, the investor takes advantage of new opportunities and options that only an offshore entity can provide.

Establishing a Presence
in a Foreign Country

You can establish a presence in a tax haven by incorporating in the country that offers you the most advantages for doing offshore business. The offshore corporation, an artificial but legal person, automatically has a presence in that jurisdiction, subject to its laws and taxes.

Once the company or trust is organized, implementing strategies, transacting business, establishing accounts, and conducting other activities can be handled swiftly and in the name of the corporation or trust. The legal entity becomes the investor's alter ego and is safely controlled at arm's length.

It may be advisable to incorporate in several different havens. This book will expose you to new ideas and a host of opportunities inherent in being offshore. Tailoring those ideas to your individual business or tax situation will help you shed light on previously unrealized possibilities.

Part 2 of this book introduces you to each prospective tax haven, allowing for comparison and analysis of their diverse aspects. Earlier chapters taught you what to look for in the selection process and why, making deduction easier and leaving you with only a handful of possibilities that truly make sense. Once you are reasonably comfortable with your choices, you can make a more thorough investigation by reading other sources and communicating with knowledgeable professionals. Undoubtedly, a logical locale for your particular needs will come to light.

The offshore world doesn't have to be a mystery. The more knowledge you possess, the better prepared you'll be to capitalize on the offshore world and improve your personal standing in life.

Privacy

Privacy is a dirty word to some, including governments who feel that citizens' private lives should be open to inspection. In the United States, deprivatization appears to be a trend. In many other countries, there is respect for an individual's right to privacy in most matters, including financial affairs. Much of this regard for privacy comes from experiencing oppressive regimes or dictatorships. For more extensive reading on this increasingly important subject, write to Eden Press (see the International Resources section) and request its free book catalog. Also see *Time* magazine's issue of November 11, 1991, entitled "Nowhere to Hide."

Preserving Confidentiality and Secrecy

Although privacy is a cornerstone of offshore activities, it can never be absolutely guaranteed. It's commonly peddled under the label "confidentiality" or "secrecy." Sounds good, doesn't it? But wait a minute. What does that really mean? Let's take a closer look.

Confidentiality is a blanket expression, leaving wide margins for interpretation. Confidentiality can be as simple as one person agreeing not to repeat something stated by someone else. The person may be a professional who claims that client matters are held in "strict confidence." By whose definition?

Secrecy is flung around just as frequently, implying the same thing as confidentiality but with an ironclad air to it. These expressions are commonly heard when entering or doing business offshore, but unless all parties understand exactly what is meant, they become meaningless terms.

Before jumping into any arrangement where others may be the recipients of your private information, always make certain that you understand what they mean by "confidentiality" or "secrecy." How well information is guarded depends entirely on how much value you place on it. If the information leaked out to the wrong person(s), how damaging would the outcome be?

Knowledge of certain information may not seem threatening today, but the world is changing quickly. Can you be totally sure that at some later point in time the information will still be secure, or that it won't have a negative impact on your future if discovered? Consider each step required to achieve the end result. Weigh it thoughtfully. Many foreigners know the importance of privacy. Here in America, we often take our physical, spiritual, and financial independence for granted.

Tax havens sell their countries and their services on confidentiality and secrecy. They know that these are major incentives, designed to attract offshore business. So important are they that countries, businesses, and individuals can be ruined if clients' secrets aren't respected. Confidentiality is one significant reason that clients went offshore to begin with, and they surely don't want to discover that, after trusting others, their deep dark secrets have been tossed around like neighborhood gossip. But it does happen. And you're the last one who wants to experience it!

The secrecy merchants include tax havens, financial institutions and professionals, marketing people, office services people, and anyone else who recognizes that your business is of a private nature by virtue of the fact that you, or the corporation you control, is offshore. Immediately, these people will appeal to your fears, insecurities, and desire for privacy. All have important services to offer offshore. So how do you separate the chaff from the wheat, as they say? Think!

A banking brochure may promise "strict bank secrecy." That does not mean that any breach in your "confidential" account will cause your banker to be fined or fired, or go to jail. On the other hand, you could be the unfortunate soul who faces these penalties.

However, that same statement may actually be trying to inform you of strict laws stipulating that all customer transactions and information held by the bank will be discreetly handled or specific legal consequences will be incurred.

When there are laws on bank secrecy, the penalties vary. Some are so ridiculously light that they amount to a slap on the wrist if laws are violated. Other tax havens place greater value on their reputation and have strong laws that intimidate bankers not to slip up. Fines may run into the tens of thousands, along with lengthy jail sentences. Still, this is no assurance that a secret will remain a secret. With enough incentive, less than scrupulous professionals everywhere will divulge anything.

For example, billions of dollars took flight following the U.S. invasion of Panama, not just because of the sudden military presence, but because of the threat that bank account information and possibly the identities of beneficial owners would be disclosed to U.S. authorities in the course of "cleaning up" the country. At the time, Panama was one of the premier offshore banking centers, providing utmost secrecy. The general response among Panama's bankers was to not betray their customers' trust under pressure, since doing so would completely undermine the country's reputation. Today Panama is rebounding, but the scenario would be different if the bankers had not taken a hard line and opposed the unwelcome intrusion. Less economically stable countries might have given in to the disclosure demands and allowed confidential bank records to be examined.

Within a tax haven country, legislation defines a clients' right to confidentiality or secrecy by limiting how an institution's account information may be treated. Ask a prospective bank or trust company exactly how much privacy can be garnered and what assurances you have.

Attorneys, banks, and trust companies in tax havens often provide support services such as incorporating, establishing trusts, and supplying nominee directors. Their dealings in these matters are also governed by law, but to what degree? Find out, if true privacy is desired. A private company or "management company" offering similar services is not necessarily regulated or subject to penalties if its representatives choose to be indiscreet.

A superb example is a group of American investors who seek privacy, among other things, when chartering an offshore bank. Instead of engaging a professional attorney, or a bank or trust company in the chosen locale, they decide to purchase their bank through an American marketing company. In order to charter the bank for the client, the marketing firm is going to be privy to highly confidential personal and financial information—information that can be easily obtained by the U.S. government or anyone else who is seriously determined to get it. Unless you don't care, it's best to go offshore to engage these services too.

Securing Anonymity

Another valuable privacy measure, linked to confidentiality and secrecy, is a desire for anonymity. The beneficial owners of a company—those who are the true owners or shareholders, not just nominee directors—can hide their identity in a number of ways (and equally they can be discovered).

For example, in America a group of promoters may not want to reveal their involvement in a company. Not that they're trying to hide something, but they feel more comfortable staying behind the scenes and letting others command center stage. So they retain control as stock-holders and employ directors and officers to manage the company. In many states, their stock ownership even in a private company would be public record, so the group decides to incorporate in Nevada to avoid having to disclose exactly who the stockholders are. By doing so, they are completely out of the picture, though still within the laws of their home country, the United States. Their primary concern wasn't absolute privacy; it was principally to remain out of the limelight. Generally speaking, this ploy works well.

Offshore, there are more ways to gain anonymity. Let's take Panama as an example again. Besides being an international banking center that provides strict bank secrecy, Panama grants full confidentiality to beneficial owners of corporations.

A Panama corporation is organized by three residents—the president, treasurer, and secretary—all of whom are directors. One of these three is a lawyer. The lawyer drafts the articles of incorporation, identifying the three individuals and describing each article. Each officer subscribes to one share of stock, as required by law. After proper signatures and notarization, the document is filed with the public registry. Although the corporation is now public information, absolutely nothing about the true beneficial owners is disclosed. The law firm that incorporated the company will provide the official document in Spanish and a certified English translation, along with signed bearer share certificates. On request, the law firm will provide a general power of attorney that's signed and certified, with a blank for the appropriate person's name. Thus not even the law firm knows who is to have power of attorney. This power is so broad that the named person will be able to conduct virtually any kind of business on behalf of the corporation.

The true beneficial owners gain privacy in several ways. First, they are not disclosed in the articles of incorporation. Second, an attorney is on the board who by law cannot disclose the beneficial owners' true identities. Third, ownership is held in the form of bearer shares.

The power of attorney is nice. It doesn't insinuate that the person is an officer, director, or shareholder, but depending on who needs to be shown the document, it does connect that person to the corporation. This may or may not matter. The person can also open bank and brokerage accounts.

Trust is a critical element in all these arrangements. Members of the law firm retained to set up the company must preserve the veil of secrecy. The person with the power of attorney and the intermediary dealing with the law firm can be carefully chosen, highly trusted outsiders thereby completely shielding the person with ultimate control.

Still, potential leaks and hazards remain. Organized crime's solution, of course, is to have trust and secrecy persuasively backed up by force.

In this regard, the individual investor is at a disadvantage. If privacy is essential in your dealings, then when going offshore or transacting business offshore, consider each course of action with regard to future outcome. Success depends on each participant's view of secrecy and the weight accorded to trust.

The Panama illustration is typical of how anonymity is achieved in an offshore corporation. The mechanics will vary a bit by tax haven, but the basic concept is the same.

The Chain of Control

The veil of secrecy disguises the steps administered in the chain of control over offshore entities, their ownership, and their dealings. The Panama corporation may be just one of a series of corporations set up to create complexity and cause blurry vision. Imagine the Panama entity setting up another company that in turn sets up another company, each in a different jurisdiction based on the advantages provided and each with bank and securities accounts in yet other countries where full bank secrecy does exist. All of them may come under a trust administered from still another country. (There may be tax benefits to a trust for non-U.S. citizens, but not Americans.) All could have total anonymity for the beneficial owners, whoever they are.

Maneuvers like these create a smokescreen. Now the activities of all these companies are fully submerged in the "gray zone" of corporate and tax laws. A professional international tax planner can show clients how to structure their offshore business affairs in such a way as to gain complete secrecy, enjoy all the other benefits of going offshore, and substantially reduce taxes.

There are costs associated with secrecy and the maintenance of corporations and their nominee management, even if minimal activity is concerned. (See Chapter 6, "International Tax Planning.") It's important to understand the differences among no-tax havens, low-tax havens, tax havens with no double-taxation agreement, and tax havens with a double-taxation agreement when deciding where to incorporate.

Forming an Offshore Corporation

The corporation is a universal concept with an American counterpart in every tax haven. It is characterized by the following:

1. Personal liability is limited to the amount of money paid into the corporation by its shareholders.

2. A corporation is more attractive to potential investors than other business forms.

3. A corporation has many more tax options than do other forms of business.

4. Favorable pensions, profit-sharing, and stock option plans may be adopted for shareholders, directors, officers, and employees.

5. In the event of an owner's death, a corporation can continue to operate without interruption.

6. Shares can be readily distributed to family members.

7. Ownership interest can be transferred without the corporation having to be dissolved.

8. Management is centralized.

9. Additional shares of stock may be issued to raise more capital.

10. Shares of stock may be used for estate and family planning.

11. Earnings may be accumulated by the corporation to ease the tax burden.

12. A corporation may own shares of stock in another corporation and receive dividends.

13. Life insurance and health programs are available to shareholders, directors, and officers at reduced group rates.

14. Corporate owners receive greater benefits than self-employed individuals.

15. Shareholders may borrow money from the corporation and pay it back at their convenience and at a preferred interest rate.

Methods of obtaining additional benefits are limited only by the owners' creativity. The corporation must first be organized, and a board of directors meeting held, before the company begins operating.

Although many tax havens recognize several types of corporations, the corporate form described above is the most common and familiar to Americans. Part 2 describes other corporate forms by country under "Legal Entities."

Tax liabilities of the corporation and its stockholders, directors, officers, and employees will depend on where the corporation is chartered, where it operates, and the citizenship and resident status of the principals and employees.

An offshore corporation offers advantages over and above the benefits enjoyed by domestic corporations. The attention-getting advantages include significant tax reductions, minimal regulations, flexibility in operations, international diversification, maximum confidentiality and secrecy, and bulletproof asset protection, all of which translate into greater net profits.

You can establish an offshore corporation much as you would a U.S. corporation. In this case, however, self-incorporation is an impractical idea, since you are not physically in the tax haven to act as an incorporator or resident agent. Even if you were a resident of the country, it would defeat your purpose to incorporate an offshore company in the same tax haven where you live. Tax havens generally have a double-tax system: Residents pay one tax and foreigners doing business with nonresidents pay another. Procedures vary from country to country.

If you can't afford the cost of professional services, you probably have no reason to go offshore in the first place. Always engage professionals who are concerned about their reputations; you will have greater assurance of getting the expertise required.

Attorneys, accountants, banks, trust companies, management companies, and corporate service companies incorporate companies and organize trusts for their clients. The services provided vary by company, but the scope of their tasks includes:

- Incorporating
- Providing legal nominee directors, officers, and shareholders
- Establishing trusts, banks, and insurance companies
- Holding corporate meetings
- Consulting on tax and legal matters
- Advising on international tax planning
- Acting as resident agent and registered office
- Opening bank and securities accounts
- Providing bookkeeping, investment-advising, and secretarial services
- Reinvoicing
- Furnishing mail-forwarding, telephone-answering, and facsimile and telex services

New companies may be incorporated at the instruction of the client, who must provide all required information and pay all fees. The following information is required in the Cayman Islands. Depending on the chosen tax haven, similar information will be requested of the beneficial owners:

1. Choice of several corporate names.
2. Ordinary or exempt company desired.
3. Authorized share capital.

4. Objects of the company.

5. Names and addresses of the beneficial owners and number of shares that each will own.

6. Names, addresses, and occupations of the directors and officers.

Incorporation time is usually quick, ranging from 24 hours to 5 days. In cases where time is of the essence and the corporate name is of little importance, an "off-the-shelf" or "shelf" company can be purchased for approximately the same amount.

In some tax havens, the above information is not a matter of public record; in other countries, confidentiality must be obtained by using nominee shareholders, directors, and officers. Even when corporate information is not available to the public, it is wise to retain the services of nominees if confidentiality is of utmost concern. Then even the public registry won't be the wiser.

When beneficial owners have to be disclosed, a trust can be inserted instead, further shielding the owners' true identity. The trust, acting through the offshore professional, would actually arrange to incorporate the company. Then, if additional corporations are required, the company immediately under the trust can make the arrangements. This combination is best in order to attain maximum secrecy.

Many tax havens require corporations to complete annual filings, which may be held in confidence by the government office or made a matter of public record. In other instances, accounts must be maintained, but there is no mandatory filing. Some tax havens require neither record keeping nor annual filing.

When offshore professionals furnish nominee directors and officers, it isn't uncommon for them to request an indemnity agreement with the beneficial owners. The agreement protects them from any potential liability, since they are acting on behalf and in the interests of the true owners. Offshore professionals may also ask for a legal or bank reference, for their benefit only, and to be held by them in confidence. Nominee arrangements are intended to give anonymity to beneficial owners, not to provide a "fall guy" in the event of legal proceedings or unforeseen political events.

Offshore agents charge an annual maintenance fee to ensure that the corporation continues in good standing with the chartering authorities. Again, the required items and related expenses vary by tax haven. In the Cayman Islands, Bruce Campbell & Company charges an annual maintenance fee under $1000 for the following corporate services:

- Maintaining the registered office
- Keeping statutory records
- Preparing minutes of the annual general meeting

- Preparing minutes of the statutory directors' meeting (exempt companies only)
- Preparing and filing annual return
- Providing nominee shareholders
- Providing a secretary or assistant secretary
- Providing post box facilities and mail forwarding
- Preparing minutes of up to two other shareholders' and/or directors' meetings

Often the professional will have the client complete an application form for corporate services that asks for client information, information required for incorporation, and stipulating the terms and conditions of the relationship.

Overseas Company Registration Agents Ltd., self-billed as "Europe's largest independent company formation agents," has affiliations worldwide. OCRA can incorporate nearly everywhere, along with providing sundry corporate services. Because of its volume of business, the agency provides incorporation and annual management functions at reasonable prices. For the address of OCRA and other companies providing similar international incorporation services, see the International Resources section in Part 3. For individual tax haven information or the name, address, and telephone of a local professional, refer to the alphabetized listing of tax havens in Part 2.

Insurance Companies

Insurance companies chartered in tax havens are often "captives"—that is, they are organized by a multinational corporation or major insurance company to insure or reinsure a particular group of people or group of companies.

The premiere havens for insurance companies include Bermuda, Bahamas, Cayman Islands, Guernsey, Isle of Man, and Luxembourg. Less-notable locations are Nauru, Vanuatu, Turks and Caicos, Netherland Antilles, and Uruguay.

Contact professionals in tax havens where insurance companies are encouraged. They will gladly assist with further information, legal requirements, and costs.

International Investment Funds

Funds are popular vehicles and require specialized investment expertise. In order to market the fund, a "private offering of fund shares" needs to be developed and written for the review of prospective clients. The fund can be administered by a management group with the ability and expertise to make it prosper.

There is growing interest among U.S. investors to operate their own fund. One advantage of controlling a fund, in addition to actually operating it as a true investment activity, is to give the appearance of having access to large amounts of capital from unidentified sources. Establishing an offshore bank offers similar benefits, but because a fund is merely a corporation, it is less expensive to start and maintain.

An ideal location for an international fund is the British Virgin Islands, where beneficial owners are permitted to issue themselves bearer shares. Other tax havens are acceptable as well. The corporation must have the power to do all that is required of a fund—namely, to function as an investment company.

If this route interests you, contact Peat Marwick or one of the other professional concerns in the British Virgin Islands. (See the listings in Part 2.) Keep in mind, however, that unless you have a genuine desire to manage a fund and are willing to assume the responsibility of investing other people's money, it's best to use another type of vehicle for conducting offshore business.

Starting an Offshore Bank

Offshore banking has developed a strong following and interest with offshore investors. It's a large step from merely maintaining an offshore bank account. Such banks have their advantages and their drawbacks.

To illustrate the growth of offshore banking: Deposits in American banks alone, and in just the Caribbean, swelled from $25 billion in 1970 to over $200 billion in 1988.

Offshore banking is banking outside one's own country, particularly in a tax haven country. Unless the bank also operates within that country, it is not subject to any jurisdictional laws. There is no legal means for an offshore bank to set up shop in the United States by opening a representative or branch office. In other, less regulated countries it may be possible. The U.S. government is highly opposed to Americans starting or owning offshore banks, on the assumption that the purpose is always tax evasion or financial fraud.

An offshore bank is designated "offshore" because the host country where the bank is chartered and licensed permits it to operate anywhere outside its borders. Offshore banks, although permitted to have a resident agent for legal and communication purposes, are not allowed to do business with residents.

This type of organization, referred to as a Class B bank, has no building of its own. Typically it shares the same quarters with other banks and corporations that are handled by a local lawyer or resident agent. Outside the local representative's office is a plaque listing the name of each bank, commonly on a brass plate—hence the less than flattering expression "brass plate" in connection with offshore banks.

A Class A bank, or one with a building and tellers as we normally know them, is an onshore bank that has maximum powers to conduct banking with residents in the jurisdiction where it is chartered. This type of bank generally operates locally, as opposed to the private, international Class B bank. There are a number of other differences, including cost to establish, minimum capitalization, and qualification requirements of the beneficial owners.

Offshore banks are permitted to conduct a wide variety of activities (such as manufacturing) in addition to exercising their banking powers. A bank's purposes vary according to the jurisdiction where it is chartered.

For example, when the Marshall Islands were readily chartering offshore banks, prior to their bank scandal in 1982, such banks were permitted to make the following offshore transactions to or for the public:

- Receive deposits
- Make personal, mortgage, industrial, or other loans
- Purchase, sell, discount, or negotiate on a regular basis notes, checks, bills of exchange, acceptances, or other evidences of indebtedness
- Issue letters of credit and negotiate drafts
- Provide trust services
- Finance foreign exchange transactions
- Purchase stock, debt obligations, or other securities for public or private distribution

The offshore bank could also engage in the insurance business, trust company business, investment banking business, broker-dealer securities business, commodities business, real estate business, and any other legal activity. Its powers in each of these areas was broad.

Today, offshore banking centers try to restrict banks to "in-house" activities, similar to those of a captive insurance company. This is called a Class B restricted license. In Vanuatu, for example, the Ministry of Finance requires a statement similar to the following:

> I/We hereby give the following undertakings: (1) the Bank will not solicit funds from the public withdrawable by cheque or otherwise; (2) the Bank will be strictly of an in-house nature; and (3) the directors in Vanuatu will be kept fully informed as to the ongoing management and affairs of the Bank.

It should be noted, however, that in Vanuatu the resident agent can modify items 1 and 2 and tailor them to the bank's individual circumstances. Similar stipulations are made in other tax havens. The major reason is the potential for abuse, especially involving the public, which could cause adverse publicity in the event of a scandal.

Offshore banking centers are not necessarily tax havens. Some of these self-described centers are attractive only because they lack adequate legislation and enforcement capabilities, a loophole of omission that allows liberal banking activities to be conducted. The party lasts until so many unscrupulous operators have exploited the jurisdiction that it comes under siege by outside regulators, usually the United States, Canada, and the United Kingdom. After the cleanup, such as in Montserrat, new legislation is enacted with proper departments to oversee licensing to qualified individuals or established banks wishing to establish a branch.

Offshore banks provide numerous unique benefits to their owners if properly managed. Here are some of them:

Save on taxes

Invest anonymously

Do third-party lending

Receive flight capital

Conduct financial transactions

Engage in manufacturing

Trade Euro dollars, Asia dollars, and Petro dollars

Perform trust functions

Deal in commodities, stocks, bonds, and precious metals

Provide merger and acquisition funding

Purchase real estate

Gain float time on bank instruments

Protect assets from creditors, lawsuits, and judgments

Borrow from depositors

Operate with minimum regulation

Conduct arbitrage

Provide cash management

Pool funds from undisclosed sources for investment

Extend liberal bank policies when advantageous

Gain instant credibility

Provide credit references

Attract lucrative deals and rich depositors

A creditworthy offshore bank may even borrow funds from other banks at favorable interbank lending rates. There are many other creative and legal benefits.

Offshore banking centers that are also tax havens include Grand Cayman, Bahamas, Anguilla, Vanuatu, Nauru, Turks and Caicos, and St. Vincent. Other locales may seem conspicuously missing from this list. Grenada, for instance, isn't mentioned because it's not a significant tax haven; in fact, Grenada has banking corporations with no bank licenses. These locales cater to private international bankers who are affluent or affluent in appearance. There are also prestigious offshore banking centers that do not allow the small-time banker to start an operation. These tax havens reserve offshore banking to sizable international banks wishing to open an offshore unit. This same caliber bank can open a branch office or at least a representative office in these tax havens.

Tax havens that welcome private international bankers have a variety of procedures to qualify applicants. In Vanuatu, for instance, the following documentation must be submitted for government approval:

1. Information required for incorporation.

2. A brief résumé on each applicant (beneficial owner), including professional qualifications and specialization in banking, trade, or industry.

3. Testimonial evidence from two internationally recognized banks on the applicant's creditworthiness and financial standing.

4. Unaudited financial statements showing a minimum net worth of $200,000.

5. Certificate of police clearance from the respective jurisdiction proving the absence of criminal convictions or arrest record.

6. Two business references, minimum, from a lawyer and other respectable source.

7. A written statement confirming the in-house undertakings of the proposed bank.

8. The ability to capitalize the bank upon incorporation and prior to operation with $150,000 minimum in paid-up capital.

The approval process can take up to 2 months. Vanuatu is faster than most other jurisdictions, requiring as short a period as 2 weeks.

The offshore bank has four components:

The bank (documents)

Registered office

Resident agent

Board of directors

The banking corporation must be incorporated and then chartered and licensed. The tax haven's financial ministry will certify the articles of incorporation, or the equivalent, and issue the bank charter and license, which is renewable each year upon payment of an annual fee. On request, a "certificate of good standing" will be issued attesting to the fact that the bank is valid and that all filings and fees are current.

The incorporator or initial director will conduct the organization meeting, at which time new directors and officers will be elected or appointed, the bylaws will be taken into consideration and adopted, registered shares of stock will be issued to the beneficial owners, and shares will be considered in exchange for assets. At the same meeting, objects of the bank will be discussed, designation of a bank where a bank or brokerage account will be established, the corporate seal will be approved, and stock certificates, minutes books, and any other important business will be discussed.

The registered agent and registered office are the liaison between the bank and the tax haven's financial authority, providing a legal address and representative for service of legal process. The board of directors may be local nominees who hold actual meetings in the tax haven. These nominees act on behalf of the beneficial owners or stockholders.

Tax havens will make exceptions to the rule of requiring owners to have satisfactory bank experience if a professional management firm demonstrating that expertise is engaged to sit on the board of directors. With modern technology, bank transactions can be handled swiftly between major international financial centers around the world, the board of directors, the agent of the bank, and the beneficial owner.

Bank Management

A common strategy used by offshore bankers is to charter their bank in a tax haven, manage it from a friendly financial center, maintain the assets in yet another country, and establish bank accounts and securities brokerage accounts in still other countries. With this strategy, no single jurisdiction can exercise too much influence over the bank. In effect, this is what the Bank of Credit and Commerce International (BCCI) accomplished on a much grander scale. And aside from a little help from its political friends, it may be a logical reason why BCCI survived so well, and for so long, undetected as a financial fraud.

Since the demise of BCCI, bank management professionals concerned about their reputations and government officials in tax havens are taking a closer look at an applicant's background, financial strength, and qualifications before issuing licenses.

Bank management professionals, acting for the beneficial owners, handle and execute the bank's transactions, including letters of credit, bank guarantees, cash deposit facilities, foreign currency management, trust services, current and savings account management, purchase of securities and real estate, insurance services, and portfolio management.

An offshore bank's board of directors need not reside in the host country. Instead, the bank can have only its resident agent in the tax haven and nominate its board elsewhere. In the case of U.S. citizens operating offshore, it's best to have a board outside the United States. A professional management group acting as board members may be based in Canada, Hong Kong, Panama City, or any other center that's conducive to bank management.

Establishing an independent management company can lend great versatility to an offshore bank. The company can be located anywhere in the world and handle bank-related affairs on behalf of the owners. The management company could be a holding company or a subsidiary of the bank, with the same board of directors. Or the beneficial owners might prefer to keep the bank's board of directors in the host country along with a separate board of directors for the management company. Professional management people can advise you on available options to suit your needs.

The services performed by bank management professionals vary from nominal duties such as acting as directors on paper to being totally absorbed in the bank's activities. These services can be retained full time or on an as-needed basis. An independent management group may be the most economical approach at the start, but as the bank's activities and responsibilities increase, one or more full-time professionals should seriously be considered.

Bank management companies maintain their own professional and clerical staff and typically handle a large volume of business. A single firm may manage dozens of banks. This has its advantages and limitations.

A management company usually charges about $2500 as an engagement fee and approximately the same amount annually to stay on board. A variety of services are offered and charged either by the hour or as a percentage of whatever is being managed. Directors' fees range from $1000 to $5000 per director.

For example, International Finance Marketing, Inc., provides a Canadian administrative base for private offshore banks. President Tej P. Thind and his associates will discuss your individual requirements, assist with establishing an administrative base, provide bank expertise, develop marketable products and marketing strategies, assist with creating financial resources, advise on legal and administrative aspects of private international banking, and profile the bank and its services.

Aston Corporate Management Ltd. provides similar bank management services and nominee directors. See the International Resources section in Part 3 for the addresses of both firms.

Foreign Trusts

Foreign trusts will be considered only briefly here since the tax benefits are too limited for most Americans to consider creating a trust.

The 1976 Tax Reform Act essentially quashed the incentive for Americans to use a foreign trust. Although there are nontax advantages, the tax penalties are significant. There are presently better mechanisms for passing an estate to the next generation.

An American granting assets to a foreign trust for the benefit of another American, such as a child, can still be taxed on the income of the trust. This tax liability is incurred until death. Further, when a U.S. grantor transfers assets, securities, real estate, and the like to the foreign trust, a 35 percent excise tax is imposed.

For other tax disadvantages to the use of foreign trusts, refer to the 1976 Tax Reform Act or consult a knowledgeable professional. To gain a solid understanding of trust planning, start with Adam Starchild's *Building Wealth* (New York: AMACOM, 1981).

5
Banking and Investing Abroad

Banking and investing offshore require owning and maintaining the necessary accounts so that transactions can be conducted at a moment's notice. Establishing these offshore accounts is another matter. Although not difficult, the procedure does require advance preparation and thought.

The simplest approach to going offshore is to open an account with a bank in the desired tax haven or international banking center. This alone may not be adequate, however. You may not wish to establish these accounts in your name. If so, the appropriate corporate entities must be established before the accounts can be set up. The latter approach, of course, produces greater versatility and privacy for the investor or offshore businessperson. Refer to Chapter 4 ("How to Use a Tax Haven") if a corporate entity is first required for your purposes.

The Nature of Foreign Banking

Foreign banking and investing is a little different from banking in the United States. The most identifiable difference is that these institutions may be thousands of miles away, and communication is a key element in doing business. You may want to visit your Liechtenstein bank because you need to transact confidential business or your Bahamas bank because it's relatively close and a trip would be a nice change of pace. Normally business will be handled by mail, fax, telex, or telephone.

Before opening an account anywhere, define what you want to accomplish. You may decide to open a bank account because of locale, strict secrecy, size or liquidity, financial services, lack of double-taxation or exchange-of-information agreements, or the presence of such agreements. After you read Part 2, additional reasons to use a particular bank or country may come to light.

Banking offshore does not necessarily mean banking with an offshore bank. This is a distinction that everyone going offshore should understand. This chapter addresses the services of the banking and financial institutions that are physically located in tax haven jurisdictions. These institutions are governed by stricter regulations than their offshore cousins, even though the restrictions vary significantly by country.

Banks chartered in tax havens fall into several categories. The Class A bank, with a building, officers, and tellers, is the type of institution you will seek for opening an account. It may be a local bank that caters to local residents or an international clientele, or a branch of an international bank like Barclays.

The offshore or "brass plate" bank is a Class B bank, licensed to conduct banking business outside the jurisdiction only. It is not permitted to transact business with local residents. Its presence in the tax haven is limited to a resident agent, lawyer, or other representative who provides the necessary legal base for the bank and may even be involved in its management.

A Class B bank may be unrestricted or restricted. If it's unrestricted, it can do business internationally and accept deposits and provide services to foreigners. If it's restricted, it can do business only with a limited clientele, usually a group of individuals and/or companies whose names are required to be listed on the banking license.

Class B banks are for certain people and certain purposes. Generally, this isn't the type of bank that you will need. The exception to this statement is if you are a beneficial owner or involved in management and have an influence over the bank's affairs, or if you know the principals well enough to feel comfortable. Also, it's important to clearly understand the offshore bank's financial position. How factual is the available information on the bank? Offshore banking should be reserved for the sophisticated investor, whether a customer or the party operating the bank.

The same applies to the offshore insurance entity, unless it is a captive insurance company that is a part of a major group. In any case, the true, underlying financial institution is the key factor as to whether a company's chances of survival are outstanding, even during uncertain times. Reflect again on the notorious Bank of Crooks and Criminals (BCCI).

A basic characteristic of foreign banks, as opposed to the American variety, is that they respect the confidentiality of the client's business. It is not common practice to divulge financial or other information about a customer to a casual inquirer. Common-law countries and British Crown colonies, which constitute approximately half of all tax havens, are bound by law to treat a bank customer's affairs in a confidential manner. Although not a bank secrecy law per se, the common-law tradition is adhered to in these jurisdictions as everyday banking policy.

Maximum privacy is possible in a few tax havens that impose strict bank secrecy laws to keep uncontrollable blabbers from spilling their beans. Secrecy laws with real teeth in them provide for criminal punishment in addition to civil penalties. These laws cover nondisclosure in regard to legal activities.

If a client's business falls into a category considered illegal by the country where the bank is located, only then is there a possibility of the bank disclosing information to authorities. However, this varies drastically by jurisdiction. In Switzerland, tax avoidance is not illegal, so Swiss bankers will not divulge account information to anyone (with exception), but they will if the investigation is for drug trafficking or money laundering. In Liechtenstein, neither of these activities is illegal and no client information will be awarded to any authorities.

Austria too extends strict bank secrecy, giving all customers a password of their own. The attitude toward privacy ranks high, with that of Liechtenstein.

Other tax havens offering utmost secrecy to customers include the Cayman Islands in the Caribbean and Vanuatu in the South Pacific.

Exceptions to secrecy laws are contained in mutual treaties that tax havens sometimes sign with other countries. The United States is a major proponent of these agreements, which offer something in exchange for something. Under the Caribbean Basin Initiative (CBI), for example, a tax haven may sign a treaty to comply with investigative authorities in certain types of criminal cases where evidence is required. If an account holder is a drug smuggler, the treaty may specifically allow pertinent client information to be turned over to the investigating body, which then uses the information to obtain an indictment.

When picking a bank it's also important to know where the institution is headquartered and where it maintains branches. This key consideration is easily overlooked. If you choose a Swiss bank that doesn't have branches outside Switzerland, there is no need for concern over outside pressures, aside from prevailing treaties that provide for exchange of information under certain circumstances.

But if your foreign bank has branches in the United States, you should know that the U.S. government can apply pressure on that bank to release normally confidential or secret information—simply because you are a U.S. citizen. Although not common, it has been known to happen. When a bank establishes a branch in another country, it subjects itself and its customers to the laws and regulations of that country and to the potential pressure of that country's regulations and investigators. This scenario applies even if the customer's account isn't actually in the U.S. branch.

In other words, an American with a bank account in Switzerland, protected by Swiss secrecy laws and not subject to the specific treaty exemptions permitting disclosure of information as a result of criminal activity, can still be subjected to the long arm of U.S. law if the bank has even one U.S. branch and succumbs to American pressure. It's something to think about.

U.S. citizens are required to report the fact that they have a foreign bank account on their income tax returns (Treasury Form TD F 90-22.1, "Report of Foreign Bank and Financial Accounts"). In keeping with the law, an individual with a foreign bank account sends up a red flag.

Types of Accounts and Services

Foreign banks typically offer a *current account*, much like the American checking account. The bank furnishes the depositor with a checkbook so that funds can be paid out of the account with ease. This account pays no interest and the funds are available on demand. The clearance time on foreign checks is considerably longer than Americans are accustomed to. This has its advantages and drawbacks. A third party may not be as likely to accept a foreign check; on the other hand, the clearance period gives the account holder longer access to the funds. The bank sends a monthly statement, with a nominal statement fee. Current accounts may be in any currency or currencies available to the bank. Some banks offer a "multicurrency" account, so that a check can be written in a variety of chosen currencies without the need to establish additional accounts. Initial minimum deposits range from $100 to $100,000.

A *deposit account* is basically a savings account that draws interest on the balance. The bank will issue a passbook. In countries like Switzerland, where stability is a primary factor, interest is usually low—often only a few percent. (In less stable countries like Mexico, where banks seek to attract depositors, up to 20 percent can be earned.) The Swiss bank will automatically deduct 35 percent withholding tax on interest earned; the deduction is reflected on the bank statement. A deposit account typically requires $100 to $10,000 to establish. A choice of currencies may be available.

In a *fixed deposit* or *time deposit* account, the funds are held on deposit for a specified length of time, as with a certificate of deposit (CD).

These types of accounts fetch higher interest returns than regular deposit accounts because the bank is assured of having the funds for a given period. The duration of the deposit is usually 3, 6, 9, or 12 months. The funds cannot be withdrawn during this time, with exceptions. The optional deposit amounts vary by bank from $1000 to $100,000. Large banks may offer a wide range of current and deposit accounts to better suit the customer.

The foreign bank is likely to have a selection of services for the international client. These services may include custodial accounts, commercial loans, consumer credit loans, foreign exchange, money transfers, traveler's checks, safe deposit boxes, purchase and/or sale of stocks and bonds, purchase and/or sale of precious metals, and managed accounts.

There are advantages to maintaining accounts in a foreign currency or having several deposit accounts in various currencies. Opportunities exist to profit from fluctuations in currencies, to hedge against fluctuations or the instability of a home country's currency, or to hedge against inflation. Profits can be made when an investor's home currency is devalued if accounts are maintained in another, more stable currency like the Swiss franc.

Highly recommended to anyone interested in Swiss banking is Harry Browne's *Complete Guide to Swiss Banks* (New York: McGraw-Hill, 1976). The book is comprehensive and good reading, and still sound after more than 15 years. Another recommended reading is Michael Arthur Jones's *Swiss Bank Accounts* (Blue Ridge Summit, PA: Liberty House, 1990). This hands-on book is thorough and current and contains loads of banking contacts.

Opening an Offshore Bank Account

Start by typing a letter to a number of banks that are likely candidates for your business. Keep the letter simple and specific.

Foreign banks accustomed to international business regularly handle large accounts. These customers are profitable for the banks, which can afford to devote more time and effort to servicing such accounts. This is why it's advisable, especially if you plan to establish a relatively small account, to approach each bank in a professional manner.

In Switzerland and Liechtenstein, you can rest assured that unless the bank is managing a million dollars or more of your money, you are considered a smaller customer. Therefore, request the minimums to open an account. That is not to say you won't get first-rate service. Smaller banks may give more personalized service to smaller account holders, but generally speaking a large bank can provide an array of services that a small bank cannot feasibly handle.

In the initial inquiry, state which type of account you wish to open. That way the bank will return the correct forms for completion.

A small bank in the Cayman Islands requires that the following documents be submitted with the initial deposit:

1. *Signature Card.* Any bank account holder is familiar with the signature card, used for verifying a signature on an instrument.

2. *Customer Information Sheet.* General information must be furnished on the customer: name, address, telephone number, and references.

3. *Certificate of Identification.* This sheet states the customer's name and requires a specimen signature to be witnessed by a notary public. Foreign banks will frequently accept verification only from a highly recognized and reputable banking institution.

4. *Verification of Account Agreement.* This form confirms the customer's understanding that the customer is obliged to verify the correctness of each statement and if the bank is not notified of error(s) or if the statement is not received, after 30 days the bank is held harmless against any claims.

5. *Agreement Regarding Operation of Account.* In this agreement, the customer accepts the terms and conditions for maintaining the account.

6. *Foreign Currency Deposit Account Agreement.* This form is required when a term account (i.e., certificate of deposit) is opened.

The Cayman Islands is an outstanding location for offshore banking if it meets your needs. The only hitch is that companies seeking to bank in the Caymans must notify the registrar's office. In effect, this is the same as "qualifying" a company to do business, as is required when a company incorporated in a U.S. state seeks to operate in another state. Unfortunately, it's rather expensive if all the company wants to do in the Caymans is open a bank account. The initial charge to register is CI $600 (US $400), with an annual fee of CI $300 (US $200). In other tax havens, registration isn't normally required of companies opening a foreign bank account.

Corporations usually have to provide a list of officers and directors and a corporate resolution authorizing the establishment of the account. Normally an officer or director will open the account, but a party with general power of attorney (either a beneficial owner or someone else) also has the authority to establish the account on behalf of the corporation. In such instances, the bank will require a copy of the general power of attorney.

A corporate applicant will often be asked to supply a copy of the articles of incorporation and bylaws or similar documents. Swiss banks usually require the signature card, an account application, and two bank reference letters addressed To Whom It May Concern. A "Declaration on Opening an Account or Securities Account" is required when depositing assets with the bank or opening a securities brokerage account. Corporations are also required to provide a copy of the articles of incorporation and bylaws. The articles must be certified by the Secretary of State or Registrar of Companies in the country of incorporation. In Switzerland, the official's signature must be notarized.

Other offshore and foreign banks will require similar forms to be completed and documents be furnished.

If the bank does not understand your inquiry, it may ask for more information before sending opening forms. Occasionally a bank will respond with a cold request for a list of bank references and for more details on how the account will be used and how much money will be deposited before furnishing information on the bank or its services. It can safely be assumed that such a bank is extremely cautious about whom it accepts as customers. The bank may be catering exclusively to an 18-karat clientele, and the delay is its way of weeding out financial lightweights. The minimum deposit requirements are probably hefty.

Occasionally, a bank will open an account on request and issue an account number, then send the opening forms for completion. In the meantime, you are expected to transfer the minimum opening deposit amount.

Tapping into Offshore Funds

Once foreign accounts are established, money can be transferred to or from them swiftly. Funds can be sent to the bank in the form of a personal or company check, cashier's check, money order, or bank draft. Personal and company checks are usually held and credited to the account when cleared. A bank draft is a collection item and must be sent to the issuing bank for payment. This is a time-consuming procedure.

For prompt credit to your account, either mail or rush by courier a cashier's check or money order or arrange a bank-to-bank wire transfer. Your bank should give immediate credit for the cashier's check or money order. A wire transfer is very efficient, but requires bank accounts between which funds can be transferred. It's an excellent means of receiving funds from overseas business customers, or gaining quick access to your offshore money.

Within the United States, funds are received by wire transfer between banks on the same day. A funds transfer between banks in two different countries—for instance, England and the United States—frequently takes up to 3 days, although banks will swear much faster times. Most banks will credit the funds instantly; others wait until a certain time of day when they normally credit deposits.

Wire transfers have been known to take much longer than 3 days, for unexplainable reasons. It's amazing when a week passes after a wire transfer has been confirmed, but the receiving bank has no knowledge of it. If the bank where you are to receive wired funds is small, the transfer will be delayed at least an extra day, since the bank depends on a large intermediary institution through which the funds are cleared. Overall, however, wire transfers provide a clean, efficient means for moving money around.

If you wish to transfer funds by wire, go to your local bank and request the wiring instruction forms. The bank will deduct the amount to be sent along with its fee and will initiate the order the same day.

In the United States, courier services like Federal Express provide next-day delivery. Packages are hand-processed to alleviate excessive damage. If a package is late or doesn't arrive, it's easy to trace the package by the airbill number. Unfortunately, "overnight" delivery from the United States is usually 2 or 3 days to Europe, 3 days or more to Hong Kong, and a week or more to the remote tax havens of Nauru, Vanuatu, and the Cook Islands. Middle East destinations can also require a week in transit. With these delays and distances, a wire transfer is preferable.

Instructions to transfer funds either by mail or wire can be sent to foreign banks in the form of a letter, fax, or telephone call. Telephone instructions should be followed up by written confirmation. If a fax is sent, the bank will compare signatures before releasing funds. Not all banks accept telephone instructions, but with fax technology it's easy to send urgent instructions.

It's advisable to have ready access to liquid offshore funds in the event they are needed on short notice. TSB Bank Channel Islands Limited, the tenth largest bank in the world, provides an excellent instrument. Its Offshore Premium Account is a high-interest-bearing checking account combined with a Visa debit card that allows instant access to offshore funds. Account balances of £2000 to £19,999 receive 11.5 percent interest per annum. Overdraft protection is also available. The minimum deposit required to open the account is £2000, or roughly US $3500. The bank has a very simple application form to complete and return with the initial deposit. TSB offers other services as well.

Finsbury Bank and Trust Company in the Cayman Islands provides similar services. The addresses of both institutions can be found in the International Resources section in Part 3.

U.S. taxpayers are expected to comply with several legal requirements when moving funds between bank and securities accounts. These financial disclosure laws assist investigative and enforcement personnel in tracking funds, particularly black and gray money that's being laundered. The information is maintained in the U.S. Treasury Department's computerized Treasury Enforcement Communications System (TECS).

These disclosures are made on several nontax Treasury forms, all of which are made available to other federal agencies on request.

Treasury Form 4789: Currency Transaction Report. CTR must be completed and filed by a financial institution whenever there is a financial transaction of more than $3000.

Customs Form 4790: Report of the International Transportation of Currency or Other Monetary Instruments. CMIR must be completed and filed whenever currency or other payment of more than $3000 is received into or sent from a bank or other financial account or when a monetary instrument (i.e., cashier's check) is purchased.

Treasury Form 90-22.1: Report of Foreign Bank and Financial Accounts. This report must be completed and filed whenever a U.S. taxpayer or U.S. stockholder of a controlled foreign corporation maintains a bank or other financial account outside the United States.

Until recently, U.S. financial institutions were required by law to report all transactions over $10,000. Today the amount has been reduced to only $3000, creating an enormous time-consuming burden for financial institutions to satisfy and a significantly bigger information-monitoring task. Banks have been known to restructure customer transactions when possible to avoid this requirement.

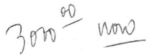

6
International Tax Planning

The typical tax haven user—whether American, Australian, Canadian, or British—is seeking some form of refuge from taxation. Taxpayers from high-tax jurisdictions often explore new means to reduce their tax liability to their homeland. In all taxing countries, new laws arise from the government's desire to curb tax avoidance by redefining what is taxed and how.

In the United States, the Internal Revenue Service (IRS) has imposed many policies and laws structured to collect more tax dollars and discourage people from trying to avoid what the government feels they should be paying. The ideal balance is to collect the maximum tax dollars from the greatest number of people and with minimal objection.

Simply going offshore does not allow taxpayers to circumvent their tax obligation. U.S. citizens are required by law to pay taxes on income regardless of its source. Unfortunately, the tax laws in the United States are very sophisticated and complex, aimed at collecting more taxes and discouraging the meek. It's advisable to hire the services of a professional accountant who possesses expertise in international tax planning.

There are certain tax laws, procedures, and loopholes that every offshore investor should be aware of. The more common ones are examined in this chapter.

Controlled Foreign Corporation (CFC) Tax

Subpart F of the Internal Revenue Code was enacted to tax U.S. shareholders on undistributed profits of foreign corporations regardless of whether a dividend is paid. This measure prevents majority owners of foreign corporations to accumulate profits and delay paying taxes until they choose to declare a dividend.

The IRS defines a CFC as a corporation having more than 50 percent of its outstanding voting shares owned by a maximum of five U.S. citizens. A U.S. stockholder is defined as an American who directly or indirectly owns 10 percent or more of the voting stock.

On the surface, this measure effectively bars tax avoidance. It subjects the U.S. shareholder's interest in a foreign corporation to federal income tax on certain profits as they are earned and as defined from foreign-based sales and services income, passive income, income from a U.S. trade or business, income from a foreign personal holding company, and income from most shipping and underwriting activities. (Passive income is produced from royalties, interest payments, rents, and dividends, as opposed to an operating enterprise.)

Activities that do *not* incur income tax in U.S.-controlled foreign corporations until profits are distributed include manufacturing, oil drilling, mining, banking, finance, and shipping. Also, a tax haven company is not immediately liable for income tax for services performed in the jurisdiction where it is chartered or if it is importing and exporting between unrelated parties. Under these circumstances a tax haven corporation can accumulate profits and defer the tax obligation indefinitely.

A third possibility for avoiding the CFC tax is for U.S. shareholders to relinquish direct control of the foreign corporation. Here, again, taxes can be deferred indefinitely or until the corporation is sold or liquidated. Thomas P. Azzara's *Tax Havens of the World* gives an example of how a U.S. shareholder can effectively own 50 percent of an offshore corporation and still retain ultimate control over its management.

Consider Azzara's suggestion for a moment. The U.S. shareholder is permitted to own up to and including 50 percent of the voting stock of the corporation. Although still not majority control, it is considerable interest. The U.S. shareholder brings in another stockholder, a foreign person or corporation, to take possession of the remaining 50 percent of the voting shares. The bylaws of the offshore corporation call for the shareholders to elect two directors who will sit on the board and manage the corporation's affairs. The articles also stipulate that an additional, nonelected director may be appointed by the U.S. director. Although the U.S. director-shareholder cannot influence the third director's decisions or vote, he or she does have the power to replace this party or appoint another one. This strategy amounts to indirect rather than direct control, but ultimately gives the U.S. director the upper hand.

Azzara's book is suggested reading for every serious offshore investor.

It may be purchased by sending $50 to Tax Haven Reporter, P.O. Box SS-6781, Nassau, Bahamas, (809) 327-7359. *Tax Haven Reporter,* edited by Azzara, is a monthly newsletter covering tax havens, taxes, and strategies. An annual subscription is just 100 well-invested dollars.

There are two other acceptable methods for a U.S. stockholder to own shares in a foreign corporation. They fall under the attribution of ownership rule [IRC 958(a)] and the constructive ownership rule [IRC 958(b)].

Foreign Personal Holding Company (FPHC) Tax

The foreign personal holding company derives its income from passive sources such as dividends, interest, royalties, annuities, profits from stock sales, securities, certain commodity profits, rents, income from sale of an estate or trust, certain personal service contract monies, and a few other sources.

A U.S. shareholder is taxed on a proportionate share of the undistributed income if a maximum of five U.S. citizens owns 50 percent or more of the value of the outstanding stock and if at least 60 percent of the gross income is FPHC income.

As with the CFC, the FPHC tax can be circumvented by not directly controlling the corporation or by attribution, which allows the shareholder to own more than a controlling interest in the corporation through family. Of course, the stock could be owned by still another corporation, or a trust could be inserted to avoid ownership control.

Remember, if you are paying taxes now on the undistributed profits, you are not immediately receiving the money, and you will pay taxes again when a dividend is declared.

Passive Foreign Investment Company (PFIC) Tax

Regardless of the number of shares held by Americans, if 75 percent of a foreign corporation's income is from passive sources or more than half its assets contribute to the creation of that income, the U.S. citizen owning shares will pay taxes on the proportionate amount along with interest when profits are no longer deferred.

Accumulated Earnings (AE) Tax

The AE tax is intended to discourage accumulated earnings so that funds will be reinvested or distributed and/or taxed. U.S. and foreign corporations are subject to the AE tax, but it applies only on U.S. income. The IRS computes the tax at 27.5 percent up to the first $100,000 of accumulated income and 38.5 percent over this amount.

Effectively-Connected-with-U.S. Tax

If a foreign corporation is "effectively connected with a U.S. business" and has U.S. stockholders, a tax is incurred on the company's U.S. income.

Foreign Source and U.S. Income

By establishing a tax haven corporation, U.S. shareholders can acquire assets and income in the company, protect themselves from creditors, exercise control at arm's length, and gain favorable treatment from foreign tax laws and government regulations.

A tax haven corporation is not subject to U.S. federal taxes unless it maintains a presence (office or branch) in the country. However, if that same corporation earns income from U.S. sources, regardless of whether it has a presence there, its U.S.-sourced income is subject to the prevailing withholding tax. Of course, if the incorporating jurisdiction has tax treaties with the United States (see below), it is likely that the tax liability will be less or eliminated by exemption.

Foreign-Earned Income of an Individual

A U.S. citizen who is a foreign resident meeting the IRS foreign residency test can be exempt on up to $70,000 in foreign earned income per year. The amount depends on the citizen's personal status. This exemption is especially attractive to an expatriate or patriot living abroad who has interests in one or more foreign corporations. In some countries, a person can live lavishly on the exempt amount.

Tax Treaties

There are numerous tax treaties between the United States and other countries. Commonly referred to as double-taxation agreements, they provide that American taxpayers living within the United States can receive a foreign tax credit for all foreign taxes that qualify.

The treaties come in different shapes and sizes, stipulating different terms and conditions. But they are useful in tax planning. You may take the foreign tax as a foreign tax credit or as a deduction. The credit directly offsets your U.S. income, whereas a deduction brings down the taxable amount.

Consult with a tax haven accountant to learn more about the conditions and restrictions of a tax treaty in effect with the United States. Non-Americans should inquire about existing treaties with their own country too.

Tax treaties sometimes include exchange-of-information clauses that allow three possible methods for the exchange of information between countries: routine or automatic transmittal of information, requests for specific information, and spontaneous exchange of information. Fortunately, the exchange of information between most treaty signers has not been perfected, and there are still some obstacles to a home government's efforts to freely obtain what otherwise is regarded as confidential and safeguarded by local laws and judicial practices.

U.S. Taxpayers

U.S. taxpayers engaging in international transactions are required to report certain income(s), profit(s), transfer(s), and other information to the IRS. The following IRS forms are involved:

Form 5471—used when acquiring or disposing of an interest in a foreign corporation, when a controlled foreign corporation conducts certain transactions, and when declaring income received from a foreign corporation. Previously, there were five forms for reporting the same information (Forms 959, 958, 2952, 957, and 3646).

Forms 926 and 3520—used when transferring property as a foreign entity.

Form 3520A—used to declare income of a foreign trust when a U.S. taxpayer holds an interest.

Forms 1042 and 1042S—used when payments are made to a foreign person.

Forms 1020NR (corporation) and 1040NR (individual)—used for receipt of U.S. income or foreign effectively-connected-with income by a resident or nonresident alien, respectively.

International tax laws are far too extensive to be adequately covered in this book. Although plenty complex, they are not totally incomprehensible to a person willing to spend the time and energy to learn more. Thomas Azzara's informative book and newsletter, mentioned earlier, are a good beginning. Another fine resource for timely tax information is Marshall J. Langer's *Practical International Tax Planning*, which is regularly updated with supplements. The subscription is several hundred dollars per year, but worth the price. Write or call Practising Law Institute, 810 Seventh Avenue, New York, NY 10019. Or check the public library for a copy. If your accountant doesn't subscribe to this publication, it's doubtful that he or she is making a livelihood from international tax planning.

The best approach is to stay abreast of the laws by subscribing to such tax information services *and* to retain knowledgeable professionals. Then you can function intelligently and be able to contribute your own suggestions and ideas so that the end results match or exceed your expectations. The financial gains will more than reward the energy you expend.

7
Traveling to Your Tax Haven Country

A side benefit to doing business from a tax haven is the option of traveling to it, for pleasure or business. The word *option* should be stressed, since it's unnecessary to visit your chosen oasis simply because you bank there or because your offshore company is incorporated or managed from there.

But if you do enjoy traveling, it's a good excuse to take a trip. This will depend, of course, on which tax haven you've selected to do business in. You most likely won't want to go to Nauru (Guam), since there is absolutely nothing to see. For that matter, officials probably won't allow you to visit.

The information provided in this chapter, including the currency and international time of a country, will always prove handy when doing business with a tax haven. The chapter also gives tourist office addresses and telephone numbers, passport and visa requirements, and airline service information for planning a trip.

Travel Guides and Advisories

The U.S. State Department issues travel advisories and warnings for Americans contemplating entering certain countries where political or other conditions could be dangerous to their well-being. The advisories describe the situation and in some instances make recommendations for those who must travel regardless of the instability of the country.

Although few tax havens are on this list (Malaysia, Cyprus, and Sri Lanka in the early 1990s), they are usually the more obscure locales. These advisories and warnings change and are regularly updated. For more information, call the State Department's hotline (202-647-5225) from a touch-tone telephone.

Travel books are useful tools for planning a trip. Fodor's publishes travel guides that cover the most desirable tax havens mentioned here. Read up before taking off. Remember, though, that your experiences will likely seem different from those described by a travel writer. Travel guides have a tendency to sell tourism rather than paint a straightforward picture.

Plan the trip in a season that you'll enjoy. A travel guide will provide a good description of the seasons in a given country. Prior to departure, get a weather report. This will influence how you pack.

USA Today's WeatherTrak system is an information service providing weather reports, forecasts, currency exchange, and State Department advisories on over 700 cities worldwide. The system is completely computerized. To select a city, you merely input a three-digit code on a touch-tone phone. A prerecorded message provides you with the access code. Call 900-370-8725. Since this is a 900 number, there will be a per-minute charge on your telephone bill.

Tourist offices gladly send inquirers colorful brochures, lists of accommodations and rates, helpful guides, and other promotional pieces. Write them well in advance of your trip. The information will likely be interesting and useful for planning local activities.

Credit cards are a convenient way to spend money when abroad, alleviating the necessity to take along large amounts of cash. Carry most of your cash in the form of traveler's checks for peace of mind and protection. Convert only a reasonable amount to the local currency upon arriving. Prepay accommodations and other anticipated expenses if possible to reduce the need to carry cash.

Before leaving, advise a family member or friend of where you are going in the event of an emergency—which includes running low on funds.

Visas, Customs, and Insurance

Know the passport and visa requirements of each country you propose visiting. The requirements listed in this chapter for 32 tax haven countries are courtesy of the U.S. State Department and are current as of June 1990.

Whenever you travel abroad, it is wise to take adequate identification, including a valid passport, other proof of citizenship, and a second photo ID (i.e., driver's license). Although some countries require only proof of citizenship, as is the case for Americans going to the Bahamas, a passport is still advisable. It is the best form of identification when traveling. Some countries also require proof of return passage—in other words, a round-trip or onward ticket.

Know whether a visa or visitor's permit will be required for the intended stay. If so, make arrangements to get it prior to departure from your home country. If it is impossible to obtain a visa before leaving because you are hopping from country to country, you can often secure one after arrival from the local U.S. or other embassy.

Medical requirements also vary from country to country. A vaccination or AIDS test may be mandatory, depending on the length of stay. Call the host country's embassy in the United States or consult a travel agent. For a current health advisory, call the International Traveler's Hotline of the U.S. Centers for Disease Control (404-332-4559) from a touch-tone phone.

Before making too many purchases, always tempting in a foreign land, know the customs limits and the duties associated with various items. An American returning from the Bahamas can bring back up to $400 worth of Bahamian merchandise duty-free—if the stay was longer than 48 hours. Travelers over 21 years old can also return with a liter of booze and 200 cigarettes. Every country has its own restrictions.

If you plan to drive, know something about the rules and be prepared for the unexpected. In the Bahamas, motorists drive on the left-hand side of the street. This can be very confusing to an American pedestrian. Unsuspecting sightseers are often shocked when they look one way, step into the street thinking it's safe, and discover a speeding Bahamian coming from the other direction. Before renting a car, decide whether you want to take the risks. Public transportation, if adequate, may be a better alternative. Numerous American travelers have been killed in auto accidents abroad because of their unfamiliarity with local custom.

If you do decide to drive, you must first obtain an international driving permit from a local AAA office (the national motor club). Two-color or black-and-white passport-size photos are required, along with a modest fee. The permit is issued on the spot. This official-looking document must accompany a valid driver's license in order to operate a vehicle abroad. It's good for one year.

American travelers abroad can benefit from AAA membership. The club publishes informative material for foreign travelers and also provides postal service abroad, so that you can receive mail while on the go.

Decide if insurance will be necessary. Several companies offer accident, health, lost luggage, and trip cancellation coverage. Refer to Fodor's travel guide or a local travel agent for further details.

If you are traveling on business, contact local businesspeople in advance of your arrival. Most likely they will be very cordial and will look forward to meeting you. A business lunch or dinner may even be appropriate and can help cement a relationship better than long-distance communications. It's always nice to meet the people you do business with. Bring corporate papers, business information, a telephone directory, or whatever else may be useful, so that everything needed to do business is at hand. There's nothing more frustrating than forgetting something important!

Study the locale where you're headed. If you are traveling to Europe to visit a tax haven, you can safely anticipate a reasonable level of sophistication, particularly in the business world. This comment extends to the neighboring tax havens that cater to rich Europeans and international professionals and businesspeople.

Professionals in the Caribbean and South Pacific tax havens are also accustomed to a sophisticated clientele from abroad. Local residents, however, may be less polished and less motivated. In most of these locales, people operate on "island time," which basically means that they're in no rush. For someone who's unaccustomed to their ways, the experience can be exasperating. Unfortunately, that won't change tradition. It's safe to say, "When in Rome, do as the Romans." You'll enjoy your trip more.

Tax Havens to Visit

The British Embassy in the United States is a primary resource for passport and travel information on tax havens, since more than half are current or former British dependencies. Local embassies can also provide colorful information. All international times are given in relation to Eastern Standard Time (EST).

Anguilla

Tourist Offices: Anguilla Tourist Office, The Valley, Anguilla, BWI. Tel: (809) 497-2759. Fax: (809) 497-2751.
USA—Anguilla Tourist Information and Reservation Office, c/o Medhurst & Associates, Inc., 271 Main Street, Northport, NY 11768. Tel: (212) 869-0402, (516) 261-1234, (800) 553-4939. Fax: (516) 261-9606.
United Kingdom—Anguilla Tourist Office, 3 Epirus Road, London SW6 7UJ. Tel: 44-71-937-7725. Fax: 44-71-938-4793.

Passport and Visa Information: Proof of U.S. citizenship, photo ID, onward/return transportation, and sufficient funds to stay up to 6 months.

For additional information, consult British Embassy, 3100 Massachusetts Avenue NW, Washington, DC 20008. Tel: (202) 462-1340.

Currency: Eastern Caribbean dollar. U.S. currency is generally accepted
throughout the island.

International Time: 1 hour ahead of EST.

Airline Service: American Eagle, Windward Islands Airways, Air BVI,
LIAT, Air Anguilla, Tyden Air.

Antigua and Barbuda

Tourist Offices: Antigua and Barbuda Tourist Office, Box 373, St. Johns,
Antigua, BWI. Tel: (809) 463-0480.
USA—610 Fifth Avenue, Suite 311, New York, NY 10020. Tel. (212) 541-
4117.
Canada—60 St. Clair Avenue, Suite 205, Toronto, Ontario MT4 1N5.
Tel: (416) 961-3085.
United Kingdom—Antigua House, 15 Thayer Street, London W1. Tel:
44-71-486-7073.

Passport and Visa Information: Proof of U.S. citizenship and onward/re-
turn ticket or funds required for tourist stay up to 6 months. AIDS test
required for university students and others suspected of having HIV
virus; U.S. test accepted. For further information, contact the Embassy
of Antigua and Barbuda, Intelsat Bldg., 3400 International Drive NW,
Suite 4M, Washington, DC 20008. Tel: (202) 362-5122/5166/5211.

Currency: Eastern Caribbean dollar.

International Time: 1 hour ahead of EST.

Airline Service: Local and regional—daily LIAT flights from Antigua
and Barbuda. International destinations—American Airlines, Eastern
Airlines, BWIA, Air Canada, British Airways, Lufthansa. Charter service
is also available.

Aruba

Tourist Offices:
USA—Aruba Tourist Information, 521 Fifth Avenue, 12th Floor, New
York, NY 10175. Tel: (212) 246-3030, (800) TO-ARUBA.
Canada—1801 W. Englington Street, Toronto, Ontario M6E 2H7. Tel:
(416) 782-9954.

Passport and Visa Information: Visas are not required. An American entering for a temporary visit must have a valid passport, birth certificate,
or other proof of citizenship and a ticket indicating onward passage.
Departure tax when leaving Aruba is $9.50. For further information,

consult Royal Netherlands Embassy, 4200 Linnean Avenue NW, Washington, DC 20008. Tel: (202) 244-5300.

Currency: Aruban florin.

International Time: 1 hour ahead of EST.

Airline Service: ALM, Continental Airlines, BWIA.

Austria

Tourist Offices:
USA—Austrian National Tourist Office, 500 Fifth Avenue, Ste. 2009, New York, NY 10110. Tel: (212) 944-6880.
Canada—1010 W. Sherbrooke Street, Suite 1140, Montreal, Quebec H3A 247. Tel: (514) 849-3709.
United Kingdom—30 St. George Street, London W1R 0AL. Tel: 44-71-629-0461.

Passport and Visa Information: Passport required. Visa not required for stay up to 3 months. For longer stays, check with Embassy of Austria, 2343 Massachusetts Avenue NW, Washington, DC 20008. Tel: (202) 232-2674.

Currency: Schilling.

International Time: 6 hours ahead of EST.

Airline Service: Air Canada, British Airways, Austrian Airlines, TWA.

Bahamas

Tourist Offices:
USA—150 E. 52nd Street, New York, NY 10022. Tel: (212) 758-2777.
Canada—1255 Phillips Square, Montreal, Quebec PQ H3B 3G1. Tel: (514) 861-6797. Or 121 Block Street East, Toronto, Ontario M4W 3M5. Tel: (416) 968-2999.
United Kingdom—10 Chesterfield Street, London W1X 8AH. Tel: 44-71-629-5238.

Passport and Visa Information: Proof of U.S. citizenship, photo ID, and onward/return ticket required for tourist stay up to 8 months. Passport and residence/work permit needed for residence and business. Permit also required to import pets. Departure tax of $5 is paid at airport. For further information, contact Embassy of the Commonwealth of the Bahamas, 600 New Hampshire Avenue NW, Suite 865, Washington, DC 20037. Tel: (202) 944-3390.

Currency: Bahamian dollar.

International Time: EST.

Airline Service: From USA—Delta, Eastern Airlines, Midway, TWA, Bahamasair, Aero Coach, Chalk's International, Carnival Airlines, Comair. From Canada—Air Canada.

Barbados

Tourist Offices: Barbados Board of Tourism, P.O. Box 242, Harbour Road, Bridgetown, Barbados, WI. Tel: (809) 427-2623/4. Telex: WB 2420. Fax: (809) 426-4080.
USA—800 Second Avenue, New York, NY 10017. Tel: (212) 986-6516/8, (800) 221-9831. Telex: 023-666-387. Fax: (212) 573-9850.
Canada—Suite 1508, Box 11, 20 Queen Street West, Toronto, Ontario M2N 6L9. Tel: (416) 512-6569, (800) 268-9122. Telex: 021-06-218247. Fax: (416) 512-6581.
United Kingdom—263 Tottenham Court Road, London W1P 9AA. Tel: 44-71-636-9448/9. Telex: 051-262081. Fax: 44-71-637-1496.

Passport and Visa Information: Travelers coming directly from the USA to Barbados may enter for up to 3 months with proof of U.S. citizenship, photo ID, and onward/return ticket. A passport is required for longer visits and other types of travel. Business visas are $25 single entry, $30 multiple entry (may require work permit). Departure tax of $10 is paid at airport. Check information with Embassy of Barbados, 2144 Wyoming Avenue NW, Washington, DC 20008. Tel: (202) 939-9200.

Currency: Barbadian dollar.

International Time: 1 hour ahead of EST.

Airline Service: Local and regional—LIAT, Aeropostal, Air Martinique. International—American Airlines, Air Canada, British Airways, BWIA, Canadian Holidays.

Bermuda

Tourist Offices: Bermuda Department of Tourism, Global House, 43 Church Street, Hamilton HM BX, Bermuda.
USA—310 Madison Avenue, Suite 201, New York, NY 10017. Tel: (800) 223-6107.
Canada—1200 Bay Street, Suite 1004, Toronto, Ontario M5R 2A5. Tel: (416) 923-9600.
United Kingdom—Bermuda Tourism, BCB Ltd., 1 Battersea Church Road, London SW11 3LY. Tel: 44-71-734-8813.

Passport and Visa Information: Proof of U.S. citizenship, photo ID, and onward/return ticket required for tourist stay up to 6 months. Departure tax of $10 is paid at airport. For further information, consult British Embassy, 3100 Massachusetts Avenue NW, Washington, DC 20008. Tel: (202) 462-1340.

Currency: Bermuda dollar.

International Time: 1 hour ahead of EST.

Airline Service: From USA—Delta, USAir, American Airlines, Continental. From Canada—Air Canada. From United Kingdom—British Airways.

British Virgin Islands

Tourist Offices: BVI Tourist Board, P.O. Box 134, Road Town, Tortola, BVI. Tel: (809) 494-3134.
USA—370 Lexington Avenue, Suite 511, New York, NY 10017. Tel: (212) 696-0400.
Canada—BVI Information Office, 801 York Mill Road, Suite 201, Don Mills, Ontario M3B 1X7. Tel: (416) 283-2235.
United Kingdom—26 Hockerill Street, Bishops Stortford, Herts, CM23 2DW. Tel: 44-279-45969. Fax: 44-279-506616.

Passport and Visa Information: Proof of U.S. citizenship, photo ID, onward/return ticket and sufficient funds required for tourist stay up to 3 months. AIDS test required for residency or work; U.S. test accepted. For further information consult British Embassy, 3100 Massachusetts Avenue NW, Washington, DC 20008. Tel: (202) 462-1340.

Currency: U.S. dollar.

International Time: 1 hour ahead of EST.

Airline Service: American Eagle, Air BVI, LIAT, Eastern Metro, VI Seaplane.

Cayman Islands

Tourist Offices:
USA—Cayman Islands Department of Tourism, 420 Lexington Avenue, Suite 2733, New York, NY 10017. Tel: (212) 682-5582.
Canada—234 E. Edington Avenue, Suite 306, Toronto, Ontario M4P 1K5. Tel: (416) 485-1550.
United Kingdom—Trevor House, 100 Brompton Road, Knightsbridge, London SW3 1EX. Tel: 44-71-584-4463.

Passport and Visa Information: Proof of U.S. citizenship, photo ID, onward/return transportation and sufficient funds required for stay up to 6 months. For additional information, consult British Embassy, 3100 Massachusetts Avenue NW, Washington, DC 20008. Tel: (202) 462-1340.

Currency: Cayman Islands dollar.

International Time: EST.

Airline Service: Cayman Airlines, Northwest Airlines, American Airlines, Air Jamaica.

Channel Islands

Tourist Offices: States of Jersey Tourism Committee, Weighbridge, St. Helier, Jersey. Tel: 44-534-24779. States of Guernsey Tourist Information Bureau, Crown Pier, St. Peter Port, Guernsey.
United Kingdom—Jersey Tourism Office, 35 Albemarle Street, London. Tel: 44-71-493-5278.

Passport and Visa Information: Passport required. Visa not required for stay up to 6 months. For additional information, consult British Embassy, 3100 Massachusetts Avenue NW, Washington, DC 20008. Tel: (202) 462-1340.

Currency: Jersey pound and Guernsey pound.

International Time: 5 hours ahead of EST.

Airline Service: British Airways via London to Jersey; Guernsey Airlines from London to Guernsey.

Cook Islands

Tourist Offices: Cook Islands Tourist Authority, P.O. Box 14, Rarotonga, Cook Islands. Tel: 682-29435. Fax: 682-21435.

Passport and Visa Information: Passport, onward/return ticket, and confirmed reservations required. Visa not needed for visit up to 30 days. For longer stays and other information, contact Consulate, Kamehameha Schools, #16 Kapalama Heights, Honolulu, HI 96817. Tel:(808) 847-6377.

Currency: New Zealand dollar.

International Time: 16½ hours ahead of EST.

Airline Service: Air New Zealand, Cook Islands International, Hawaiian Airlines, Polynesian Airlines.

Costa Rica

Tourist Offices: Costa Rican Tourist Board, Plaza de la Cultura, 5th Street, Central and 2nd Avenue, San José, Costa Rica. Tel: 506-23-1733, ext. 277.
USA—1101 Brickel Avenue, Boulevard Tower, Suite 801, Miami, FL 33131. Tel: (305) 358-2150.

Passport and Visa Information: Passport and visa or tourist card required. Tourist cards for stay up to 30 days may be purchased from most airlines or at airport on arrival. U.S. citizens must have onward/return ticket and $300 as proof of solvency. Business travelers must register with local authorities. Visitors staying over 60 days must have AIDS test performed in Costa Rica. For travel with children or pets, contact Embassy of Costa Rica, 1825 Connecticut Avenue NW, Suite 211, Washington, DC 20009. Tel: (202) 328-6628, 234-2945.

Currency: Colon.

International Time: 1 hour behind EST (CST).

Airline Service: Eastern Airlines, LASCA (national airline).

Gibraltar

Tourist Offices: Gibraltar Tourist Office, Cathedral Square, Gibraltar. Tel: 350-4623.
United Kingdom—Arundel Great Court, 179 The Strand, London WC2R 1EH. Tel: 44-71-836-0777.

Passport and Visa Information: Passport required. Visa not required for tourist stay up to 6 months. For further information, consult British Embassy, 3100 Massachusetts Avenue NW, Washington, DC 20008. Tel: (202) 462-1340.

Currency: Gibraltar pound.

International Time: 6 hours ahead of EST.

Airline Service: British Airways, Gibraltar Airways.

Hong Kong

Tourist Offices: Macao Tourist Information Board (better information than tourist board in Hong Kong), Arrival Wharf, Shun Tak Centre. Tel: (852) 540-8180/8196.
USA—Hong Kong Tourist Association, 590 Fifth Avenue, New York, NY 10036. Tel: (212) 869-5008.
Canada—Hong Kong Tourist Association, 347 Bay Street, Suite 909, Toronto, Ontario M5H 2R7. Tel: (416) 366-2389.
United Kingdom—Macao Tourist Information Board, 22A Devonshire Street, London W1N 1RL. Tel: 44-71-224-3390.

Passport and Visa Information: Passport and onward/return transportation by sea or air required. Visa not required for tourist stay up to 1 month; may be extended to 3 months. Confirmed hotel and flight reservations recommended during peak travel months. Departure tax of $7 is paid at airport. Visa required for work or study. For other types of travel, consult British Embassy, 3100 Massachusetts Avenue NW, Washington, DC 20008. Tel: (202) 462-1340.

Currency: Hong Kong dollar.

International Time: 13 hours ahead of EST.

Airline Service: United Airlines, Cathay Pacific, 36 other international airlines.

Ireland

Tourist Offices: Bord Failte, Irish Tourist Board, P.O. Box 273, Dublin 8, Ireland. Tel: 353-1-765871. Telex: 93755. Fax: 353-1-7674764.
USA—Irish Tourist Board, 757 Third Avenue, New York, NY 10017. Tel: (212) 418-0800.
Canada—Irish Tourist Board, 10 King Street East, Toronto, Ontario M5C 1C3. Tel: (416) 364-1301. Telex: 06-22084.
United Kingdom—150 New Bond Street, London W1Y 0AQ. Tel: 44-71-493-3201. Telex: 266410. Fax: 44-71-493-9065.

Passport and Visa Information: Passport required. Visa not needed for stay up to 90 days, but onward/return ticket may be requested. For further information, consult Embassy of Ireland, 2234 Massachusetts Avenue NW, Washington, DC 20008. Tel: (202) 462-3939.

Currency: Irish pound (punt).

International Time: 5 hours ahead of EST.

Airline Service: Aer Lingus, Delta, charter flights.

Isle of Man

Tourist Offices: British Tourist Authority, 40 W. 57th St., 3rd Fl., New York, NY 10019. Tel: (212) 581-4700.

Passport and Visa Information: Passport required. Visa not required for stays up to 3 months.

Currency: Isle of Man pound.

International Time: 5 hours ahead of EST.

Airline Service: British Airways, Manx Airlines.

Liechtenstein

Tourist Offices: Liechtenstein National Tourist Office, FL-9490 Vadus, Liechtenstein. Tel: 41-75-21443. Telex: 889488. Fax: 41-75-66460.

Passport and Visa Information: Passport required. Visa not required for tourist or business stay up to 3 months. For further information, consult

Embassy of Switzerland, 2900 Cathedral Avenue NW, Washington, DC 20008. Tel: (202) 745-7900.

Currency: Swiss franc.

International Time: 6 hours ahead of EST.

Airline Service: Excellent air service from Austria or Switzerland.

Luxembourg

Tourist Offices: National Tourist Office of the Grand Duchy of Luxembourg, Aerogare bus depot, Place de la Gare 51, Luxembourg City, Luxembourg. Tel: 352-48-79-99.
USA—Luxembourg Tourist Information Office, 801 Second Avenue, New York, NY 10017. Tel: (212) 370-9850.
United Kingdom—36-37 Piccadilly, London W1V 9PA. Tel: 44-71-434-2800.

Passport and Visa Information: Passport required. Visa not required for tourist or business stay up to 3 months. For additional information, contact Embassy of Luxembourg, 2000 Massachusetts Avenue NW, Washington, DC 20008. Tel: (202) 265-4171.

Currency: Luxembourg franc.

International Time: 5 hours ahead of EST.

Airline Service: Luxair, Air France, British Airways, Icelandair, Lufthansa.

Malta

Tourist Offices: National Tourism Organization, 280 Republic Street, Valletta, Malta. Tel: 365-224444/5. Telex: 1105 Holiday MW. Fax: 356-220401.
USA—Maltese Consulate, 249 E. 35th Street, New York, NY 10016. Tel: (212) 725-2345.
United Kingdom—Malta National Tourist Office, Suite 300, Mappin House, 4 Winsley Street, London W1N 7AR. Tel: 44-71-323-0506. Fax: 44-71-323-9154.

Passport and Visa Information: Passport required. Visa not required for stay up to three months. For additional information, consult Embassy of Malta, 2017 Connecticut Avenue NW, Washington, DC 20008. Tel: (202) 462-3611/2.

Currency: Maltese lira.

International Time: 6 hours ahead of EST.

Airline Service: Air Europe, Air Malta, British Islands Airways, Monarch Airlines.

Monaco

Tourist Offices: 2a Boulevardes Moulins, Monte Carlo, Monaco.
USA—Monaco Government Tourist and Convention Bureau, 845 Third Avenue, New York, NY 10022. Tel: (212) 759-5227.
United Kingdom—3/18 Chelsea Garden Market, Chelsea Harbour, London SW10 0XE. Tel: 44-71-352-9962.

Passport and Visa Information: Passport required. Visa not required for visit up to 3 months. For further information, consult French Embassy, 4101 Reservoir Road NW, Washington, DC 20007. Tel: (202) 944-6000.

Currency: French franc.

International Time: 6 hours ahead of EST.

Airline Service: Serviced by airport at Nice, France, only 10 minutes away.

Montserrat

Tourist Offices: Montserrat Tourist Board, P.O. Box 7, Plymouth, Montserrat, WI. Tel: (809) 491-2230. Cable: Tourism. Telex: 5720 MNT GOVT.MK.
USA—Tromson Monroe Public Relations, 40 East 49th Street, New York, NY 10017. Tel: (212) 752-8660.
United Kingdom—High Commission for Eastern Caribbean States, 10 Kensington Court, London W8 5DL. Tel: 44-71-937-9522.
Germany—Caribbean Tourism Association, Guteutrabe 45/V1, D-6000 Frankfurt Main 1, Germany.

Passport and Visa Information: Proof of U.S. citizenship, photo ID, onward/return transportation, and sufficient funds required for stay up to 6 months. For additional information, consult British Embassy, 3100 Massachusetts Avenue NW, Washington, DC 20008. Tel: (202) 462-1340.

Currency: Eastern Caribbean dollar.

International Time: 1 hour ahead of EST.

Airline Service: LIAT, Montserrat Air via Antigua.

Nauru

Tourist Offices: Consulate of the Republic of Nauru in Guam, 1st Floor, ADA Professional Building, Marine Drive, Agana, Guam 96910. Tel: 671-649-8300. Or Honorary Consulate, 841 Bishop Street, Suite 506, Honolulu, HI 96813. Tel: (808) 523-7821.

Passport and Visa Information: Passport and visa required. Passengers must have onward/return ticket. For specific information, contact the consulate.

Currency: Australian dollar.

International Time: 16½ hours ahead of EST.

Airline Service: Air Nauru from various points in the Pacific.

Netherlands

Tourist Offices: Central Station, Amsterdam, The Netherlands. Tel: 31-20-24 92 22.
USA—Netherlands Board of Tourism, 355 Lexington Avenue, New York, NY 10017. Tel: (212) 370-7367.
Canada—25 East Adelaide Street, Suite 710, Toronto, Ontario M5C 142. Tel: (416) 363-1577.
United Kingdom—25-28 Buckingham Gate, London SW1E 6LD. Tel: 44-71-630-0451.

Passport and Visa Information: Passport required. Visa not required for tourist or business stay up to 90 days. Tourists may be asked to show onward/return ticket or proof of sufficient funds for stay. For further information, contact Royal Netherlands Embassy, 4200 Linnean Avenue NW, Washington, DC 20008. Tel: (202) 244-5300.

Currency: Dutch guilder.

International Time: 6 hours ahead of EST.

Airline Service: KLM, Northwest Airlines, TWA.

Netherlands Antilles

Tourist Offices: Curaçao Tourist Board, Peater Maai 19, Willemstad, Curaçao. Tel: 599-9-616-000.
USA—Netherlands Board of Tourism, 355 Lexington Avenue, New York, NY 10017. Tel: (212) 370-7367.

Passport and Visa Information: Passport or proof of U.S. citizenship required. Visa not required for stay up to 14 days; may be extended to 3 months after arrival. Tourists may be required to show onward/return ticket or proof of sufficient funds for stay. Departure tax is $10 when leaving Bonaire and Curaçao. For further information, consult Royal Netherlands Embassy, 4200 Linnean Avenue NW, Washington, DC 20008. Tel: (202) 244-5300.

Currency: Netherlands Antilles florin.

International Time: 1 hour ahead of EST.

Airline Service: American Airlines, ALM from New York.

Nevis

Tourist Offices: St. Kitts and Nevis Department of Tourism, P.O. Box 132, Church Street, Bassetarre, St. Kitts, WI. Tel: (809) 465-2620. Or Main Street, Charlestown, Nevis, WI. Tel: (809) 469-5521.
USA—414 E. 75th Street, New York, NY 10021. Tel: (212) 535-1234. Fax: (212) 879-4789.
Canada—11 Yorkville Avenue, Suite 508, Toronto, Ontario M4W 1L3. Tel: (416) 921-7717. Fax: (416) 921-7997.

Passport and Visa Information: Proof of U.S. citizenship, photo ID, and return/onward ticket required for stay up to 6 months. AIDS test required for work permit or residency; U.S. test accepted. For further information, consult Embassy of St. Kitts and Nevis, 2501 M Street NW, Washington, DC 20037. Tel: (202) 833-3550.

Currency: Eastern Caribbean dollar.

International Time: EST.

Airline Service: To St. Kitts—Air St. Kitts–Nevis, Air BVI, American Airlines, American Eagle, BWIA, LIAT, Winair. To Nevis—Air St. Kitts–Nevis, BWIA, Carib Aviation, LIAT, Winair.

Panama

Tourist Offices: Panama Tourist Board, ATLAPA Convention Center, Via Israel, Panama City, Panama. Tel: (507) 26-4002, 26-7000.
USA—2355 Salzedo Street, Suite 305, Coral Gables, FL 33134. Tel: (305) 442-1892/3.

Passport and Visa Information: Passport, tourist card, and onward/return ticket required. Tourist card for 30 days available from Air Panama for $2 fee. For official or diplomatic travel and other information, contact Embassy of Panama, 2862 McGill Terrace NW, Washington, DC 20008. Tel: (202) 483-1407.

Currency: US dollar; Panamanian coins.

International Time: EST

Airline Service: Air Panama, Eastern, Pan Am from Miami.

St. Vincent

Tourist Offices: St. Vincent and Grenadines Tourist Board, P.O. Box 834, Kingstown, St. Vincent, WI. Tel: (809) 457-1502.
USA—801 Second Avenue, New York, NY 10017. Tel: (212) 687-4981.
Canada—100 University Avenue, Suite 504, Toronto, Ontario M5J 1V6. Tel: (416) 971-9666.
United Kingdom—1 Collingham Gardens, London SW5 0HW. Tel: 44-71-370-0925.

Passport and Visa Information: Proof of U.S. citizenship, photo ID, and return/onward ticket required for tourist stay up to 6 months. For further information, check with Consulate of St. Vincent and the Grenadines, 801 Second Avenue, 21st Floor, New York, NY 10017. Tel: (212) 687-4490.

Currency: Eastern Caribbean dollar.

International Time: EST.

Airline Service: LIAT, Air Martinique, Mustique Airways.

Singapore

Tourist Offices: Singapore Tourist Promotion Board, Raffles City Tower, 250 North Bridge Road, Singapore. Tel: 65-339-6622.
USA—590 Fifth Avenue, 12th Floor, New York, NY 10036. Tel: (212) 302-4861.
Canada—175 Bloor Street East, Suite 112, North Tower, Toronto, Ontario M4W 3R8. Tel: (416) 323-9139.

Passport and Visa Information: Passport required. Visa not required for tourist or business stay up to 2 weeks, extendable to 3 months maximum. For further information, contact Embassy of Singapore, 1824 R Street NW, Washington, DC 20009. Tel: (202) 667-7555.

Currency: Singapore dollar.

International Time: 13 hours ahead of EST.

Airline Service: Singapore Airlines, United Airlines.

Switzerland

Tourist Offices: Swiss National Tourist Office, Bahnhofplatz 15, Zurich, Switzerland. Tel: 41-1-211-4000.
USA—608 Fifth Avenue, New York, NY 10020. Tel: (212) 757-5844.
Canada—154 University Avenue, Suite 610, Toronto, Ontario M5H 3Y9. Tel: (416) 971-9734.
United Kingdom—Swiss Centre, 1 New Coventry Street, London W1V 8EE. Tel: 44-71-734-8681.

Passport and Visa Information: Passport required. Visa not required for tourist or business stay up to 3 months. For further information, consult Embassy of Switzerland, 2900 Cathedral Avenue NW, Washington, DC 20008. Tel: (202) 745-7900.

Currency: Swiss franc.

International Time: 6 hours ahead of EST.

Airline Service: Swissair, British Airways, TWA.

Turks and Caicos

Tourist Offices: Turks and Caicos Islands Tourist Board. 425 Madison Avenue, 14th Fl., New York, NY 10017. Tel: (800) 441-4419. Turks and Caicos reservations: (800) 282-4753.

USA—Caribbean Organization, 20 E. 46th Street, New York, NY 10017. Tel: (212) 682-0435.

United Kingdom—West Indian Committee, 48 Albermarle Street, London W1X 4AR. Tel: 44-71-629-6353.

Passport and Visa Information: Proof of U.S. citizenship, photo ID, onward/return transportation, and sufficient funds required for stay up to 6 months. For additional information, consult British Embassy, 3100 Massachusetts Avenue NW, Washington, DC 20008. Tel: (202) 462-1340.

Currency: US dollar.

International Time: EST.

Airline Service: Atlantic Gulf Airlines, British Caribbean Airways.

Vanuatu

Tourist Offices: Tourist Information Bureau, P.O. Box 209, Vila, Vanuatu.

Passport and Visa Information: Passport required. Visa not required for stay up to 30 days. For further information, contact Permanent Mission to the U.N., 416 Convent Avenue, New York, NY 10031. Tel: (212) 926-3311.

Currency: Australian dollar.

International Time: 16 hours ahead of EST.

Airline Service: Air Vanuatu, Air New Guinea.

Western Samoa

Tourist Offices: Western Samoan Visitors Bureau, P.O. Box 2272, Apia, Western Samoa. Tel: 685-20471. Tel./Fax: 685-20886.

Passport and Visa Information: Passport and onward/return ticket required. Visa not required for stay up to 30 days. For longer stays, contact Embassy of Western Samoa, 1155 15th St. NW, Ste. 510, Washington, DC 20005. Tel: (202) 833-1743.

Currency: Tala.

International Time: 16 hours ahead of EST.

Airline Service: Polynesian Airlines, Air Pacific, Air New Zealand, South Pacific Island Airways, Hawaiian Airlines.

PART 2
Profiles of Tax Havens

Major
Tax Havens

Introduction

Part 2 provides indispensable information to assist you in making an intelligent decision on which tax haven(s) will best suit your present requirements. As you review each choice carefully, you will gain an insight into the unique characteristics of these locales. The following areas are spotlighted: geographical, political, legal, economic, financial, and business.

Some countries are faced with domestic circumstances that can very well influence, positively or negatively, the decision to use them as tax havens. Panama, Hong Kong, and Montserrat are notable examples. To a lesser extent, all other countries and sovereignties have internal problems and challenges to contend with.

"Profiles of Tax Havens" covers 32 major tax havens around the world and another baker's dozen of marginal and incidental havens. This last group offers benefits in special circumstances. Adequate information is furnished to make an immediate judgment, so that the most impractical choices can be eliminated without further, time-consuming investigation. Certain countries will stand out as favorable, and it is these havens that should be explored in greater depth.

The profiles are divided into two parts for easier reference. Country profiles begin with a brief introduction describing the location, geography, population, and climate of the jurisdiction in focus. Occasionally, this lead-in will go into greater length when warranted. The country information is broken down to highlight government, legal system, economy, and communications. Business Profiles delve into banking; money and foreign exchange; legal entities; banks, trusts, and insurance companies; taxation; financial and investment incentives; tax treaties; and business contacts.

A closer look at each of these categories will aid in understanding the information provided.

Country Profile

Introduction.   The introduction to each profile describes where the tax haven is located. Frequently, tax havens are tiny islands situated in remote areas that are unfamiliar to many people. The description gives a sufficient bearing to locate the place on a map. Travel time and climate information is supplied to assist those planning a trip.

Government.   Most tax haven islands are British Crown colonies with their own legal systems and autonomy in their daily affairs. The general stability of these jurisdictions is of paramount interest to the offshore investor. Other forms of government may provide the necessary stability as well, but in some countries, if the wind were suddenly to change direction, so would your investments. As you read each description, you will likely form a favorable or unfavorable impression. Tax havens are highly dependent on people's perceptions of their stability.

Legal Systems.   The most popular legal system among tax havens is based on English common law. Its long tradition has great appeal to the offshore investor. In addition, common law stipulates that banks and their employees maintain secrecy regarding the affairs of customers. Trusts are the product of English common law, as opposed to civil or other law.

Economy.   Information is provided on the country's economic stability, which industries it is most dependent upon, and in which direction it may be headed.

Communications.   Excellent communications are important in dealing with a tax haven. Frequently, important information must be transmitted without delay between various international points. Any wrinkles in the line of communications can be expensive. Most tax havens provide good communication and recognize its importance. Unfortunately, there are no guarantees. People, language, time zones, and cultures don't always keep pace with modern-day technology. All of these can affect business progress.

Business Profile

Banking, Money, and Foreign Exchange.   Onshore banking is discussed and the number, size, and names of major banks are identified. Specific bank secrecy laws may be pointed out as an additional attraction. The monetary unit is given, along with any exchange control regulations or requirements. The ability to freely move money in and out of a tax haven may be an important aspect of your decision.

Legal Entities. The corporation, particularly the exempt or offshore corporation, is the principal tax haven vehicle. Pertinent information and instructions are provided. Other, less useful forms of business enterprise may be mentioned as background information. Offshore banking and offshore insurance, when available, are included with organizational information and requirements. Trusts can be established in many havens, but are not of primary importance to most U.S. investors due to lack of tax incentives.

Taxation. Many tax havens have no income or capital gains taxes that affect offshore business. A no-tax haven has none, and a low-tax haven usually exempts tax on offshore activities and profits. A high-tax country that is also considered a tax haven (typically, an industrialized nation) generally offers no tax or low tax on a specific type of entity, thereby creating a unique situation within its tax system.

Financial and Investment Incentives. Tax havens offer financial and investment incentives by the sheer uniqueness of their corporate and tax legislation. These incentives are inviting to foreign business that are accustomed to greater legal restrictions and higher taxes. In addition, some countries offer specific incentives to encourage onshore development and investment. All such opportunities are mentioned.

Tax Treaties. Any relevant tax treaties, such as double-taxation agreements between the tax haven and other countries, are described. Such agreements can provide certain advantages in tax planning. On the other hand, as noted in Part 1, there may be times when a no-tax-treaty country is preferable.

Business Contacts. Names, addresses, and telephone and fax numbers are given for each tax haven. The listings include attorneys, accountants, trust companies, and government offices. These contacts can furnish valuable information on the locale and the nature of their professional services. Additional contacts may be found in Part 3.

For further, in-depth reading on many countries, refer to *Countries of the World* (Detroit, MI: Gale Research, Inc.). This set of directories includes background notes, comprehensive information, and facts and statistics on selected countries compiled by the U.S. State Department. The directories should be available at any large public or university library.

Anguilla

> ### Fast Facts
>
> *Population:* 6883 (1990)
> *Capital and Largest City:* The Valley
> *Language:* English

Country Profile

Anguilla is a stable British colony and cousin to the British Virgin Islands and Montserrat, located in the Leeward Islands intersecting the Greater Antilles and Lesser Antilles in the British West Indies, 170 miles east of Puerto Rico.

Christopher Columbus may have sailed by her, but it was historian Thomas Southey in 1564 who first made reference to the island. English settlers colonized the island in 1650, and it has remained a British colony ever since.

The literacy rate is 80 percent, and the dominant religions are Methodist and Anglican, with a small percentage of other Christian denominations.

The tropical climate of this coral island features modest annual temperature variations of 72° to 85°F and an average rainfall of approximately 30 inches.

Flying time from St. Maarten is 7 minutes; San Juan and Antigua, 1 hour; St. Thomas, 45 minutes; and St. Kitts, 35 minutes.

Government.   This British-associated state is administered by the Anguilla Constitution Order of 1982 and a constitution that went into effect on April 1, 1982. The government structure is similar to that of the British Virgin Islands.

Legal System.   The primary judicial body is the Eastern Caribbean States Supreme Court. It is subject to English common law.

Economy.   During the 1980s, Anguilla experienced steady economic growth, principally from an increase in services and tourism. Salt exports are second to tourism as a chief source of revenue.

Communications.   The direct-dialing system affords instant communication with the world. Central telex and fax services are available.

Business Profile

Banking, Money, and Foreign Exchange. Four commercial banks serve residents on Anguilla: Barclays Bank International PLC, National Bank of Anguilla, Caribbean Commercial Bank, and The Scotia Bank.

The official currency is the East Caribbean (EC) dollar. There is no exchange control. A 2 percent government fee is charged when exchanging East Caribbean dollars for U.S. currency. Bank accounts can be opened in any currency offered by the bank.

There are strict confidentiality laws punishable by large fines and jail terms. Only information needed for a criminal proceeding that would be a triable offense in Anguilla can legally be disclosed. Fines range from $10,000 to $50,000 and a 12-month jail term, depending on whether the violator is a nonprofessional, professional, or corporation. A bank would receive the maximum penalty.

Legal Entities. Anguilla distinguishes between private and public companies.

A private company requires two incorporators. The right to transfer shares must be restricted, and securities may not be offered to the public. A maximum of 50 shareholders is permitted, excluding employees and former employees.

Nominee shareholders are acceptable. Annual financial audits are not required, but disclosure of capital and names of directors, including the number of shares held by each, must be made annually. The company may have limited or unlimited liability.

A public company requires at least five incorporators. Nominee shareholders are permitted, and beneficial owners are held in strict confidence. Detailed, audited financial statements must be disclosed annually.

Corporations may issue different classes of stock, such as common and preferred. Bearer shares may be issued only by a public company. All companies with limited liability must end their name with "Limited." Directors' meetings may be held anywhere, but all companies must maintain a registered office in Anguilla.

Costs are $185 to file for incorporation and $400 annually, making Anguilla one of the best bargains in the Caribbean. Attorneys or management companies will also charge for their services to incorporate and to provide the registered office. Expect to pay an additional $600 and $300, respectively.

Although a private corporation is the most popular form for utilizing Anguilla as an offshore financial center, establishing an insurance company or a bank is another option. Unlike many other tax havens, Anguilla encourages offshore banking. A Class B bank cannot transact business with residents; however, it may maintain an office on the island and employ residents. Minimum capitalization is US $148,000. A bank of this nature pays an annual license fee of $3700. If the bank has no presence on the island other than its resident agent or office, the annual fee is approximately doubled, or $7462. Financial information must be published annually in the *Official Gazette*. The Registrar of Companies also requires an annual return. A restricted Class B license can be obtained, limiting banking business to clients listed on the license. Minimum capitalization is $7400.

A domestic insurance company can be incorporated and licensed at a cost of less than US $7000. Minimum capitalization is $74,000. A marine insurance company costs less to organize. These figures include all government fees, professional and agency fees, and related charges. There is no specific offshore insurance legislation.

For further information and costs for starting a corporation, insurance company, or offshore bank, contact Mitchell's Chambers (Supreme Court Barristers and Solicitors).

Taxation. There is no personal income, capital gains, gift, estate, inheritance, sales, capital transfer, or corporate income tax.

Financial and Investment Incentives. Anguilla has no financial or investment incentives.

Tax Treaties. Anguilla continues its United Kingdom Tax Convention with Denmark, New Zealand, Norway, Sweden, and Switzerland. This treaty provides a maximum withholding tax of 15 percent on dividends. Royalties and technical fees are generally affected.

Double-taxation treaties exist with Barbados, Guyana, Jamaica, Trinidad, and Tobago.

Under the Caribbean Basin Initiative, Anguilla is considering an exchange-of-information agreement with the United States.

Business Contacts

Banking

Charter Bank & Trust Ltd.
P.O. Box 197
The Valley, Anguilla, BWI
Tel: (809) 497-5082/3
Fax: (809) 497-5138
Telex: (809) 497-5138

Swiss-Arab Bank & Trust Co. (WI)
P.O. Box 100
The Valley, Anguilla, BWI

Legal

Mitchell's Chambers
P.O. Box 174
The Valley, Anguilla, BWI

Antigua and Barbuda

```
┌─────────────────────────────────────────────────┐
│                  Fast Facts                      │
│  Population: 100,000 (1990)                       │
│  Capital and Largest City: St. Johns, 30,000 (1988) │
│  Language: English                                │
└─────────────────────────────────────────────────┘
```

Country Profile

Nestled amongst the Leeward Islands, Antigua and Barbuda are separated by 30 miles of Caribbean sea. These low-lying twin islands are made up of limestone and volcanic formations laced by reefs and shoals.

The literacy rate is 90 percent and the dominant religions are Anglican and Roman Catholic.

The tropical climate produces low humidity, with an average year-round daytime temperature of 76°F.

The picturesque, British-influenced islands are readily accessible by air. Expect 2½ hours from Miami, 3½ hours from New York, 4½ hours from Toronto, and 8 hours from London.

Government. Once a stopover for wayward souls of the sea, Antigua and Barbuda gained their independence from Britain on November 1, 1981. The larger of the two islands received its name in 1493 from discoverer and globetrotter Christopher Columbus, who affectionately called her "Santa Maria de la Antigua."

Hundreds of years later, the islands have developed into a constitutional monarchy and British form of parliamentary government. The government is divided into three branches: legislative, executive, and judicial.

The free election process is well established and continues with stability.

Legal System. Magistrate's Court handles minor offenses, while the High Court deals with major offenses, upholding local parliamentary law. The highest judicial body is the Eastern Caribbean States Supreme Court.

Economy. Today, a significant portion of the economy (roughly 40 percent) is dependent on the lucrative tourist trade, which generates more than 100,000 visitors annually, principally from the United States.

The service industry has replaced agriculture as the leading economic producer. Condominium and time-sharing arrangements account for a good share of the increase; however, renewed emphasis is being placed on agriculture and on manufacturing.

In the past decade, Antigua has emerged as a highly competitive no-tax haven, fully equipped with attractive legislation aimed at international corporations, banks, and insurance companies.

The stable economy produces an annual real growth average of 4.6 percent. Coupled with a sound infrastructure, reliable work force, modern air and port facilities, and state-of-the-art communications, Antigua and Barbuda offer investors a solid foundation to build on.

Communications.   There is international direct dialing from either island, 24 hours a day. Telephone, telex, cable, facsimile, and data services are available.

Business Profile

Banking, Money, and Foreign Exchange.   Full commercial banking services are available on Antigua and Barbuda through Antigua Commercial Bank, Bank of Antigua, Bank of Nova Scotia, Barclays Bank of Commerce, Royal Bank of Canada, and Swiss-American National Bank of Antigua.

Other banks include Antigua Cooperative Bank, Antigua-Barbuda Savings Bank, Antigua International Trust, and Swiss-American Bank Ltd.

The East Caribbean dollar floats against other currencies. Residents may freely purchase sterling pounds, but permission is necessary to purchase other currencies.

Offshore companies can obtain permission to maintain external accounts.

Legal Entities.   The International Business Corporation Act, passed in 1982, is the legislation responsible for encouraging offshore activities. The IBC is empowered to operate outside the islands. This limited-liability corporation is organized by one or two incorporators, residents of Antigua, one of whom must be a lawyer or trust company. In addition, the IBC must have a registered office and resident agent in the country.

Benefits of an IBC include full tax exemption, exemption from exchange control, no minimum capital requirement, no mandatory audit, bearer shares allowed, automatic 50-year tax-free guarantee, and redomiciliation for both Antigua companies and foreign companies desiring to change jurisdiction.

The articles of incorporation are filed with the Director of International Business Corporations along with a US $250 filing fee. The corporation's license must be renewed, and the fee paid, annually.

The corporation can begin operations upon issuance of the certificate of incorporation.

The corporate name must end in a word or abbreviation that is acceptable in any country that identifies the company as having limited liability (Corporation, Corp., Incorporated, Inc., Limited, Ltd., Sociedad Anonima, SA, or some other appropriate choice).

The capital structure of the IBC allows for a minimum of one nonresident shareholder, bearer shares if desired, no minimum capitalization, par or no-par stock, various classes of stock, shares with or without preference, and preemptive rights favoring existing shareholders. Bearer shares must be fully paid up, and registered shares may be paid with a negotiable promissory note.

The board of directors must consist of at least one member. Corporate minutes and resolutions of director(s) must be maintained in Antigua and Barbuda; however, there is no residency requirement. Officers may be elected, or a managing director may substitute.

The annual shareholder meeting and director meetings must be conducted in Antigua and Barbuda; other meetings may be held elsewhere. Telephone meetings are also permitted. Although annual financial statements are not disclosed to the government, shareholders are expected to be given a copy.

Antigua International Trust Ltd. and its affiliate, Swiss-American Bank Ltd., will provide incorporators; the trust also provides full management services. (See the Business Contacts section for complete names and addresses.) An IBC can be organized through a trust company or management company for under US $1000.

IBCs wishing to transact financial business—such as offshore banking, trust company services, or offshore insurance—are required to procure the necessary license. The Supervisor of International Banks and Trust Corporations is responsible for licensing IBCs for offshore banking and trust company activities.

Antigua is not a popular offshore banking center for the simple reason that the capitalization requirements are hefty. An offshore bank must have a minimum capitalization of US $10 million, unless the applicant is a foreign bank with an equal or greater paid-up capital, in which case the offshore Antigua bank must have a minimum $1 million capitalization. The annual license fee is $5000, plus required management fees. Quarterly reports must be filed.

An IBC trust company furnishing trustees or managers must have a minimum paid-up capital of US $500,000. Antigua and Barbuda do not restrict accumulations, and there is no rule against perpetuities. A quarterly return must be filed.

Bank secrecy is very strong, and disclosure of a bank or trust transaction can fetch up to US $18,850 in fines and up to a year in prison under the 1982 Bank and Trust Confidentiality Act.

Offshore insurance companies may provide any form of insurance or conduct any type of insurance business outside the islands. The minimum capitalization is US $250,000. Annual audited reports must be filed with the Supervisor of International Insurance Companies and maintained in strict confidence. Formation costs through a trust or management company are less than $1000.

From the standpoint of organizational costs, Antigua and Barbuda are very reasonable, and annual maintenance and management fees are highly competitive.

Taxation. Antigua and Barbuda effectively became no-tax entities, joining a handful of other no-tax havens worldwide, with the 1982 International Business Corporations Act. A 20-year exemption from taxes, beginning from the day of incorporation, applies to IBCs, offshore banks, qualified trusts, and insurance companies.

Nonresidents can rest assured that they will not be taxed on income, capital gains, or inheritance held by an IBC trust. This tax holiday is for a maximum of 20 years from the incorporation date of the trust company.

Financial and Investment Incentives. Antigua and Barbuda offer numerous financial and investment incentives for businesses directly involved in economic development. These fall under government programs, trade incentives, and regional organizations.

Government programs include fiscal incentives under the Fiscal Incentives Act, reductions on local value-added tax, export allowances, an industrial estates program administered by the Ministry of Economic Development, repatriation of profits granted by the Ministry of Finance, import duty exemptions to foreign investors, and the Hotel Aids Ordinance.

Tax Treaties. Antigua's double-taxation agreements are a major attraction for IBCs. These agreements alleviate being taxed in two jurisdictions, or at least reduce certain income tax. Treaties with industrialized countries include Australia, Canada, Hong Kong, New Zealand, Singapore, the United Kingdom, and the United States.

Business Contacts

Government

Ministry of Economic
  Development and Tourism
Administration Building
Queen Elizabeth Highway
St. Johns, Antigua, WI
Tel: (809) 462-0099
Cable: External Antigua
Telex: AK 2122

Embassy of Antigua and Barbuda
Investment Promotion Office
3400 International Drive NW,
  Suite 2H
Washington, DC 20008
Tel: (202) 362-5122
Telex: 7108 221130
  ANTIBARMISWSH

Government of Antigua and
  Barbuda
Department of Trade and
  Investment
121 SE First Street, Suite 508
Miami, FL 33131
Tel: (305) 381-6762

Antigua Industrial Development
  Board
Newgate Street
St. Johns, Antigua, WI
Tel: (809) 462-1038

Ministry of Finance
Long Street
Antigua, WI
Tel: (809) 462-0092

Banking

Swiss-American Bank Ltd.
Affiliate of Antigua International
  Trust Ltd.
St. Johns, Antigua, WI
Tel: (809) 462-4460
Fax: (809) 462-0274

Bank of Antigua Ltd.
High and Thames streets
St. Johns, Antigua, WI
Tel: (809) 462-4282/3
Nelson's Dockyard
Tel: (809) 463-1367
Fax: (809) 462-0040

Royal Bank of Canada
High and Market streets
St. Johns, Antigua, WI
Tel: (809) 462-0325

Barclays Bank International
High and St. Mary's streets
Antigua, WI
Tel: (809) 462-0432/3/5

Bank of Nova Scotia
High Street
Antigua, WI
Tel: (809) 462-1104/06/08/10

Antigua Overseas Bank Ltd.
High Street and Corn Alley
St. Johns, Antigua, WI
Tel: (809) 462-1652/53
Fax: (809) 462-0804

Canadian Imperial Bank of
  Commerce
High Street and Corn Alley
St. Johns, Antigua, WI
Tel: (809) 462-0998/0836/7

Trust Services

Antigua International Trust Ltd.
P.O. Box 230
St. Johns, Antigua, WI

Antigua Management and Trust
  Ltd.
P.O. Box 1407
St. Johns, Antigua, WI

Accounting

Investor Service Program
Coopers & Lybrand
1800 M Street NW
Washington, DC 20036
Tel: (202) 822-4050
Telex: 440-241-C-LINT

Price Waterhouse
14 Radcliffe Quay
St. Johns, Antigua, WI

Aruba

Fast Facts

Population: 60,000
Capital: Oranjestad
Languages: Papiamento, English, Dutch, and
   Spanish

Country Profile

This lively, resort-dotted southern Caribbean playground rests peacefully in the blue-green sea 12 miles off the Venezuela coast.

The literacy rate is 95 percent. The Roman Catholic, Protestant, and Jewish religions are represented.

Summertime is year round with Aruba's dry and sunny climate. The median temperature change from day to night and from summer to winter is only 3.6 degrees.

Aruba is well connected by air travel between major cities in the United States, Latin America, and Europe.

Government.   Originally one of the islands in the Netherland Antilles, Aruba became a separate entity within the kingdom of the Netherlands on January 1, 1986.

The parliamentary democracy has 21 members. The governor represents the queen of the Netherlands. The Council of Ministers forms the executive power. Aruba offers political stability as a component of the kingdom of the Netherlands.

Legal System.   Aruba's laws and well-developed legal structure are based on the Dutch legal system of civil and penal law.

Economy.   Gold and oil were once the leading economic producers, but today these industries are pages in history. Aruba now works to develop tourism and attract light industry.

Aruba's structure as a tax haven was elevated with the passing of new legislation designed to attract offshore business. More favorable legislation is in the works.

Communications.   Telecommunications are excellent.

Business Profile

Banking, Money, and Foreign Exchange.   There are numerous international and local banks, law firms, accounting firms, and trust companies to service the offshore sector. The monetary unit is the Aruba florin (Afl).

Numbered bank accounts are not permitted. The identity of an account holder must be known. Secrecy is a way of doing business; however, no specific laws enforce it.

Legal Entities.   The passing of the zero-tax-company law gave birth to the Aruba exempt company (AEC), which is limited by shares. Previously, the NV, or *naamloze Vennootschop*, was the vehicle of choice for offshore activities.

The Aruba exempt company has significant advantages over its predecessor, which is still employed for onshore activities, including less regulation and no taxes, making the AEC the best method for utilizing this offshore center.

The AEC has limited liability, may issue different classes of shares (including registered or bearer), and may maintain an office in Aruba. It may not conduct business with residents, however.

One incorporator must have the deed of incorporation, containing the articles of association, notarized in Aruba. This document is then published in the *Official Gazette*. A management company or professional residing on the island should handle this procedure.

Minimum capitalization is Afl 10,000, or approximately US $5600. One share of stock must be issued at the time of incorporation. Shares must be fully paid.

The AEC must always be maintained in good standing by remaining current on all legal requirements of the corporation and by having a local legal representative.

There are no audit requirements or annual financial reporting.

The annual government registration fee for an AEC is Afl 500, or approximately US $285. The company must also be registered at the Commercial Registrar of the Chamber of Commerce; the fee is $40.

Taxation.   There is no corporate income tax on an AEC or personal income tax on its shareholders. There are no withholding taxes of any kind. The zero-tax-corporation law makes Aruba an attractive and competitive tax haven.

Financial and Investment Incentives.   The government offers numerous incentives to new industry.

Tax Treaties.   Aruba's main attraction as a tax haven over the past 30 years rested on a number of treaties that have since terminated. As a result, Aruba took action and implemented offshore legislation. Today, Aruba is a rising tax haven through law rather than mutual agreements with other countries.

Contacts

nt

U.S. Department of Commerce
Desk Officer for Aruba
Room H 3314
Washington, DC 20230
Tel: (202) 377-2527

American Consulate General
Santa Ana Boulevard
P.O. Box 158
Williamstad, Curaçao
Tel: 599-9-613066

Chamber of Commerce and
  Industry
Zoutmanstraat 21
Oranjestad, Aruba
Tel: 2978-21566

Department of Economic Affairs
Commerce and Industry
L. G. Smith Boulevard 82
Oranjestad, Aruba
Tel: 2978-21181

Department of Foreign Affairs
L. G. Smith Boulevard 76
Oranjestad, Aruba
Tel: 2978-24900

Aruba Foreign Investment Agency
85 Nassaustraat
Oranjestad, Aruba
Tel: 2978-26070

Management

European American Management
  Trust NV
Aruba
Tel: 2978-33728

Banking

Aruba Bank NV
41 Nassaustraat
P.O. Box 192
Oranjestad, Aruba
Tel: 2978-21558

Legal

Mr. R. A. Brown
Dominicanessenstraat 2
Oranjestad, Aruba

Mr. C. A. Hese
Emanstraat 112
Oranjestad, Aruba

Austria

Fast Facts

Population: 7,600,000 (1990)
Capital and Largest City: Vienna, 1,550,000
Language: German

Country Profile

Austria is situated in the heart of the European continent. Slightly smaller than Maine, this culturally rich country borders Germany and Czechoslovakia to the north, Italy and Yugoslavia to the south, Switzerland to the west and Hungary to the east.

The hilly lowlands are similar to that of the northeastern United States, with snow in the winter and rain in the summer. The terrain climbs skyward to the peaks of the snow-laden Alps.

The literacy rate is 98 percent, and 89 percent of the population is Roman Catholic.

Government. This politically stable parliamentary democracy consists of nine provinces (Bundeslander) and is divided into three branches. The executive branch includes the federal president, chancellor, and cabinet. The legislative branch is represented by a bicameral federal assembly. Judicial bodies include the Constitutional Court, Administrative Court, and Supreme Court. Executive and legislative powers are divided between the federal government and the provinces.

Political parties represented in the legislature include the Socialist Party, People's Party, and Freedom Party, along with the Green-Alternative Movement, an environmental and antiestablishment group.

Legal System. The legal system is based on the Federal Constitutional Act of 1920, which provides for separate judicial and administrative functions.

Economy. Austria has emerged as one of the wealthiest industrial nations in the world. As the face of Europe changes, Austria is fast gaining recognition as the gateway to eastern Europe. Of course, it is the established hub of international political diplomacy and important business conferences.

The stable economy has demonstrated consistent growth and strength. Investments and exports are directly attributed to economic success.

The investment activity in 1986 accounted for 22.4 percent of the GDP (gross domestic product), high by international standards. Tax incentives help stimulate manufacture of high-technology, consumer, and finished products.

Exports bearing the quality-associated label "Made in Austria"—60 percent of which are destined for EC countries—contribute a whopping 40 percent to the GDP.

Communications. As with most major European countries, communications are excellent.

Business Profile

Banking, Money, and Foreign Exchange. Austria has a highly developed banking system. The Austrian National Bank functions as the country's central banking institution, with power to influence the economy and markets.

The banking system includes savings banks, mortgage banks, postal savings banks, specialized banks offering various types of financing, and commercial banks with a full range of banking services.

Austria is known for its high level of bank secrecy. Over the past decade, it has attracted depositors away from Switzerland, mainly because of negative publicity and pressure applied on that country by the U.S. government. Through it all, Austria has remained untarnished, refusing to divulge confidential information about account holders. Rather than numbered accounts, password accounts provide extra secrecy.

Bank secrecy is regulated by Section 23 of the Austrian Banking Act, which states that

> the banks, their shareholders, their partners, members of their various bodies, employees as well as all other persons in any way acting for the banks may not disclose or make use of secrets which have been entrusted or made accessible to them solely due to the business relationships with customers or pursuant to section 16 subsection 2 [bank secrecy]. If facts which are subject to bank secrecy come to the attention of functionaries of the authorities or of the Austrian National Bank in the course of their professional activities, they shall keep such banking secret as an official secret from which they may be released only in the instances set forth in subsection 2. The obligation to maintain secrecy shall apply without time restriction.

As in most countries, however, exceptions are incorporated in the statutes that permit disclosure of information under certain extreme conditions.

Creditanstalt and other commercial banks that cater to foreigners offer a wide range of services, including interest-bearing individual or joint current and savings accounts in either schillings or a foreign currency.

Investments that can be arranged through an Austrian bank include bearer bonds and bearer mortgage and local-authority bonds, certificates of deposit, mutual funds, stocks, participation certificates, and profit-sharing certificates.

Security accounts may be registered in the name of the depositor or maintained anonymously. In the latter case, the purchase price is deposited in cash with the security order, and a numbered voucher is given as a receipt. A password may be used to protect against unauthorized sales of securities.

Bankhaus Daghofer, with 104 years of service in Salzburg, rigorously protects the anonymity of account holders. A signature is not required to establish an anonymous or deposit account; instead a password is arranged between the client and the bank. This bank extends many diverse services to its clientele.

Foreign exchange controls have been liberalized in capital transactions and in exchange of currencies with countries that are members of the International Monetary Fund (IMF) and the Organization for Economic Cooperation and Development (OECD). However, there are extensive reporting requirements to the Austrian National Bank.

Commercial banks offer many services. Contact individual banks directly for complete information.

Legal Entities. There is no offshore entity in Austria along the lines of the international business corporation (IBC), adopted by many progressive tax havens. However, under special circumstances there may be reason for establishing an Austrian company. Unfortunately, it will be subject to certain taxes.

The limited-liability company (*Gesellschaft mit beschrankter Haftung*), or GesmbH, and the stock corporation (*Aktiengesellschaft*), or AG, are the preferred choices for foreign companies operating in Austria.

Since Austria is not a desirable offshore center for the purposes of incorporation, formation requirements need not be discussed. For further information or professional services, call or write Price Waterhouse in Austria. (See the Business Contacts at the end of this section.) Also request a copy of the informative booklet *Doing Business in Austria.*

Taxation. With regard to bank accounts, nonresidents are not required to pay income tax or tax on net assets (bank balances.) In Switzerland, by contrast, there is a 35 percent withholding tax on all interest earned.

There are no taxes on interest from Austrian bonds or local-authority bonds, or on income from foreign securities. There is a 20 percent withholding tax on share dividends and participation capital dividends. However, if Austria has a double-taxation agreement with the customer's own country, the tax is normally reduced.

Limited-liability corporations and stock corporations are subject to relevant Austrian taxes.

Financial and Investment Incentives. The Austrian government offers various financial and investment incentives in the form of special financing, loan guarantees, and tax relief. Investors interested in establishing an Austrian company should check into which incentives are applicable. Price Waterhouse can advise.

Tax Treaties. Austria has a wide range of tax treaties with other countries. Most are with industrialized countries and primarily cover personal income and corporation profits taxes.

The model treaty of the Organization for Economic Cooperation and Development (OECD) is the standard form for agreements between Austria and other countries. The treaties cover withholding taxes, permanent establishment, industrial and commercial profits, shipping and aircraft, dividends and royalties, real estate rentals, personal services, elimination of double taxation, exchange of information, and competent authority.

Presently, Austria has treaties with Argentina, Australia, Belgium, Brazil, Bulgaria, Canada, Czechoslovakia, Denmark, Egypt, Finland, France, Germany, Greece, Hungary, India, Indonesia, Ireland, Israel, Italy, Japan, Korea, Liechtenstein, Luxembourg, Malta, Netherlands, Norway, Pakistan, Philippines, Poland, Portugal, Romania, Spain, Sweden, Switzerland, Thailand, Tunisia, Turkey, the USSR, the United Kingdom, and the United States.

Business Contacts

Information Services

Interaudit Prufungs und Wirt-schaftsberatungsgesellschaft mbH (IPW)
Traungasse 12
A-1030 Vienna, Austria
Tel. (222) 713-4561-0
Fax: (222) 713-45-61-22
Cable: Interaudit

IPW is the Price Waterhouse representative and correspondent firm in Austria. Price Waterhouse publishes *Doing Business in Austria.*

Salzburger Betriebsansiedlungs-gesellschaft mbH (BAG)
Karajan House
Schwartzstrasse 9
A-5020 Salzburg, Austria
Tel: (662) 88-27-41 or 88-27-42
Fax: (662) 88-27-43

The Salzburger Business Settlement Association publishes *Investment in Austria.* Call or write for a copy.

ICD-Austria Company
Chrysler Building
405 Lexington Avenue
New York, NY 10174
Tel: (212) 370-0717
Telex: 421018/ICD-AUST

ICD promotes the establishment of industries and industrial co-operation.

Bundeskammer der gewerblichen Wirtschoft
Stubenring 8-10
A-1010 Vienna, Austria
Tel: (222) 514 50-0

The Federal Chamber of Commerce of Industrial Affairs provides business information services.

Banking

Creditanstalt
Schottengasse 6
1011 Vienna, Austria
Tel: 222-531-31-0
Telex: 133030 Series

For questions concerning securities investments, call Konrad Petter or Albert Beronneau. Tel: 222-531-31-1960 or 1961. For questions concerning current and savings accounts, call Gerhard Losch. Tel: 222-531-31-18.

Bankhaus Daghofer & Co.
Postfach 16
A-5010 Salzburg, Austria
Telex: 63 3267 BHDA
Fax: 662-80-48-333
Teletex: 3622347 BHDA

Centro Internationale
Handelsbank AG
P.O. Box 272
A-1015 Vienna, Austria

Citibank (Austria) AG
P.O. Box 90
A-1015 Vienna, Austria

Bahamas

Fast Facts

Population: 246,491 (1990)
Capital: Nassau
Largest City: New Providence, 110,000
Language: English

Country Profile

The proximity of the Bahamas to the United States has contributed to their popularity with Americans as a standby vacation mecca for shopping, gambling, sport fishing, entertainment, and plain old-fashioned relaxation.

This archipelago of about 700 islands lies 50 miles off the Florida coast in shallow turquoise waters, drawing millions of Americans and others to enjoy its sandy white beaches and abundantly pleasant year-round climate.

The literacy rate is 93 percent, and the dominant religious groups are Baptist, Anglican, Methodist, and Roman Catholic.

Although negative publicity and scandals relating to drug trafficking and money laundering have marred the Bahamas' public image in the past decade, the islands remain a favorite and inviting playground.

The Bahamas are 30 minutes by air to the U.S. mainland, and in the same time zone as New York and Toronto.

Government.　An independent member of the British Commonwealth with a multiparty parliamentary democracy, the politically stable Bahamian government is headed by the Progressive Liberal Party (PLP).

Legal System.　Laws are enacted under the 1973 Bahamian constitution by a bicameral parliament. Legislation is created from English common law and Bahamian statute law. The Supreme Court handles major civil and criminal cases, while the Magistrate's Court handles minor cases. The Court of Appeals is the highest judicial body.

Economy.   The tourism industry is the thrust of the Bahamian economy and employs nearly half the work force. Finance runs a close second. The 400 or so licensed banks and trust companies maintain assets of US $170 billion.

The Bahamian economy is stable, but to continue its pattern of growth, the government is concentrating on further developing tourism and resorts; capturing and recapturing more international offshore business; and promoting investment in industry and export trade.

Other important industries include ship registration, cement, petroleum refining, rum, and fishing.

The Bahamas hope to gain favored-nation status by the end of the decade.

Communications.   First-rate telecommunications afford direct dialing, cable, telex, and fax services. The 809 area code requires only a 1 in front of the number for direct dialing from the United States.

Business Profile

Banking, Money, and Foreign Exchange.   The Central Bank of the Bahamas supervises and promotes the integrity of the modern and sophisticated Bahamian banking system. The monetary unit is the Bahamian dollar.

Major banks include Atlantic Bank of Commerce, Barclays Bank, Bankers Trust Co., Bank of Boston, Bank of New Providence, Bank of Nova Scotia, Canadian Imperial Bank of Commerce, Chase Manhattan Trust, Cititrust, Royal Bank of Canada, Security Pacific Trust, Fidelity Bank, Riggs National Bank of Washington DC, Toronto-Dominion Bank, and Finance Corporation of the Bahamas.

The offshore banking community is self-regulated through the code of conduct enforced by the Association of International Banks and Trust Companies in the Bahamas.

The Bahamas offer high standards of local expertise and sophisticated skills in banking, trust, law, and accounting. Bahamian banks are free from statutory reserves and liquidity requirements, permitting greater flexibility. A host of excellent banking and trust facilities is available.

The present "It's better in the Bahamas" promotional campaign to attract more tourists and new business, coupled with recent internal housecleaning, should draw favorable attention to the islands.

The island group has grown and matured over the past 30 years into an offshore financial center and has come to be considered "America's tax haven." Unfortunately, like Switzerland, its reputation for privacy has diminished as a direct result of the erosion of bank secrecy and adverse publicity.

A paramount example is the Dennis Levine case, in which bank secrecy laws were quickly violated under pressure from U.S. authorities, even though insider trading was not illegal in the Bahamas at the time. This single event sent a negative signal to the financial world.

The Bahamas still advocate bank secrecy (with certain exceptions, as in most countries), but the question remains whether some future turn of events could cause the country to succumb to the whims of outside influences.

In addition to bank secrecy, the Bahamas offer many attractive and competitive benefits as an offshore financial center.

There are no exchange controls affecting nonresidents.

Legal Entities.   The Bahamas are home to many types of offshore business activities, including international business companies, banks, and insurance companies as well as trust services, ship registration, personal investment companies, and mutual funds.

International Business Companies.   The International Business Companies Act of 1989 was enacted by the Bahamian government to enhance and regain offshore business lost over the past 15 years to the Cayman Islands, British Virgin Islands, and Turks and Caicos.

Bahamian international business companies (IBCs) offer distinct advantages:

1. Two subscribers can incorporate an IBC.

2. The company cannot do business with residents except for seeking professional services.

3. The company may issue bearer shares, no-par-value shares, and unnumbered shares.

4. The company may purchase or acquire its own shares.

5. The board of directors can consist of only one subscriber to the memorandum. Anyone can be elected a director.

6. Telephonic or electronic board meetings are permitted.

7. Director(s) may take action by a resolution, by written consent, or by telex, fax, telegram, cable, or other electronic means without giving notice.

8. Meetings may be held anywhere at any time.

9. A director can be present at a board meeting via telephone or other electronic means.

10. The company may open any accounts desired with no filing or registration requirements.

11. A parent company may merge with a subsidiary or subsidiaries incorporated in the Bahamas without the authorization of the members of any company involved. Companies incorporated in other jurisdictions may do the same to the extent that it is permitted by local law.

12. Members who dissent to a merger, consolidation, redemption of shares, or any other engagement approved by the court are entitled to be paid a fair value for their shares.

13. A company incorporated in another jurisdiction may continue in the Bahamas as an IBC if it satisfies the legal requirements.

14. By board resolution, a company incorporated outside the Bahamas may continue in the same manner as prescribed by law.

15. A shareholder will not be subject to any business license fee, income tax, corporation tax, capital gains tax, or any other tax on income or distributions accruing to or derived from an IBC.

16. Exchange control regulations do not apply between shareholders and their shares and the IBC company.

The tax and exchange control exemptions described above are granted for a period of 20 years from the date of incorporation.

Registration fees to incorporate an IBC are payable to the registrar as follows: US $100 for authorized capital with par value shares of $5000 or less; $350 for capital with no par value. If the authorized capital is higher than $5000, the fees are greater.

An IBC can be formed within 24 hours. It has limited liability. No minimum capital is required. The corporation must have a registered office and agent in the Bahamas. Nominee directors are permissible.

The company name may be in any language but must end in a word internationally understood to signify limited liability: Limited, Corporation, Incorporated, Societé Anonyme, Sociadad Anonima, or the abbreviations Ltd., Corp., Inc., or SA.

The cost to organize an IBC depends largely on whose services are engaged. For example, the Bahamas International Trust Company Limited charges US $900, including government fees, to incorporate an IBC. The annual basic management fee (for serving as an agent or registered office) is $400, and the annual government license fee is $100.

Banks. The Bahamians have guarded their banking system for over 25 years by carefully screening applicants to keep out pirate bankers. In contrast to tax havens that have no requirements for banks, specific legislation is in place. The Bahamas and Trust Companies Regulations Act No. 64 of 1965, as amended by No. 20 of 1969, discourages unscrupulous operators from choosing the Bahamas as their base.

Although the criteria imposed make it difficult for the small-time banker to qualify, they have been very successful at keeping the Bahamian banking system clean. The success rate (compared to other tax havens) is very good, considering that some 400 banks have been chartered. As a result, the Bahamas have a more respectable banking reputation than most tax havens. Credibility is important to any banker. In Montserrat, by contrast, more than 200 banks have had their licenses suspended or revoked.

Banks fall into several categories. The two types pertinent to offshore investors are unrestricted and restricted.

Type of bank	Minimum capitalization	License fee
Unrestricted	$1,000,000	$25,000
Restricted	100,000	5,000

An unrestricted bank can operate only outside of the Bahamas, and a restricted bank can operate only with persons named in its license.

The filing fees and stamp duty for incorporation of an unrestricted bank come to US $3291. The organizers of the new bank must submit an application form to the Central Bank of the Bahamas for evaluation and approval.

All shareholders, officers, and directors must provide reference letters, including two character references and two banking references, along with a police certificate and a personal financial statement. The bank must have a minimum of five shareholders, and one of the directors must have banking experience.

In addition to the above costs, the organizers will likely incur expenses for professional assistance in the Bahamas. For example, International Investment Management Ltd. will establish a bank for a client for US $7000—over and above all other costs. In addition to providing consulting services, completing all required filings and disclosures, dispersing fees, and performing all necessary tasks associated with chartering the new bank, IIM will provide maintenance and office facilities for the first year.

Insurance Companies.   Captive insurance companies are popular in the Bahamas. Normally captives are established by large multinational corporations. Insurance activities are also well regulated.

For further information, contact one of the captive management companies listed in the Business Contacts section.

Taxation. There are no taxes on income, profits, earnings, capital gains, distribution, estates, probate, or inheritance. There are no withholding taxes on dividends, interest, royalties, or payroll.

Financial and Investment Incentives. The Bahamian government offers investment incentives beyond tourism and offshore financial services in order to promote certain industries and diversify the economy.

Tax Treaties. There are no double-taxation treaties. A tax treaty with the United States does permit access to bank accounts if tax evasion or drug smuggling is suspected.

Business Contacts

Government

Registrar of Insurance Companies
Ministry of Finance
P.O. Box N-3017
Nassau, Bahamas

Bahamas Chamber of Commerce
P.O. Box N-665
Nassau, Bahamas
Tel: (809) 322-2145
Publishes an annual directory.

The Registrar General's
 Department
Registry of Companies
P.O. Box N-532
Nassau, Bahamas
Tel: (809) 322-3316/7
Fax: (809) 322-5553
Publishes *International Business Companies of the Bahamas.*

Management

International Investment
 Management Limited
Nassau Shop Building, 2nd Floor
284 Bay Street, P.O. Box N-4826
Nassau, Bahamas
Tel: (809) 325-1226 or 322-1038
Fax: (809) 322-3919

Financial Management
 Corporation Ltd.
Nassau Shop Building, 2nd Floor
284 Bay Street, P.O. Box N-4826
Nassau, Bahamas
Tel: (809) 325-1126
Telex: 20-275
Cable: Transcon

United Management Services Ltd.
Marlborough and Cumberland
 streets
P.O. Box N-529
Nassau, Bahamas

Bahamas Company Formations
72 New Bond Street
London, WIY 9DD
Tel: 44-71-4955145
Fax: 44-71-4953924
                   or
Tower Street Centre
Ramsey, Isle of Man
Tel: 44-624-813571
Fax: 44-624-815697

Bahamas International Trust
 Company Ltd.
P.O. Box N-7768
Nassau, Bahamas
Tel: (809) 322-1161
Fax: (809) 326-5020

Equity Corporate Management
Limited
Nassau Shop Building, 2nd Floor
284 Bay Street
Nassau, Bahamas
Tel: (809) 322-3183/4 or 323-3093
Fax: (809) 323-7130

Corporate Management
(Bahamas) Ltd.
23 Delancy Court
P.O. Box N-4432
Nassau, Bahamas
Tel: (809) 322-6238
Fax: (809) 322-5422

LMP Corporate Services Limited
Claughton House
Charlotte Street
P.O. Box N-4875
Nassau, Bahamas
Tel: (809) 328-0563
Fax: (809) 328-0566

Worldwide Trust Service Ltd.
Nassau Shop Building, 2nd Floor
284 Bay Street, P.O. Box N-4826
Nassau, Bahamas
Tel: (809) 326-6437

Captive Insurance Management

British American Insurance
Company of the Bahamas
Limited
P.O. Box N-4815
Nassau, Bahamas

Bahamas Underwriters Services
Limited
P.O. Box N-6341
Nassau, Bahamas

J. S. Johnson & Company Limited
P.O. Box N-8337
Nassau, Bahamas

Bank America Trust and Banking
Corporation (Bahamas) Limited
P.O. Box N-9100
Nassau, Bahamas

Banking
Here are only a few of the many
major banks.
Credit Suisse (Bahamas) Ltd.
Rawson Square
P.O. Box N-4928
Nassau, Bahamas
Tel: (809) 322-8345

Goltardo Bank
IBM House
P.O. Box 6312
Nassau, Bahamas
Tel: (809) 325-1531
Fax: (809) 323-8561

Handels Bank NatWest (Overseas)
Ltd.
Beaumont House
P.O. Box N-4214
Nassau, Bahamas
Tel: (809) 325-5534
Fax: (809) 326-8807

Hang Seng Bank (Bahamas) Ltd.
A Hong Kong Bank
Euro Canadian Centre, 2nd Floor
P.O. Box N-3019
Nassau, Bahamas
Tel: (809) 322-2173

Deltec Panamerica Trust
Company Ltd.
Deltec House, Lyford Cay
P.O. Box N-3229
Nassau, Bahamas
Tel: (809) 362-4549
Fax: (809) 362-4623

Paribas Suisse (Bahamas) Ltd.
East Bay Street
P.O. Box N-8323
Nassau, Bahamas
Tel: (809) 393-3460
Fax: (809) 393-8424

Security Pacific Trust (Bahamas)
Ltd.
The Hotel Corporation Building,
2nd Floor
P.O. Box CB-10976
Nassau, Bahamas
Tel: (809) 327-7798
Fax: (809) 327-8700

Barclays Bank
Bay Street
P.O. Box N-8350
Nassau, Bahamas
Tel: (809) 322-4921

Lloyds Bank International
(Bahamas) Limited
P.O. Box N-1262
Nassau, Bahamas
Tel: (809) 322-8711/6
Fax: (809) 322-8719

Laurentian Bank & Trust
Company Limited
Euro Canadian Centre
Marlborough Street
P.O. Box N-4392
Nassau, Bahamas
Tel: (809) 326-5935
Fax: (809) 326-5871

Bank of New Providence
P.O. Box N-4723
Nassau, Bahamas
Tel: (809) 322-1291

Canadian Imperial Bank of
Commerce
P.O. Box N-7125
Nassau, Bahamas
Tel: (809) 322-8455

Chase Manhattan Bank NA
P.O. Box N-4921
Nassau, Bahamas
Tel: (809) 322-8721

Citibank NA
P.O. Box N-8158
Nassau, Bahamas
Tel: (809) 322-4240

Commonwealth Industrial Bank
P.O. Box SS-5541
Nassau, Bahamas
Tel: (809) 322-1154

ENI International Bank Ltd.
P.O. Box SS-6377
Nassau, Bahamas
Tel: (809) 322-1928

First Trust Bank
P.O. Box N-7776
Nassau, Bahamas
Tel: (809) 326-4308

Gothard Bank International Ltd.
P.O. Box SS-6052
Nassau, Bahamas
Tel: (809) 325-1531

Hentsch Private Bank & Trust Ltd.
P.O. Box N-4232
Nassau, Bahamas
Tel: (809) 325-4485

L.M.T. Banking Corp.
P.O. Box N-100
Nassau, Bahamas
Tel: (809) 322-7481

Natwest International Trust Corp.
Bank (Bahamas) Ltd.
P.O. Box N-7788
Nassau, Bahamas
Tel: (809) 322-4500

Overseas Union Bank & Trust
Bank (Bahamas) Ltd.
P.O. Box N-8184
Nassau, Bahamas
Tel: (809) 322-2476

People's Penny Savings Bank Ltd.
P.O. Box N-1481
Nassau, Bahamas
Tel: (809) 322-4140

Royal Bank of Canada (Bahamas)
Ltd.
P.O. Box N-3024
Nassau, Bahamas
Tel: (809) 322-4980

Swiss Bank Corp. (Overseas)
P.O. Box N-7757
Nassau, Bahamas
Tel: (809) 322-7570

Legal

Callender, Sawyer, Klonaris &
  Smith
P.O. Box 7117
Nassau, Bahamas
Tel: (809) 322-2511

Charles Barnell
P.O. Box N-5759
Nassau, Bahamas
Tel: (809) 322-1686

Graham Thompson & Co.
P.O. Box N-272
Nassau, Bahamas
Tel: (809) 322-4130

Higgs & Johnson
P.O. Box N-3247
Nassau, Bahamas
Tel: (809) 322-8571

Higgs & Kelly
P.O. Box N-1113
Nassau, Bahamas
Tel: (809) 322-7511

Harry B. Sands Chambers
P.O. Box N-624
Nassau, Bahamas
Tel: (809) 322-2670

Maynard & Co.
P.O. Box N-7525
Nassau, Bahamas
Tel: (809) 322-8956

McKinney, Turner & Co.
P.O. Box N-8195
Nassau, Bahamas
Tel: (809) 322-8914

Toothe, Unwala & Leonard
P.O. Box N-9360
Nassau, Bahamas
Tel: (809) 328-7404

Mossack Fonseca & Co.
Bitco Building, 3rd Floor
P.O. Box N-8188
Nassau, Bahamas
Tel: (809) 322-7601
Fax: (809) 322-5807

Accounting

Arthur Young & Co.
P.O. Box N-3231
Nassau, Bahamas
Tel: (809) 322-3805

Deloitte, Haskins & Sells
P.O. Box N-7120
Nassau, Bahamas

Publishing

Bahamas Handbook
P.O. Box N-7513
Nassau, Bahamas

A softback edition of the handbook is US $23.45, Canada
  $23.85, UK $28.70, sent by air-
  mail, and is essential for anyone
  seriously interested in the Bahamas.

Barbados

```
┌────────────────────────────────────────────────────┐
│                     Fast Facts                      │
│  Population: 300,000 (1990)                          │
│  Capital and Largest City: Bridgetown, 102,000      │
│     (1988)                                           │
│  Language: English                                   │
└────────────────────────────────────────────────────┘
```

Country Profile

The easternmost island in the Lesser Antilles, Barbados rests serenely in the Atlantic waters, clutching the chain of Caribbean islands to the west.

The literacy rate is 99 percent. The dominant religion is Anglican, with small Methodist and Roman Catholic representations.

Approximately the size of San Antonio, Texas, this 166-square-mile island is embraced by cool and dry northeasterly trade winds from December to June. The remainder of the year is marked by rainfall, which fluctuates with the elevation, but 40 inches annually can be expected.

The moderately tropical Barbadian climate permits a thriving sugarcane harvest and supports an ever-growing tourist trade. Daytime temperatures generally range from 80° to 85°F with year-round humidity levels of 71 to 76 percent.

Most Caribbean islands are within 500 nautical miles of Barbados. The far points of Haiti and Jamaica are nearly 1100 nautical miles away. Due south, Georgetown, Guyana, on the South American coast is a distance of only 389 nautical miles.

Air travelers will appreciate the relatively short flying times to other Caribbean destinations. Puerto Rico, nearly 500 miles northwest, is only 1½ hours away. Regional airlines such as LIAT, Aeropostal, and Air Martinique provide good service.

International cities are serviced daily by American Airlines, Air Canada, British Airways, British West Indian Airways (BWIA), and Canadian Holidays. Air travel time to Miami is 3 hours and 40 minutes; New York, 4 hours and 20 minutes; Toronto or Montreal, 5 hours; London, Brussels, or Frankfurt, 9 hours; Rio de Janeiro, 8 hours.

Government. Barbados became known as "Little England" over the years as a result of its stature as one of Britain's first overseas possessions. The island is also home to the second oldest parliament outside of England.

The island was settled in 1627, but not until 1885 did it become a Crown colony. England reigned over Barbados until November 1966, when it gained independence as a self-governing state within the British Commonwealth.

The essential powers granted the governor in 1652 became the basis for the constitution that went into effect in 1966. It remains the foundation for today's Westminster parliamentary system of government.

The governor general is appointed by the British monarch, both of whom are members of the Barbadian parliament. The senate has 21 appointed members and the house of assembly, 27 elected members.

Legal System. The mature legal system is the product of English common law enacted by local parliament and upheld by local courts. The Privy Council in England is the highest judicial body, responsible for handling final appeals from Barbadian courts.

Economy. Political and social stability gives Barbados a competitive edge over other tax havens. Harmonious transitions between the two opposing parties contribute to its all-important reputation for being stable and help create an ideal base to expand free enterprise.

Today the economy is diversified into four primary industries: agriculture, tourism, offshore financial services, and manufacturing.

Communications. Modern communications afford direct dialing worldwide, including facsimile and telex capabilities. High-speed electronic data transmission is available. Overnight courier services are offered by the postal system and by major air carriers.

Business Profile

Banking, Money, and Foreign Exchange. The Central Bank of Barbados was organized in 1972 to stabilize the economy, maintaining proper levels of foreign exchange reserves, controlling the money supply, providing rediscount facilities for lending to industry, and overseeing bank activities, including establishment of reserve minimums. The monetary unit is the Barbadian dollar (Bd).

The Central Bank's effectiveness in assisting with economic development and functioning as intermediary in domestic and international financial activities has earned it the reputation of being one of the strongest financial institutions in the Caribbean.

Major international commercial banks and locally owned financial institutions provide funding and other services. International banks include Bank of Nova Scotia, Bank of Nova Scotia Trust Company (Caribbean) Limited, Barclays Bank International (offshore), Canadian Imperial Bank of Commerce, Chase Manhattan, Royal Bank and Trust Company (Barbados) Limited, and the Royal Bank of Canada (offshore). Locally owned are Barbados National Bank, Barbados International Bank and Trust Co. Ltd. (offshore), and Barbados Savings Bank (national). A few others also exist.

In June 1987 the Securities Exchange of Barbados was established for companies with gross earnings or assets in excess of US $500,000, so their shares could be easily traded. To be listed on the exchange, a company must have a satisfactory track record for the preceding 3 years and meet some other basic requirements.

Certain exchange control regulations apply to residents and to other circumstances; however, there are no exchange controls concerning offshore banks and insurance companies.

Legal Entities

Corporations.   The Companies Act of 1982 identifies two distinct types of entities.

A *company* (formerly, a private company) is considered a "small enterprise" if its gross reserves or assets do not exceed US $500,000. Liability is limited by shares. The company has the right to restrict shares. Information disclosure is minimal. A single shareholder, director, and incorporator are permitted.

A *public company* sells stocks and bonds to the public as opposed to being held by a limited number of people. Most tax havens do not make the public company distinction; then again, most do not have their own stock exchange for trading shares.

The incorporation procedure is similar to incorporating in the States. Generally, a management, accounting, or law firm performs the function, increasing the costs well above the nominal US $375 registration fee. One major accounting firm quotes Bd 2500 to Bd 5000, or $1250 to $2500.

Duplicate copies of the articles of incorporation are filed with the Registrar of Companies. Upon acceptance, generally within 2 days, the company can begin business.

In adhering to the requirements of the Companies Act, a new company must include the following information in the articles of incorporation:

1. Name of corporation, followed by the word (or abbreviation for) "Limited," "Corporation," or "Incorporated."
2. Maximum authorized number of shares and the classes of stock, complete with appropriate legal classifications.
3. Any restrictions on the right to transfer shares.
4. Number of directors.
5. Any limitation on business activities.

In the case of a company, the articles, along with a notice of directors and registered office, are the only information for public disclosure.

Anonymity can be achieved by purchasing an "off the shelf" corporation or engaging local professionals to form the company. In either case, an incorporator will be provided. The management firm will appoint local directors for an additional annual fee. Names of actual principals need not be disclosed.

Shareholders too can gain anonymity—by allowing nominees to hold shares, using share warrants, or establishing a trust in another country with superior secrecy laws.

Offshore Banks and Exempt Insurance Companies.   As of December 31, 1986, Barbados was home to 46 exempt insurance companies, but only a few offshore banks. At a casual glance, this indicates that exempt insurance companies are encouraged and offshore banks are discouraged by strict requirements. The few offshore banks presently in operation are subsidiaries of foreign banks. If offshore banking is your interest, find a jurisdiction with favorable legislation.

However, Barbados should be a serious consideration if you wish to establish an offshore insurance company. The exempt insurance business is thriving. The stated capital of those 46 companies in 1986 was US $144.1 million, and retained premium income was estimated at US $570 million. Numerous insurance management companies can assist principals with establishing and operating their own insurance company.

Here are a few of the attractions of an exempt insurance company in Barbados:

- Exemption from exchange control regulations
- Provision for incorporation of mutual insurance companies
- Simplified corporate mobility
- Up to 35 percent of earnings tax-free for resident expatriate employees
- Minimum capitalization of US $125,000
- Flat annual license fee of US $2500
- Competitive startup and running costs
- Reasonable solvency requirements
- Freedom to acquire real estate
- Government guarantee that the company will not pay taxes for 15 years

- Exemption from all corporate, capital gains, or other direct tax, or any tax on the transfer of assets or securities to any person
- Exemption from withholding tax on any dividends, interest, or other returns to shareholders

An exempt insurance company is licensed only to do business off-shore. It cannot generate premiums or incur risk within Barbados.

The procedure for application includes submitting a business plan, a pro forma application, and a copy of the company's articles of incorporation to the Supervisor of Insurance. The fee is US $250.

The booklet *Barbados: A Guide for Investors in the Exempt Insurance Industry* provides valuable information on the subject, including eligibility requirements and the recommended application procedure. It is available from the Supervisor of Insurance at the Ministry of Finance.

Taxation. Although Barbados has its own share of taxes designed to produce revenue to fuel its economy, the five areas of the offshore financial sector pay relatively no taxes. In particular:

1. Offshore banks are taxed at a maximum rate of 2.5 percent on net income.
2. Exempt insurance companies pay no taxes on income.
3. Foreign sales corporations (FSCs) pay no taxes on income.
4. International business companies (IBCs) are taxed at a maximum rate of 2.5 percent on net income.
5. Shipping corporations receive a 10-year tax holiday.

Financial and Investment Incentives. Barbados offers numerous tax incentives to attract investment capital. These programs have directly contributed to the growth of the economy. Tax concessions are the primary form of investment incentive available to all foreign investors.

The government is encouraging foreign investment into Barbados, with particular emphasis on manufacturing, tourism, and low-tax off-shore business.

Tax Treaties. Double-taxation treaties presently exist with Canada, Denmark, Norway, Switzerland, the United Kingdom, and the United States. There is talk that similar treaties will be negotiated with Sweden, Japan, and Germany.

The U.S. treaty with Barbados is one of the few tax-reducing treaties that the United States has with a low-tax jurisdiction. Although not as compelling as the favorable Antilles treaty that was terminated, it holds many of the same benefits.

Business Contacts

Information Services

Barbados Hotel Association
P.O. Box 711C
Bridgetown, Barbados, WI
Tel: (809) 426-5041
Telex: 2314WB HOBARS
Fax: (809) 429-2845

The association provides a complete directory of all hotels in Barbados, including first-class convention and meeting facilities.

Barbados Industrial Development Corporation
Barbados:
Harbour Road
Bridgetown, Barbados, WI
Tel: (809) 427-5350
New York:
800 Second Avenue
New York, NY 10017
Tel: (212) 867-6420

Call or write for further business, investment, and economic information on Barbados.

Institute of Chartered Accountants of Barbados
BAPO Professional Center
Lower Collymore Rock
St. Michael, Barbados, WI

Write for information on accountants.

Barbados Bar Association
Lexis Chambers
Whitepart Road
St. Michael, Barbados, WI

Write for information on attorneys.

Ministry of Finance and Economic Affairs
Government of Barbados
Office of the Supervisor of Insurance
Treasury Building, 6th Floor
Bridgetown, Barbados, WI
Tel: (809) 426-3815

Call or write for *Barbados: A Guide for Investors in the Exempt Insurance Industry,* which includes a comprehensive list of insurance management companies, accountants, and attorneys.

Registrar of Companies
Coleridge Street
St. Michael, Barbados, WI
Tel: (809) 426-3461

Legal

David King & Co.
United Insurance Center, 1st Floor
Lower Broad Street
Bridgetown, Barbados, WI
Tel: (809) 427-3174

Accounting

Price Waterhouse
Collymore Rock
St. Michael, Barbados, WI
Tel: (809) 436-7000
Telex: 2456
Fax: (809) 436-7057
Mailing Address:
P.O. Box 634 C
Bridgetown, Barbados, WI

This major accounting firm can provide a full range of accounting services. Upon request, it will furnish a copy of the informative guide *Doing Business in Barbados.*

Arthur Young
Arthur Young Building
Bush Hill
Bay Street
Bridgetown, Barbados, WI
Tel: (809) 427-5260
Telex: (0392) 2464 ARTHYOUNG WB
Fax: (809) 426-9551

This major accounting firm can provide a full range of services as well as informative booklets on offshore, taxation, corporate,

and other aspects of Barbados business.

Ernst & Young
Bay Street, P. O. Box 261
Bridgetown, Barbados, WI
Tel: (809) 427-5260
Telex: 2255 ERNSTYOUNG WB
Fax: (809) 426-9551/429-6446

This major accounting firm can provide invaluable services as well as informative booklets such as *Barbados: A Unique Offshore Business Centre.*

Bermuda

Fast Facts

Population: 56,000
Capital: Hamilton, 1676
Language: English

Country Profile

The oldest self-governing body in the British Commonwealth is the island of Bermuda, a string of seven main islands, all bound by bridges, plus some 150 smaller islands and islets.

The literacy rate is 98 percent. The Anglican, Roman Catholic, and African Methodist Episcopal religions are represented.

Situated 650 miles east of North Carolina in the Atlantic Ocean, Bermuda is the world's northernmost coral island. Its hilly green landscape appears naturally manicured, and the warming effect of the Gulf Stream gives it a semitropical climate. Rarely does the temperature exceed 90°F in the summer or drop below 50°F in the winter.

This world-class vacation destination is host to many of today's rich and famous. In business circles, Bermuda is known as a leading, prestigious offshore business center that caters to a sophisticated clientele. Polished professionalism is customary etiquette in Bermuda's daily business life.

New York is 774 miles northwest, and the Bahamas are 900 miles south. Scheduled airline flights connect Bermuda with major U.S. and Canadian cities. International airlines directly link to London and Far East destinations.

Government. Bermuda has the oldest parliamentary system outside of the United Kingdom. Representative government was first introduced in 1620. The Bermuda Constitution Order became effective in 1968, providing internal self-government. Bermuda's democratic structure provides for a sound political system and contributes to a stable and growing economy based on free enterprise.

Legal System. English common law is applicable. The judicial system incorporates the Court of Appeals, Supreme Court, Magistrate's Court, and Special Court.

Economy. The stable local economy is subsidized principally by tourism, which contributes 60 to 70 percent of the annual gross national product (GNP) and employs a majority of the work force.

The second major force acting on the economy is the international financial center, fostered by the presence of more than 6000 international companies.

Communications. Excellent worldwide telecommunications afford direct dialing, telex, fax, and cable. Overnight courier services are available to points in North America and Europe.

Business Profile

Banking, Money, and Foreign Exchange. The three major banks are Bank of Bermuda Ltd., Bank of N. T. Butterfield & Son, and Bermuda Commercial Bank Limited. All provide a wide range of commercial banking services and maintain correspondent relations with major banks in financial centers worldwide. Financial transactions can be handled in any currency or in Euro dollars.

Exempt or nonresident companies incorporated in Bermuda are not subject to any currency controls. Bank accounts may be maintained in any currency or in any country and funds may be freely transferred. Nonresidents are permitted to maintain accounts in any currency except Bermuda dollars.

There are no bank secrecy laws. The government will not allow disclosure of confidential bank information in cases strictly involving tax evasion.

Legal Entities. The most common types of business operations in Bermuda are mutual funds, insurance companies, trusts, investment holding companies, and trading companies.

Incorporation. Two types of companies may be incorporated in Bermuda: local and exempt. A local company may conduct business within

Bermuda, provided a Bermudian owns 60 percent. The exempt company is a nonresident or offshore company that can conduct business only outside Bermuda. The exempt company is generally the choice for those wishing to take advantage of Bermuda as a tax haven.

Exempt companies must get special permission to transfer shares, do business with other exempt companies, or hold mortgages on Bermuda real estate.

Application to form a new company must be submitted to the Bermuda Monetary Authority, which scrutinizes the principals to determine their integrity and financial standing.

The exempt company must have a minimum share capital of US $12,000. All authorized capital stock must be subscribed, but does not have to be fully paid up.

At least two directors must hold office, and each must own at least one share of stock. Every exempt company must have at least two Bermudian directors so that meetings may be held in Bermuda.

Exempt companies pay an annual fee of US $1200—unless they are in the business of insurance, mutual funds, or finance, or manage any unit trust schemes.

Incorporations are handled by local law firms and take approximately 6 weeks.

Bermuda has achieved the dignified reputation of being a premiere offshore financial center that courts a high-caliber clientele by carefully investigating the background and financial standing of prospective beneficial owners of all companies or partnerships.

When an ultimate beneficial owner is an individual, the following information is usually required by the Bermuda Monetary Authority and is held in strict confidence:

- Name, address, nationality, and occupation of the applicant
- Reference from a bank with which the applicant has had a banking relationship for not less than 3 years, stating in general terms the person's financial standing as known to the bank and such other information as is available to the bank concerning the integrity of the applicant

When an insurance company is being formed with individuals as the beneficial owners, each individual must also provide a statement of net worth.

Similar disclosure requirements are necessary when the beneficial owner is a public or private company, trust, partnership, or nonprofit association.

Insurance Companies. Bermuda is the world's largest "captive" insurance market. Some 20 percent of companies in Bermuda are insurance-related.

In addition to filing, applicants wishing to form an insurance company must have the application reviewed by the Registrar of Companies under the Insurance Act of 1978.

The Ministry of Finance is the ultimate regulator under the 1978 Insurance Act and has a host of industry experts at its disposal. Under the auspices of the Insurance Advisory Committee, advisers determine and insure the financial viability of the proposed company and its reputable ownership.

The minimum share capital of an insurance company is US $120,000 for general business, $250,000 for long-term business, or $370,000 in fully paid-up capital for a combination of general and long-term business.

Government fees are US $2250 per year for insurance companies, excluding management and brokerage firms. The same fee applies to mutual funds, finance companies, and management companies of any trust scheme.

In addition, under the 1978 Insurance Act an insurer must pay the following business fee by March 31 of each year:

Nonresident insurance undertaking under the Nonresident Insurance Undertakings Act of 1967	$2500
Exempt company	2000
Overseas company with the legal right to do business in or from Bermuda	2000
Other	1500

A nonresident insurance undertaking is an insurance company incorporated outside Bermuda, but managed from Bermuda.

Banks. Presently, there is no offshore banking legislation.

Generally speaking, professional fees in Bermuda are expensive compared with costs in other tax havens. For instance, in 1989 the total cost to incorporate an exempt company through Richards, Francis & Francis, Barristers and Attorneys, was US $3545 for an "ordinary" company or $7215 for a "special" company.

A special company is identified by the law firm as a company whose "principal business is insurance or an open-ended company with mutual fund business, financed by raising money from the public or managing unit trusts, or shipping, oil, pharmaceutical, and chemical companies."

The cost breakdown for an ordinary company is US $1720 in professional fees and $1825 in disbursements. For a special company, costs are $1920 in professional fees and $5295 in disbursements.

Taxation.   There are no taxes on income, profit, sales, value added, withholding, or capital gains.

Financial and Investment Incentives.   There are no specific financial incentives for onshore investments.

Tax Treaties.   There is no tax treaty to avoid double taxation. However, a treaty ratified in July 1986 provides U.S. law enforcement agencies with financial information only concerning civil and criminal tax cases.

Business Contacts

Government

Bermuda Monetary Authority
Hamilton HM 12, Bermuda
Tel: (809) 295-5278
Fax: (809) 292-7471

Chamber of Commerce
P.O. Box HM 655
Hamilton HM CX, Bermuda
Tel: (809) 295-4201

Registrar of Companies
30 Parliament Street
Hamilton HM 12, Bermuda
Tel: (809) 295-5151
Fax: (809) 292-8152

Ministry of Finance
Government Administration
  Building
30 Parliament Street
Hamilton HM 12, Bermuda

Management

Argonaut Ltd.
Argus Insurance Building
Wesley Street
P.O. Box 20001
Hamilton, Bermuda
Services are provided for incorpo-
  ration and management of insur-
  ance, trading, banking, trust, and
  shipping companies.

Ardon Management Services Ltd.
Warner Building
King and Reid streets
P.O. Box HM 181
Hamilton HM 5-23, Bermuda

Banking

Bermuda Commercial Bank
  Limited
(affiliated with Barclays)
Barclays International Building
44 Church Street
Hamilton HM 12, Bermuda
Mailing address:
P.O. Box HM 1748
Hamilton HM CX, Bermuda
Tel: (809) 295-5678
Fax: (809) 295-8091

Bermuda Provident Bank Ltd.
Barclays International Building
P.O. Box 1748
Hamilton 5, Bermuda
Tel: (809) 295-5678

Bank of Bermuda Ltd.
6 Front Street
Hamilton 5-31, Bermuda
Tel: (809) 295-4000

Trust Services

International Trust Co. of
  Bermuda Ltd.
Barclays International Building
P.O. Box 1255
Hamilton 5, Bermuda

Legal
Richard, Francis & Francis
Barristers and Attorneys
Cedarpoint Centre
48 Cedar Avenue
Hamilton HM 11, Bermuda
Mailing address:
P.O. Box HM 191
Hamilton HM AX, Bermuda
Tel: (809) 295-0790
Fax: (809) 292-1394

Accounting
S. Arthur Morris
Chartered Accountants
Century House
Richmond Road
P.O. Box HM 1806
Hamilton HM HX, Bermuda
Tel: (809) 292-7478
Fax: (809) 295-4164
Write or call for *Doing Business in Bermuda.*

British Virgin Islands

Fast Facts

Population: 13,000 (1990)
Capital and Largest City: Road Town (Tortola), 2500 (1990)
Language: English

Country Profile

Some 50 islands, rocks, and cays encompass the Sir Francis Drake Channel just 60 miles east of Puerto Rico to form the tranquil British Virgin Islands.

The literacy rate is 95 percent. About 73 percent of the population is Methodist and 16 percent is Anglican.

Palms and mangoes thrive in the subtropical climate, where the temperature range is 77°–85°F in the winter and 80°–90°F in the summer.

American Eagle, Air BVI, LIAT, Eastern Metro, and VI Seaplane shuttle-hop from BVI to neighboring islands, including Anguilla, Antigua, Puerto Rico, St. Croix, St. Kitts, St. Maarten, Dominica, Dominican Republic, and St. Thomas, where further connections can be made.

Government. The British Virgin Islands is a stable, self-governed British Crown colony under the 1967 constitution.

Legal System. The legal system is based on English common law.

Economy. The economy is very stable and based primarily on tourism and tax haven operations.

In recent years BVI has transformed into a prominent no-tax haven attracting considerable offshore business. Presently, there are more than 13,000 international business corporations (IBCs) registered on the islands. The simple corporate offshore legislation, zero tax status, excellent communications, and stable economic and political environment have encouraged corporations from other tax havens to redomicile in the British Virgin Islands. Thousands of corporations fled from Panama to BVI during the Noriega downfall.

Communications.   There are excellent telecommunications, including direct dialing, fax, telex, and cable.

Business Profile

Banking, Money, and Foreign Exchange.   Banking is an important aspect of the economy, with approximately $300 million held on deposit. Six major banks operate on the islands with a general license that permits them to take deposits from residents. The monetary unit is the US dollar.

Confidentiality is upheld by the government and banks. Numbered accounts are nonexistent. An additional and very attractive advantage over other locales is that no exchange-of-information agreement has been signed between BVI and the United States. There are no exchange controls.

Legal Entities.   Corporations, trusts, insurance companies, and banks can all be chartered in the British Virgin Islands.

Although several types of corporations exist for various purposes—resident companies, nonresident companies, and international business companies, among them—the IBC is preferred in most instances for offshore purposes.

Resident companies can do business with residents and pay taxes. Nonresident companies cannot do business within BVI and are exempt from income taxes or profits made offshore, but they are taxed on interest income derived from the islands. IBCs can operate only outside BVI, with these exceptions: They can maintain a BVI bank account, use the local professional services, hold shareholder and director meetings, and lease office space. IBCs are totally exempt from income tax.

Private companies may have limited or unlimited liability, with or without share capital. A minimum of two directors and a maximum of 50 shareholders are required.

A public company may have limited or unlimited liability, with or without share capital. The only distinction between private and public companies is that a public company must have a minimum of five shareholders.

The registered agent will draft the memorandum of association and file it in triplicate with the Registrar of Companies along with payment of the appropriate filing fee based on the amount of authorized capital.

All capital stock must indicate a par value. Fully or partially paid shares of stock may be issued for cash, services, or other consideration. Classes of stock are permissible.

The minimum annual license fees are $250 for nonresident companies and $25 for resident companies.

The same requirements apply to IBCs, with some variation: The corporate name must contain the word "Limited," "Corporation," "Incorporated," "Societé Anonyme," "Sociedad Anonima," or the appropriate abbreviation. Bearer shares are permitted. A foreign company can register as an IBC.

The registration fees are as follows:

Authorized share capital up to $50,000	$ 300
Authorized share capital exceeding $50,000	1000
No-par-value stock	1000

Trusts, Insurance Companies, and Banks. Trusts are commonly administered from BVI for business purposes and tax planning.

New legislation governs the issuance of insurance licenses and the organization and administration of insurance companies.

Banking is strictly regulated and governed by the Banking Ordinance of 1972. There are several categories of licenses, but BVI is not a practical tax haven for offshore banking. The financial requirements are steep. The Bahamas and Caymans offer maximum credibility to offshore bankers without the high capitalization and other requirements imposed in the British Virgin Islands.

Taxation.   BVI is characterized as a zero tax haven.

Financial and Investment Incentives.   Limited incentive is offered to attract new industry. Incentive comes mainly in the form of relief from customs duty and income tax.

Tax Treaties.   There is no double-taxation treaty with the United States; however, one is being considered and is expected to be ratified. Also, there are no such treaties with Denmark, Japan, Norway, Sweden, and Switzerland.

Business Contacts

Management

International Trust BVI Ltd.
Columbus Centre Building
P.O. Box 659
Road Town, Tortola, BVI
Tel: (809) 494-3215/2368

Peat Marwick
Bank of Nova Scotia Building
P.O. Box 438
Road Town, Tortola, BVI
Tel: (809) 494-2616
Fax: (809) 494-2704

Banking

Barclays Bank PLC
P.O. Box 70
Road Town, Tortola, BVI

Bank of Nova Scotia
P.O. Box 434
Road Town, Tortola, BVI

Trust Services

Trust Co. of the Virgin Islands Ltd.
Bank of Nova Scotia Building
P.O. Box 438
Road Town, Tortola, BVI

Legal

Mossack Fonseca & Co. (BVI) Ltd.
Attorneys
Skelton Building, Main Street
P.O. Box 3136
Road Town, Tortola, BVI
Tel: (809) 494-4841

Accounting

Peat Marwick
Bank of Nova Scotia Building
P.O. Box 438
Road Town, Tortola, BVI
Tel: (809) 494-2616
Fax: (809) 494-2704

Write or call for *Investment in the British Virgin Islands.*

Deloitte & Toucher
P.O. Box 362
Road Town, Tortola, BVI
Tel: (809) 494-2868
Fax: (809) 494-6247

Write or call for *International Tax and Business Guide—British Virgin Islands.*

Cayman Islands

Fast Facts

Population: 26,356 (1990)
Capital and Largest City: George Town (Grand Cayman), 10,000 (est. 1987)
Language: English

Country Profile

The Cayman Islands, one of the more recognized and well-regarded tax havens of the past 15 years, is situated in the Western Caribbean just south of Cuba.

The literacy rate is 97.5 percent. The dominant religion is Protestant.

The Caymans are a popular vacation destination for shoppers, sight-seers, divers, and sport fishermen, and a port-o'-call to thousands of cruise passengers annually.

Approximately 480 miles south of Miami and 150 miles west of Jamaica, the Caymans are well connected to neighboring islands and major cities courtesy of Cayman Airways, Northwest Airlines, American Airlines, and Air Jamaica. Travel time is 1 hour to Miami, 2½ hours to Houston, 3½ hours to New York, 4½ hours to Toronto, and 5½ hours to San Francisco.

Government.   This British Crown colony consisting of three small islands enjoys a very stable political, economic, and social environment.

The Caymans are self-governed under a constitution. Executive and legislative power are divided among the governor, executive council, and legislative assembly.

Legal System.   The legal system is based on English common law. Laws and statutes are initiated and passed locally and upheld by the Cayman court system.

Economy.   Both the well-developed tourist trade and the offshore sector are major forces in the economy. Revenue is principally derived from registration license fees for corporations and banks, import duties, postage stamp sales, and stamp duty on conveyances, mortgages, and other legal documents.

Communications.   An important feature of any first-rate tax haven is a superb communication system. The Caymans are no exception.

Business Profile

Banking, Money, and Foreign Exchange.   Major commercial banks include Barclays Bank PLC, Royal Bank of Canada, Canadian Imperial Bank of Commerce, and Bank of Nova Scotia.

Over 600 banks, including Class A and Class B types, are chartered in the Caymans. Its importance as an offshore banking center make it an excellent locale for offshore bankers wishing to gain maximum credibility.

The Cayman dollar was adopted in 1972 and is tied into the US dollar.

Cayman banks adhere to the practice of confidentiality. English common law and the Banks and Trust Companies Regulations Law impose a duty upon bankers to keep customer information confidential. In addition, the Confidential Relationships (Preservation) Law prohibits disclosure of confidential information regarding customers and their accounts, including credit inquiries. Such disclosures are punishable by laws. The restriction extends to trust companies and to anyone coming in contact with information of a proprietary nature of anyone attempting to procure such information. In some instances, penalties are doubled.

On the other hand, the law does not extend to activities that are considered crimes in the Caymans. Illegal drug activities, theft, and fraud are among them.

Through its exchange-of-information agreement with the United States, concluded under the Caribbean Basin Initiative (CBI), confidential information can be released in specific circumstances to various law enforcement agencies.

Presently, there are no exchange controls.

Legal Entities.   The most common means of utilizing the Caymans as an offshore base is to organize an ordinary nonresident or exempt company.

The *ordinary nonresident company* must have at least one director and three shareholders. Shareholders are not public record. Annual financial returns need not be filed. There is no minimum capitalization requirement.

The *exempt company* is permitted to have only one shareholder and must have at least one director. The shareholder is not on public record, and the shareholder and director can be the same person. The company does not file an annual financial return. Shares may be in bearer form or have no par value. It cannot solicit shares to the public. There is no minimum capitalization requirement.

Incorporation is a simple procedure. The memorandum of association is drafted containing the company name, registered office address, purpose, capital structure, and liability status (limited or unlimited). A professional will handle drafting the memorandum along with the articles of association and will complete the filings and disbursements to the appropriate government bodies.

The minimum incorporation fee for an ordinary nonresident company is CI $500 (approximately US $375); for an exempt company, CI $850 (approximately US $637.50).

In 1990, the Cayman International Trust Company Limited incorporated an ordinary nonresident company for US $1400 or an exempt company for US $1950. If management services are required, there is an additional annual management fee.

The Banks and Trust Companies Regulations Law (Revised) stipulates the requirements for the issuance of bank and trust licenses. The

Insurance Law of 1979, as amended, provides for the licensing of insurance companies. For all these entities, a Class A license permits the conduct of business within the Caymans. A Class B license permits business transactions only outside the Caymans.

These classes are further divided into restricted and unrestricted, each providing specific powers and limitations. An unrestricted bank license provides maximum banking powers to a Class A or Class B bank. For instance, a Class B restricted bank license permits the offshore bank to provide services only to specified persons in the bank license, thereby limiting potential abuses.

Capitalization requirements also vary. An unrestricted license requires a minimum paid-up capital of CI $400,000; a restricted license requires a minimum of only CI $27,500.

Licensing fees for a 12-month period are as follows:

Class A unrestricted	CI $20,000
Class B unrestricted	8,500
Class B restricted	5,500

An insurer must have a minimum net worth of CI $100,000 if providing general but not long-term business. CI $200,000 is required for insurers of strictly long-term business, such as life insurance. When both general and long-term business is written, CI $300,000 net worth is required.

A restricted Class B license is intended for captive operations that underwrite for the parent group. The capitalization requirements vary by individual situations.

Applicants for bank, trust, or insurance licenses must possess satisfactory credentials and references. Supporting documentation will be required with the application, and the appropriate government body will verify all information provided.

Taxation.   There are no corporation taxes. The Cayman Islands are characterized as a no-tax haven.

Financial and Investment Incentives.   Other than incentives to attract hotel business, financial incentives come in the form of advantages offered by the Caymans as a tax haven, international financial center, and banking center.

Tax Treaties.   No double-taxation treaties exist, since there are no taxes. As noted, under the CBI, the Caymans have signed an exchange-of-information agreement with the United States.

Business Contacts

Incorporation and Management

Euro Bank Corporation
P.O. Box 1183
Grand Cayman, BWI

IncoBank and Trust Company
P.O. Box 970
Grand Cayman, BWI
Tel: (809) 949-7807

Washington International Bank
and Trust Ltd.
P.O. Box 609
Grand Cayman, BWI

Swiss Bank & Trust Corp. Ltd.
P.O. Box 852
Grand Cayman, BWI
Tel: (809) 949-7344
Fax: (809) 949-7308

Government

Registrar of Companies
Government Administration
  Building
Grand Cayman, BWI
Tel: (809)949-4844

Management

Bruce Campbell & Co.
Attorneys at Law
Bank of Nova Scotia Building
P.O. Box 884
Grand Cayman, BWI
Tel: (809) 949-2648
Fax: (809) 949-8613

Cayman International Trust
  Company Limited
P.O. Box 500
Grand Cayman, BWI
Tel: (809) 949-4277
Fax: (809) 949-8293

International Management
  Services, Ltd.
P.O. Box 61
Grand Cayman, BWI

Banking

Midland Bank Trust Corporation
  (Cayman) Limited
P.O. Box 1109
Grand Cayman, BWI
Tel: (809) 949-7755
Fax: (809) 949-7634

Finsbury Bank and Trust Company
Transnational House
West Bay Road
P.O. Box 1592
Grand Cayman, BWI
Tel: (809) 947-4011
Offers debit Gold Mastercard.

Bank of Nova Scotia
P.O. Box 689
Grand Cayman, BWI
Tel: (809) 949-7666

First Cayman Bank Ltd.
P.O. Box 1113
Grand Cayman, BWI
Tel: (809) 949-5266
Fax: (809) 949-5398
Requires a minimum $50 deposit
  to open a savings account.

Barclays Bank PLC
P.O. Box 68
Grand Cayman, BWI
Tel: (809) 949-7300

CIBC Bank and Trust Company
  (Cayman) Ltd.
P.O. Box 695
Grand Cayman, BWI
Tel: (809) 949-2366

Cayman National Bank and Trust
  Co.
P.O. Box 1097
Grand Cayman, BWI
Tel: (809) 949-4655

Royal Bank of Canada
P.O. Box 245
Grand Cayman, BWI
Tel: (809) 949-4600

Cititrust (Cayman) Ltd.
P.O. Box 309
George Town, Grand Cayman, BWI
Tel: (809) 949-5405

Canadian Imperial Bank Ltd.
P.O. Box 695
George Town, Grand Cayman, BWI
Tel: (809) 949-2366

Chase Manhattan Trust Ltd.
P.O. Box 190
George Town, Grand Cayman, BWI
Tel: (809) 949-2081

Legal

Myers & Alberga
P.O. Box 472
Grand Cayman, BWI

Maples & Calder
P.O. Box 309
George Town, Grand Cayman,
  BWI
Tel: (809) 949-2081
Telex: 4212

Truman Bodden & Co.
P.O. Box 866
George Town, Grand Cayman, BWI

W. S. Walker & Co.
Swiss Bank Building
P.O. Box 265
George Town, Grand Cayman, BWI
Tel: (809) 949-2444

Accounting

Coopers & Lybrand
P.O. Box 219
Grand Cayman, BWI
Tel: (809) 949-9700

Deloitte, Haskins & Sells
P.O. Box 1787
Grand Cayman, BWI
Tel: (809) 949-7500

Ernst & Whinney
P.O. Box 1567
Grand Cayman, BWI
Tel: (809) 949-8444

Price Waterhouse
First Home Tower
British-American Centre
Jenner Street
P.O. Box 258
George Town, Grand Cayman, BWI
Tel: (809) 949-2944
Fax: (809) 949-7352

Channel Islands

Fast Facts

Population: 137,000 (1990)
Capital and Largest City: St. Peter Port
  (Guernsey); St. Helier (Jersey)
Language: English

Country Profile

The four main Channel Islands are Jersey, Guernsey, Alderney, and
Sark, in order of size. They rest approximately 40 miles north of France
and 110 miles south of Britain in the English Channel.

The literacy rate is 99.5 percent.

Frequent flights and ferry service connect the Channel Islands with the United Kingdom and Europe.

Government. The Channel Islands were once part of the Duchy of Normandy and have been politically stable for hundreds of years. Although they are possessions of the British Crown, they maintain their own legal systems. Their constitution dates back to 1066. Alderney and Sark are independent jurisdictions with their own constitution.

Jersey and Guernsey are effectively part of the European Economic Community (EC), thanks to negotiations by the United Kingdom, but the islands retain their independence and fiscal autonomy.

Legal System. The legal system of Jersey and Guernsey is based on Norman law. However, the local legislature enacts laws, regulations, and statutes that are directly influenced by English common law.

Economy. The two economies of Jersey and Guernsey depend on tourism, agriculture, and international finance. Guernsey also has light industry.

Communications. There are excellent communications on Jersey and Guernsey, including 24-hour direct dialing to any part of the world and data link, facsimile, and telex services.

Business Profile

Banking, Money, and Foreign Exchange. Dozens of registered, deposit-taking institutions are located on the islands for use by residents and offshore business.

Westpac Banking Corporation (Jersey) Limited, the first bank in Australia with offices worldwide, performs banking, corporate, and trust services. Westpac can establish deposit accounts in major currencies, organize and manage corporations, set up and administer trusts, and manage international investments.

English common law requires banks and their employees to maintain secrecy, but no specific local legislation has been passed. However, nominees may be engaged by corporations to shield the identity of the actual beneficial owners. Also, numbered bank accounts are available. Professionals cannot disclose information requested by a foreign court order.

Exchange controls in Jersey and Guernsey are invalid at present, but could be reimposed on short notice.

The monetary unit for international purposes is the pound sterling

(£). Jersey and Guernsey have their own currencies that freely circulate between islands.

Legal Entities

Jersey. Sole proprietorships, partnerships, corporations, trusts, societies, mutual funds, insurance companies, banks, and trust companies can be chartered and licensed under Jersey laws.

Corporations are limited and organized by at least three members, each with a minimum of one share. Nominees may be engaged to secure privacy. Incorporation takes approximately 10 to 14 days.

The attorney or trust company handling the incorporation will file the incorporation application, provide nominees, and draft the memorandum of association. This document will contain the name of the company, stated capital, number of shares and value, terms of payment for shares and related penalties, shareholder liability, and perpetuity of the corporation.

The company name must end with "Limited" or "Ltd."

No-par-value stock is not permitted. Par value may be any stated amount. Form of payment is optional and is stated in the memorandum. A minimum of nine paid or unpaid capital shares must be issued. Each unpaid amount for shares is the shareholder's maximum individual liability.

The corporation must maintain a minimum of three shareholders, and all have to be residents. The names and addresses of the shareholders must be open for public inspection and maintained at the registered office of the corporation. Nominee shareholders are not identified as such.

The names of the directors and the individual or company handling the incorporation need not be disclosed in the memorandum or filed with the Registry of Companies. Nor do their names have to be displayed on the company's letterhead (as required on the Isle of Man).

A company that holds director meetings in Jersey is subject to income tax on profits; otherwise, the flat corporate tax rate applies. Annual returns are filed and open to public inspection.

Incorporation fees charged by the government are a minimum of £50 or .5 percent of the authorized capital stock, and a stamp duty of £100 is imposed.

Sole proprietorships and partnerships are of little or no use in the offshore world.

Mutual funds can be a trust or corporation.

The Finance and Economics Committee has limited the entrance of new banks by restricting applicants to internationally recognized banks that wish to establish a subsidiary.

Guernsey. Under Guernsey law, partnerships, societies, trusts, and corporations may be established.

There are two types of corporations. The *noncorporation tax company* is considered a resident and is subject to income tax. The *corporation tax company* is a nonresident that pays an annual fixed-rate duty. Both carry limited liability.

Unlike Jersey or most other jurisdictions, Guernsey has no established procedure or authority for incorporating companies. Permission must be obtained from the Royal Court. After the court conducts a name search and issues its approval, the memorandum and articles of association can be registered.

Seven shareholders are required to incorporate, each holding a minimum of one share. Nominee shareholders are usually furnished by a local lawyer or trust company. Other stipulations and information are required prior to making application.

If Guernsey is of interest, contact a local professional for complete details, costs, and formalities. But Jersey is a better alternative.

The following incorporation costs can be anticipated in Jersey or Guernsey:

Westpac	£1000
Castle Trust	600
Croy Trust	700

Alderney. Various historical events have left Alderney somewhat dependent upon Guernsey under the Government of Alderney Law 1948 and the Alderney (Application of Legislation) Law 1948, and their amendments.

There are two important points worth mentioning here. Guernsey tax laws apply to Alderney, and Guernsey legislates for Alderney. However, any actions are generally taken in consultation with Alderney.

Alderney has its own company law, and professionals can assist with incorporation.

Sark. There is no method or procedure for incorporation in Sark. Generally, a Guernsey corporation is managed from Sark. There is no tax system. Guernsey corporations are taxed by Guernsey according to its own tax laws. Communications go through Guernsey, and travel is restricted by irregular sea passage.

Sark is best known in financial circles for the $40-million Bank of Sark swindle perpetrated in the 1960s by Phil Wilson. The story is graphically detailed in Jonathan Kwitney's *The Fountain Pen Conspiracy* (New York: Alfred A. Knopf, 1973). Definitely worth reading.

Taxation. A Jersey "corporation tax" company pays a flat £500 per year. This type of company is similar to the exempt company in other jurisdictions. It is the preferred choice for offshore purposes.

A Guernsey corporation controlled from Guernsey does not pay corporation tax. Otherwise, it is subject to an annual flat tax of £500.

Financial and Investment Incentives. There are no incentives to establish industries. Incentives come in the form of benefits offered by the Channel Islands as an offshore financial center.

Tax Treaties. Double-taxation agreements are in effect between the United Kingdom and Jersey and Guernsey.

Business Contacts

Management

Croy Trust Limited
Belmont House, 1st Floor
2–6 Belmont Road
St. Helier, Jersey, CI
Tel: 44-534-78774
Fax: 44-534-35401

Castle Trust Company Limited
P.O. Box 226
Weighbridge House
Lower Pollet
St. Peter Port, Guernsey, CI
Tel: 44-481-23372
Fax: 44-481-711354

Beresford Trustees Ltd.
White Lodge
Wellington Road
Jersey, CI
Tel: 44-534-79502
Fax: 44-534-33405

Channel Trust Ltd.
P.O. Box 203
St. Johns House
Union Street
St. Peter Port, Guernsey, CI
Tel: 44-481-721896
Fax: 44-481-724800

Jordan & Sons (Jersey) Ltd.
P.O. Box 578
17 Bond Street
St. Helier, Jersey, CI
Tel: 44-534-30579
Fax: 44-534-26430

Calder, Vlieland-Boddy
P.O. Box 70
Abacus House
Newton, Alderney, CI

Schroder Financial Management
  International
P.O. Box 273
Schroder House
The Grange
St. Peter Port, Guernsey, CI

Banking

Westpac Banking Corporation
  (Jersey) Limited
Charles House
Charles Street
St. Helier, Jersey, CI
Tel: 44-534-27421/79500
Fax: 44-534-77717

Lombard Banking (Jersey) Limited
P.O. Box 554
39 La Motte Street
St. Helier, Jersey JE4 8XH, CI
Tel: 44-534-27511

Citibank (Channel Islands) Ltd.
Channel House
Green Street
St. Helier, Jersey, CI

Hill Samuel (Channel Islands)
Trust Co. Ltd.
7 Bond Street
P.O. Box 63
St. Helier, Jersey, CI

Kleinwort, Benson (Channel
Islands) Ltd.
Church Street
P.O. Box 76
St. Helier, Jersey, CI

Guiness Mahon
P.O. Box 188
La Vieille Cour
St. Peter Port, Guernsey, CI
Tel: 44-481-23506
Fax: 44-481-20844

TSB Bank
25 New Street
St. Helier, Jersey, CI
Tel: 44-534-27306
Fax: 44-534-23058

Legal

Mossack Fonseca & Co.
P.O. Box 168
St. Helier, Jersey JE4 8RZ, CI
Tel: 44-534-42800
Fax: 44-534-42054

Accounting

Deloitte, Haskins & Sells
Guernsey:
Albert House, South Esplanade
St. Peter Port, Guernsey, CI
Jersey:
Whitely Chambers
41 Don Street
St. Helier, Jersey, CI

Lince, Salisbury, Meader & Co.
Avenue House
St. Julian's Avenue
St. Peter Port, Guernsey, CI

Cook Islands

Fast Facts
Population: 21,000 (1990)
Capital: Avarua (Rarotonga)
Languages: English, Maori

Country Profile

Some 15 islands sprawled across 850,000 square miles of Polynesian waters in the South Pacific are joined under the auspices of the Cook Islands. The Samoas lie to the west, and the French Polynesian chain to the east.

The remote Cook Islands are connected to major points like Auckland (New Zealand), Honolulu, Los Angeles, and numerous neighboring destinations by indirect weekly flights operated by Air New Zealand, Cook Islands International, Hawaiian Airlines, and Polynesian Airlines. Anticipate lengthy travel time.

Government.   Previously a British protectorate, the Cook Islands were annexed into New Zealand territory in 1901. The islands became self-governing under a "Westminster model" constitution in 1965. Since that time, the islanders have been tied to New Zealand by common citizenship.

The two-party system—the Cook Islands Party and the Democratic Party, whose ideologies are similar—fosters political stability. Elections are conducted every 5 years.

Legal System.   The legal system is based on English common law. The Cook Islands parliament has complete law-making authority, supported by a court system.

Economy.   The economy is fueled by tourism and by the offshore finance sector, both of which have surpassed agriculture in generating business growth. Postage-stamp sales also bring in important revenue.

Tax haven legislation is supported by both political parties. In recent years, the Offshore Banking Act (1982), Offshore Insurance Act (1981–82), International Trusts Act (1984), and Trading Companies Act have spurred the island economy.

Communications.   Courtesy of an earth satellite station located in the financial center of Rarotonga, 24-hour international direct-dialing, telex, fax, and cable services are available.

Business Profile

Banking, Money, and Foreign Exchange.   The two major banks in the Cook Islands are ANZ and Westpac Banking Corporation Limited. The Exchange Control Regulations of 1948 apply only to New Zealand dollars, the primary legal tender. International companies are exempt from exchange controls. Banks are subject to secrecy laws.

Legal Entities.   An international company with limited liability can be incorporated quickly. A name check can be conducted by telephone, and within 24 hours of filing, the memorandum of association will be incorporated.

A one-page standard memorandum of association may be adopted, or the incorporators may choose to draft a new version.

The company name must end with "Corporation," "Incorporated," "Limited," or the appropriate abbreviation.

Shares may be in bearer form or registered, have a par value or no par value, and be divided into more than one class. Bearer debentures can be issued in lieu of stock, allowing the debt holder to control the corporation.

The international company must have a registered office in the Cook Islands. One director and one resident secretary are required. An annual return must be filed.

The government fee for incorporating is US $1000, with a $500 annual renewal fee. Trust companies will charge an additional $1000 to $2000 for their incorporation services.

European Pacific Trust Company (Cook Islands) Limited can provide organization and management services. Its charge to incorporate a company is US $2650. This amount includes the $1000 government registration fee and professional fees of $1650. The annual renewal fee for government registration and professional services is $1600.

The inaccessibility of the Cook Islands is a two-edged sword. Although generally considered a disadvantage, it also offers distinct benefits. There is less regulation and adverse influence from the outside world. For example, the Cook Islands have no direct tax treaties, and the Registry of Companies has relatively no knowledge of a corporation's activities. Also, in the case of an asset protection trust (see below), a litigant is needed to commence new litigation in the Cook Islands in order to secure a judgment against the trust or parties to it.

The Offshore Insurance Act of 1981–82 offers favorable legislation for the establishment of a captive or reinsurance company.

An insurance company must first be incorporated under the International Companies Act of 1981–82. The application for an insurance license is then submitted to the Cook Islands Monetary Board. The application includes the following pertinent information: certified copy of the memorandum of association, license fee, nature and character of company's business, company's financial standing, stock ownership, management, corporate address within the islands, and professional and character references.

Satisfactory asset backing for an insurance company is stipulated as follows:

An applicant for, and a holder of, a license—
a) shall have such surplus of tangible assets over liabilities as may from time to time be prescribed by regulation, and
b) if required at any time in writing by the Board so to do, shall demonstrate to the satisfaction of the Board its financial standing.

An annual report and audited accounts are required.

Strict secrecy laws apply to insurance companies and their auditors.

European Pacific Trust Company will arrange for the insurance license. The total cost is US $5300, which covers the government license fee of $2000 and the professional fee of $3300. The annual renewal fee is $2700.

Offshore banking is encouraged under the Offshore Banking Regulations of 1982. The procedure for securing a license is similar to that for insurance companies.

Two classes of banking licenses are available. The Class A license permits offshore banking and allows the holder to maintain a permanent operation within the islands; upon approval, the bank may transact business with residents. The minimum paid-up capital is US $10 million. The license fee is $10,000.

The Class B license permits only offshore banking activities. Annual license fees are determined by the number of foreign currencies the bank will handle.

One currency	US $2000
Two to five currencies	4000
Unrestricted number of currencies	6000

Annual returns must be filed. Secrecy laws apply to offshore banks and their account holders. The minimum capitalization is US $2 million.

Trusts are administered in the Cook Islands under the International Trusts Act (1984).

An attractive trust touted by European Pacific is the *offshore asset protection trust*. It is inexpensive to establish and administer and has several distinct advantages over trusts in other jurisdictions. To quote the literature:

> The law includes:
> a) Provision to ensure the validity of Trusts notwithstanding the subsequent bankruptcy of the Settler;
> b) Modification of common law presumptions as to intent to defraud creditors, for the purpose of protecting the validity of Trusts and dispositions of property to Trusts by Settlers;
> c) Modification of the common-law rule which voids Trusts where significant control or interest is retained by the Settler;
> d) The nonrecognition of foreign judgments in the Cook Islands.

European Pacific Trust Company quotes the following:

Annual fee payable to the Registrar of International Trusts	US $100
Provision of settler and settlement	500
Provision of trustee	800

Taxation.   There are no taxes.

Financial and Investment Incentives.   Tax incentives to manufacturers and income tax holidays are offered.

Tax Treaties.   Indirectly, the Cook Islands have an income tax treaty with the United States, since they fall under the Income Tax Convention of 1948 initiated between New Zealand and the United States.

Business Contacts

Incorporation and Management

European Pacific Trust Company
  (Cook Islands) Limited
European Pacific Centre
Tutakimoa Road
P.O. Box 25
Rarotonga, Cook Islands
Tel: (682) 22680
Fax: (682) 20566

Cook Islands Trust Corporation
  Limited
Australia:
The Rocks
29 George Street
P.O. Box 4858 GPO
Sydney, Australia
Cook Islands:
P.O. Box 666
Mercury House
Rarotonga, Cook Islands

Costa Rica

Fast Facts

Population: 2,851,000 (1990)
Capital and Largest City: San José, 277,800
Language: Spanish

Country Profile

The Republic of Costa Rica is a little-known tax haven in the heart of Latin America. This narrow strip of land with its majestic mountains pressed between Nicaragua to the north and Panama to the south has been described as the "Switzerland of the Americas."

The literacy rate is 88 percent. About 93 percent of the population is Roman Catholic.

An oasis flanked by the glistening Caribbean Sea and the bountiful Pacific Ocean, Costa Rica is the beneficiary of natural beauty and a pleasantly moderate climate.

Eastern Airlines and LACSA (national airline) connect San José daily with flights to several major U.S. cities. Air service is also available to other Central American and Caribbean cities.

Government.   This stable democratic republic has a presidential head
of state with full executive powers. The government is divided into three
bodies: executive, legislative, and judicial.

The present constitution has been in force since 1948.

Legal System.   Although based on a Spanish civil law system, Costa
Rican law has counterparts similar to those found in U.S. commerce and
industry regulations.

Economy.   Although the economy has suffered some major challenges
in the recent past, Costa Rica remains one of the more economically stable countries in the region.

After restructuring with the aid of the International Monetary Fund
and the World Bank, Costa Rica has gradually bolstered its economy
each year as it transforms into more of a market-oriented climate with
special emphasis on exports.

Communications.   Telecommunications are excellent.

Business Profile

Banking, Money, and Foreign Exchange.   The continuity and liquidity of Costa Rica's foreign exchange are attributable to the strong Central Bank and the country's progressive banking system. The monetary
unit is the colon, which is tied to the U.S. dollar.

Although Costa Rica has mild exchange controls, they do not affect
any foreigner or foreign entity wishing to maintain an account in the
country in a currency other than colons. Currency exchange applies to
natural citizens or legal entities.

The law stipulates total confidentiality and secrecy in bank transactions. This measure also applies to information given to attorneys. The
law follows long-standing tradition.

Legal Entities.   There are five types of legal entities: individual enterprise with limited liability, collective company, limited partnership, limited-liability company, and stock corporation or chartered company.

The stock corporation is the most commonly employed entity and
provides the greatest flexibility and diversity. Two incorporators are required, along with a minimum of three directors of any nationality.
Only one shareholder is necessary. There are no residency requirements.

The company is limited by registered shares. Bearer shares, once permitted, were eliminated in 1988. Registered shares can be endorsed in
"blank," giving the holder desired anonymity. There is a possibility of
the ruling on bearer shares being reversed. In the past, bearer shares

had to be issued and paid-in-full at the time of incorporation or be registered. No-par-value shares are not permitted.

Stock corporations are distinguished as public, close, or holding companies. Meetings may be held anywhere in the world. There is no minimum capitalization requirement except for finance companies.

The procedure for incorporation is simple but is usually best handled by a local lawyer who is familiar with the laws and procedures and who can assist the corporation in many other ways.

Once the corporate charter is drafted and notarized, it is published in the *Official Gazette* and recorded with the Registry of Companies.

Costa Rica is an outstanding offshore financial base for corporations.

Taxation. International companies operating exclusively offshore do not pay taxes. There is a 15 percent withholding tax on dividends of nonresident shareholders, but withholding can be avoided if the shareholder can show that no income tax credit was received on the tax that was paid to the home country of the shareholder.

A corporation doing business in Costa Rica will pay a moderate income tax, various indirect taxes, payroll taxes, import duties, and real estate taxes. However, exporters are exempt from most taxes. Taxes are calculated on net profits less business expenses.

Financial and Investment Incentives. Costa Rica is encouraging foreign investment and is granting tax holidays to favored industries. For example, "new industries" are extended 5-year exemptions which can be increased to 10 years. Companies exporting nontraditional products outside of Central America are granted 12-year tax holidays. There are also possibilities for international companies to do substantial business within the country.

Tax Treaties. There are no double-taxation treaties. Under the Caribbean Basin Initiative an exchange-of-information agreement has been signed with the United States, but the treaty is not yet ratified.

Business Contacts

Information Services

U.S. Department of Commerce
Desk Officer for Costa Rica
Room H 3314
Washington, DC 20230
Tel: (202) 377-2527

American Embassy—San José
Commercial Attaché
APO Miami 34020
Tel: 506-331155

Embassy of Costa Rica
1825 Connecticut Avenue NW,
  Suite 211
Washington, DC 20009
Tel: (202) 234-2945

American Chamber of Commerce
  of Costa Rica
Apartado 4946
San José, Costa Rica
Tel: 506-332133

Costa Rica Investment and Trade
  Promotion Office
Gaslight Tower, Suite 1617
235 Peachtree Street
Atlanta, GA 30303
Tel: (404) 223-5708

Chicago Association of Commerce
  and Industry
Caribbean Basin Promotion
  Center
200 N. LaSalle Street
Chicago, IL 60601
Tel: (312) 580-6930

Costa Rica Investment Promotion
  Office
36 Junting Lane, Suite 1A
Stamford, CT 06902
Tel: (203) 968-1448

Costa Rican Trade and Investment
  Promotion Office
17910 Sky Park Circle
Suite 101
Irvine, CA 92714
Tel: (714) 250-0146

Banking
Banco Credito Agricola de Cartago
P.O. Box 5572
San José 1000, Costa Rica

Banco Anglo-Costarricense
P.O. Box 10038
San José 1000, Costa Rica

Banco Nacional de Costa Rica
P.O. Box 10015
San José, Costa Rica

Banco de Santander
P.O. Box 6714
San José, Costa Rica

Banco de Costa Rica
P.O. Box 10035
San José 1000, Costa Rica

Citicorp (Costa Rica)
Edificio Plaza de la Artilleria
Avenidas Central y Primera,
  Calle 4
San José, Costa Rica

Corporation Francoamericana de
  Finanzas SA
Edificio Plaza de la Artilleria
Avenidas Central y Primera,
  Calle 4
San José, Costa Rica

Corporacion Internacional de
  Boston
P.O. Box 6370
San José 1000, Costa Rica

Ibero-Amerika Bank
P.O. Box 5548
San José, Costa Rica

First Pennsylvania SA
P.O. Box 528
San José, Costa Rica

Legal
Dr. Enrique Von Browne
Apartado 5634
San José, Costa Rica
Tel: 506-218550
Fax: 506-215910

Juan Edgar Picardo, Jr.
Apartado 2047
San José, Costa Rica

Pacheco Coto
P.O. Boxes 10 and 246
San José, Costa Rica

Gibraltar

Fast Facts

Population: 30,000 (1990)
Capital and Largest City: Gibraltar
Languages: English, French, Spanish

Country Profile

The "Rock" of Gibraltar is the tip of the Iberian peninsula that juts from the southernmost part of Spain into the Strait of Gibraltar, the narrow passage between the continents of Europe and Africa at the extreme west end of the Mediterranean Sea.

The literacy rate is 99 percent. About 75 percent of the population is Roman Catholic, with small Anglican and Muslim representations.

The importance of the airport at Gibraltar is increasing as it develops into a major European offshore financial center. Additional international airlines are expected to provide service in the near future.

Government. Although Gibraltar is connected to Spain by an isthmus, it is actually a self-governing British Crown colony.

Gibraltar has been a stable territory and a British possession since 1704, but Spain has made several attempts to claim sovereignty over the 2.25-square-mile area. In recent years Spain and Britain have agreed to resolve their differences.

The constitution provides for legislative powers and a house of assembly.

Legal System. The legal system is based on English common law and acts of parliament. But statutes are enacted by Gibraltar's own legal system.

The judicial system includes the Court of First Instance, Magistrate's Court, Supreme Court, and Court of Appeal.

Economy. Revenue is generated from tourism, customs and excise taxes, a lottery, marine-related business, and most important, offshore financial services.

The British have poured hundreds of millions of dollars into the development of a commercial shipyard, new housing, and improvements in the infrastructure and overall business conditions. Inflation and unemployment are very low.

The exempt company has attracted considerable international business. Approximately 21,000 corporations have been organized in Gibraltar; of these, 3000 received exempt certificates. The number of applications continues to increase as attorneys and accountants promote the unique advantages of this tiny haven.

Communications.   There are first-rate telecommunications in Gibraltar.

Business Profile

Banking, Money, and Foreign Exchange.   The following full-service banks possess licenses allowing them to operate offshore and to transact business with local residents: Barclays Bank PLC, A. L. Galliano Bankers Limited, Algemene Bank Gibraltar Limited, Bank Indosuez, Bank of Commerce and Credit (Gibraltar) Limited, and Metropolitan Bank.

A few of the banks that have limited licenses, allowing them to offer their services to nonresidents only, include Gibraltar and Iberian Bank Limited, Hambros Bank Gibraltar Limited, and Hong Kong Bank and Trust Co. Limited.

No exchange controls are imposed on the transfer of any currency. There is no central bank. Customer confidentiality is customary bank practice.

The Gibraltar pound is the official legal tender. It is not linked to any other currency.

Legal Entities.   The popular exempt company is granted a 25-year tax-exempt certificate by the Financial and Development Secretary. The certificate guarantees that the corporation will not pay income tax, capital gains tax, withholding tax on dividends, succession tax, or estate duty for that period.

The exempt company requires a minimum of two incorporators, each owning at least one share of stock. A maximum of 50 shareholders is allowed. An exempt company that is ordinarily resident in Gibraltar pays a flat-rate tax of £225 annually.

Before stock in an exempt company can be transferred, permission must be obtained from the Financial and Development Secretary. Suitable references from the party acquiring the stock will be required. If a trust owns the shares, however, no permission is needed to sell or transfer the interest.

Legal entities include a private limited-liability company (without the tax-exempt certificate) with or without share capital, a limited company tax-exempt by guarantee with or without share capital, an unlimited company with or without share capital, a public company, and an exempt public company.

Foreign companies may also qualify in Gibraltar with or without exempt status.

The tax-exempt Gibraltar corporation has other benefits to residents

outside Gibraltar or the United Kingdom. This is the only tax haven
that is an associate member of the European Community (EC), having
enlisted through England under the Treaty of Rome. Equally important, there are no double-taxation agreements and/or tax information
exchange agreements with any country except the United Kingdom.

Banks.   The Banking Ordinance of 1983 provides for two types of licenses: Class A (full) and Class B (limited).

The full-class license requires a paid-up share capital and reserves
equivalent to US $1,770,000. The limited-class license calls for a mini-
mum capitalization equivalent to $442,500.

Two directors are required. The shareholders and directors must
demonstrate expertise and a good reputation. Audited accounts are
open to the public.

Insurance Companies.   The Insurance Companies Ordinance of 1987
was drafted to enable insurers under the law to operate in EC countries.
Licensing and solvency margin requirements must be satisfied before a
company can begin underwriting.

Taxation.   The standard rate on corporate income tax is 35 percent.
Nonresidents, other than British subjects, are basically tax-exempt. Exempt corporations pay no taxes.

Financial and Investment Incentives.   The government grants exemptions from income tax to attract investors to certain development projects.

Tax Treaties.   There is a double-taxation treaty with the United Kingdom only.

Business Contacts

Management

Goutaland Trust Company Limited
International Commercial Centre
Suites 3 and 11, 10th Floor
2a Main Street
P.O. Box 629
Gibraltar
Tel: 350-79013 or 79038
Fax: 350-70101

Jordan & Sons (Gibraltar) Ltd.
Victoria House, Suite 31
Main Street
P.O. Box 569
Gibraltar
Tel: 350-75446
Fax: 350-79902

Riggs Valmet Corporate Services
   Ltd.
Riggs Valmet Trust Co. Ltd.
50 Town Range
P.O. Box 472
Gibraltar
Tel: 350-40000
Fax: 350-40404

International Company Service
   (Gibraltar) Limited
Manor House, Suite 2B
143 Main Street
Gibraltar
Tel: 350-76173
Fax: 350-70158

Banking

Hambros Bank (Gibraltar)
  Limited
Hambros House
Line Wall Road
P.O. Box 375
Gibraltar
Tel: 350-74850
Fax: 350-79037

Banco Español de Credito SA
Banesto Co. Management Ltd.
Banesto Trust Corporation Ltd.
Gibraltar
Tel: 350-76518
Fax: 350-73947

A. L. Galliano Bankers Limited
76 Main Street
P.O. Box 143
Gibraltar

Legal

Anthony Courtney, LLB
Chief Executive
CONSULT S.L.
Carrer Dr. Nequi No. 7 3A
Andorra
Tel: 33628-29 1 90
Fax: 33628-29 7 83

James Levy, LLB
J. A. Hassan & Partners
Barristers-at-Law
57–63 Line Wall Road
P.O. Boxes 199 and 612
Gibraltar
Tel: 350-79000
Fax: 350-71966

Allias & Levy
3 Irish Place, Suite 3
P.O. Box 466
Gibraltar

Louis W. Triay & Partner
Main Street, Suite 1
P.O. Box 147
Gibraltar Heights
Tel: 350-72712/72694
Fax: 350-71405

Accounting

Isola & Co.
Chartered Accountants
Main Street, Suite 12
P.O. Box 191
Gibraltar Heights

Hong Kong

Fast Facts

Population: 5,731,000 (1990)
Capital and Largest City: Victoria, 1,183,621
Languages: Chinese (Cantonese), English

Country Profile

The future of Hong Kong, the eminent British Crown colony since the 1800s, is wavering in the face of June 30, 1997, the date when Britain's lease over Hong Kong expires and the colony is reunited with China.

Uncertainty over Hong Kong's economic and political future was further shadowed in mid-1989 by the wave of civil unrest and the brutal response in Beijing by the hierarchy of the People's Republic of China. Migration, particularly to Singapore, Taiwan, and the Caribbean, had been increasing steadily as the countdown to 1997 continued, but the shocking events in Beijing triggered a mass exodus. Suddenly, the number of people leaving Hong Kong increased tenfold.

Hong Kong naturally commands a leading edge in the world market, providing an ideal center for trade, manufacturing, transportation, and banking. A strategic location in the Asian Pacific region and possession of one of the finest deep-water harbors in the world position Hong Kong in third place with New York and London as an international financial center.

Hong Kong's prospects have given many people the jitters. Fortunately, there is much hope and tremendous incentive for the Chinese not to tinker with this most vibrant economic and trading system, which offers the potential to bolster all of China.

In 1984, Great Britain and China signed the Sino-British Joint Declaration, in theory providing Hong Kong with a high degree of political latitude until 2047 under a policy of "one country, two systems." Most of the colony's present capitalistic and free-market attributes are not expected to change.

Slated for continuance are a freely convertible Hong Kong dollar, freely traveling residents, a free port, the right to own private property, and the present court system. These are a few of the reassuring signs that Hong Kong will experience a relatively smooth merger with China, considering the complexities of this unique situation.

Confidently, manufacturing companies have already begun to move their facilities to mainland China, jumping at the opportunity to capitalize on cheap labor and inexpensive land. This pattern is expected to continue into the next century. All the while, Hong Kong is forecast to transform into a more service-oriented climate, providing the desperately needed business acumen sought by the People's Republic of China. Increasingly, Hong Kong is viewed as the gateway to China.

This vertically structured mecca of commerce and industry promises interesting changes and new opportunity for the decades ahead.

The literacy rate is 77 percent. Some 90 percent of the population is Buddhist or Taoist; 10 percent is Christian.

Hong Kong's subtropical and monsoonal climate produces dry and cool winters (December to February), with an average temperature of 59°F. Summers are hot and rainy (May to September) with an average temperature of 82°F. Humidity runs high.

Hong Kong International Airport is serviced by 38 international airlines. Air travel times are Tokyo, 3 to 4 hours; Bangkok, Singapore, Jakarta, and Kuala Lumpur, 3 to 5 hours; India and Sri Lanka, 5 to 7 hours; California, 15 hours.

Government. The British monarch appoints a governor who represents the Royal Crown in Hong Kong and presides over an executive and legislative council.

Legal System. Hong Kong's independent judicial system consists of the Supreme Court, District Court, Magistrate's Court, Coroner's Court, and Juvenile Court as well as lesser courts.

Economy. The bustling economy stems from sheer numbers: Hong Kong is the eleventh largest trade economy in the world, the premiere container port, and Asia's number-one tourist destination. It has the sixth busiest international airport, and it is the third largest financial center. All this activity is packed into 400 square miles known as Hong Kong.

Over the past 20 years, the gross domestic product (GDP) in real terms has averaged 8.3 percent. This outstanding growth nearly doubles the world trade rate. Hong Kong has long had a hands-off posture toward business, thereby creating an atmosphere that attracts global business and stimulates bold growth.

The financial spectrum is reflected in these figures: There are over 400 foreign-owned banks with assets and liabilities exceeding US $550 billion. Some 175 overseas securities and futures firms trade actively. More than 275 insurance underwriters experienced a $987 million increase in total gross premiums between 1980 and 1987.

Communications. There are state-of-the-art communications to all parts of the world.

Business Profile

Banking, Money, and Foreign Exchange. The Banking Ordinance provides for three types of deposit-taking financial institutions: licensed banks, restricted-license banks, and deposit-taking corporations. The monetary unit is the Hong Kong dollar.

Licensed banks are Hong Kong corporations with residents controlling major interests. The minimum paid-up capital is HK $150 million. Prior to licensing, a bank must have previously accepted deposits and lent money to the public for 10 years. It must have a minimum of HK $1.75 billion in public deposits. Total assets must exceed HK $2.5 billion.

Foreign banks seeking to enter Hong Kong must demonstrate their financial strength by showing at least HK $14 billion in assets.

All licensed banks are required to join the Hong Kong Association of

Banks, which has the authority to regulate interest rates payable on accounts.

Restricted-license banks must have a paid-up capital of HK $100 million. These banks do not have interest rate limitation. They must meet the commission of banking's qualification requirements for beneficial owners and management.

Deposit-taking corporations must exhibit the minimum paid-up capital requirement of HK $25 million and must be majority-controlled by a licensed bank. Only deposits exceeding HK $100,000 are acceptable.

Typically, Hong Kong banks will offer the following types of accounts: current accounts, HK dollar savings accounts or time deposits, US dollar savings accounts, and onshore and offshore fixed-term deposits or savings accounts in major foreign currencies.

Establishing a corporate account is a simple procedure. Complete the bank's account-opening form, signature card, and mandate, and submit them with the initial deposit. The bank will also require certified copies of the corporation's memorandum and articles of association, along with any amendments, plus the certificate of incorporation, business registration certificate, and a company ordinance form providing information on the directors and acceptance and appointment.

All banks are members of the Paper (Cheque) Clearing System. There is also the Electronic Clearing System and the Clearing House Automated Transfer System (CHATS). The daily volume of items cleared is US $82 billion.

There are no exchange controls on currency movements.

Legal Entities. Sole proprietorships and partnerships are optional forms of business enterprise, but the limited-liability company is generally preferred. The Companies Ordinance, based on English statute law, governs this type of corporation.

The corporation must have a registered office and corporate secretary in Hong Kong. A minimum of two directors and one corporate secretary is required. Directors need not be residents. There is no capitalization requirement.

Approximately one month after the appropriate procedures have been satisfied, the Registry of Companies will issue a certificate of incorporation, allowing the company to commence business.

The incorporators must prepare the memorandum of association containing the name of the corporation, registered office address, purposes, authorized capital, subscription, and statement of the liability of members. Articles of association should also be prepared stating the company's internal guidelines. These two documents, along with a declaration of compliance, are then filed with the Registry of Companies.

These steps are generally handled by a lawyer or management or trust company.

Once the certificate of incorporation is received, a business registration certificate should be applied for through the Inland Revenue Department.

Because of the lengthy waiting period, many incorporators purchase a "shelf" company, so that business may commence immediately. The required documents of "shelf" companies are already incorporated. If desired, the name can be changed.

Sovereign Trust International, a member of the International Company Services Limited Group (see the Business Contacts section) will organize a new Hong Kong corporation for US $195 (HK $1500). A shelf company can be acquired for $325; a name change is $130.

For US $650 (HK $5000) annually, STI also provides domiciliary services for the required registered office, required local corporate secretary, preparation and filing of the annual return, and use of its mailing address and telephone and fax numbers.

Optional management services provide for two third-party directors and two corporate nominee-trustee shareholders acting under a declaration of trust. The annual fee is US $500.

The annual business registration fee is US $130.

Insurance companies and banks in Hong Kong are not practical for small underwriters or private international bankers to establish.

Taxation.   Taxation is straightforward.

Profits tax—16.5 percent income tax derived from Hong Kong source income

Salaries tax—15 percent tax on income gained from employment in Hong Kong

Property tax—15 percent tax on rental income generated from Hong Kong properties

Corporations doing business in Hong Kong do not pay profits tax on income that is not derived from Hong Kong sources. This single factor explains why Hong Kong not only is an enormous commercial, industrial, and financial center but also is regarded worldwide as a tax haven. Presently, 36,000 Hong Kong companies are being incorporated annually, most of them for this very reason.

Tax Treaties.   There are no double-taxation agreements.

Financial and Investment Incentives.   There are no specific incentives.

Business Contacts

Information Services

Industrial Promotion Office
Hong Kong Department of
   Industry
Hong Kong Government Office
180 Sutter Street
San Francisco, CA 94104
Tel: (415) 956-4560
Fax: (415) 421-0646

Furnishes very helpful promotional information on Hong
Kong.

Trade Department
G/F Ocean Centre
5 Canton Road
Kowloon, Hong Kong
Tel: 852-722-2333
Fax: 852-723-6135

Provides information and advice
on trade, import-export, licensing documentation, and other
matters.

Inland Revenue Department
Windsor House
311 Gloucester Road
Causeway Bay, Hong Kong
Tel: 852-894-5098
Fax: 852-576-6359

Provides tax information.

Trade Licensing Section
Trade Department
Ocean Centre
5 Canton Road
Kowloon, Hong Kong
Tel: 852-722-2333
Fax: 852-723-6135

Offers detailed information on licensing arrangements.

Hong Kong Trade Development
   Council
Convention Plaza
Office Tower, 36th–39th Floors
1 Harbor Road
Wanchai, Hong Kong
Tel: 852-833-4333
Fax: 852-824-0249

Distributes nine magazines cover-
ing the latest product news and
industry innovations.

Registrar of Companies
Queensway Government Offices,
   13th–14th Floors
66 Queensway
Hong Kong
Tel: 852-862-2600
Fax: 852-528-5423

New corporations must be registered here.

Chinese General Chamber of
   Commerce
CGCC Building, 7th Floor
24–25 Connaught Road
Central, Hong Kong
Tel: 852-525-6385
Fax: 852-584-2610

Sponsors 4300 member firms, 87
member associations, and 2800
individual members.

Chinese Manufacturers
   Association
CMA Building, 3rd–4th Floors
64–66 Connaught Road
Central, Hong Kong
Tel: 852-545-6166
Fax: 852-541-4541

Represents 2800 members.

Federation of Hong Kong
Industries
Hankow Centre, 4th Floor
5–15 Hankow Road
Tsimshatsui
Kowloon, Hong Kong
Tel: 852-723-0818
Fax: 852-721-3494

Promotes and protects Hong
Kong industries; supplies Chinese legal, financial, and technical translations; provides product design protection; conducts market surveys; and publishes *Hong Kong Industry News*, a monthly magazine.

Hong Kong Export Credit
Insurance Corp.
South Seas Centre
Tower 1, 2nd Floor
75 Moody Road
Tsimshatsui East
Kowloon, Hong Kong
Tel: 852-723-3883
Fax: 852-722-6277

Assists exporters with selling overseas on credit.

Hong Kong Exporters Association
Star House, Room 825
Tsimshatsui
Kowloon, Hong Kong
Tel: 852-730-9851
Fax: 852-730-1869

Promotes Hong Kong export
trade; 250 members.

Hong Kong General Chamber of
Commerce
United Centre, 22nd Floor
95 Queensway
Hong Kong
Tel: 852-529-9229
Fax: 852-527-9843

Independent representative organization for trade, commerce, and industry; 2800 member companies.

Hong Kong Management
Association
Fairmount House, 14th Floor
8 Cotton Tree Drive
Hong Kong
Tel: 852-526-6516
Fax: 852-868-4387

Publishes *Hong Kong Manager* and *Management and Finance Weekly,* and provides a host of services for the management field.

American Chamber of Commerce
Swire House, 10th Floor
Central, Hong Kong
Tel: 852-526-0165
Fax: 852-810-1289

Publishes several informative
books and monthly business magazines; 2250 American and non-American members.

Incorporation and Management

Sovereign Trust International
55 Connaught Road, Room 902
Central, Hong Kong
Tel: 852-5-8504422
Fax: 852-5-8505311

ICS Trust Company, Inc.
Tower III
918 China Hong Kong City
Tsimshatsui
Kowloon, Hong Kong
Tel: 852-736-9000
Fax: 852-735-7800

Mossack Fonseca & Co.
Attorneys at Law
Kowloon Centre, Room 903–5
29–43 Ashley Road, TST
Kowloon, Hong Kong
Tel: 852-3-672485
Fax: 852-3-7224308

Hall & Zyleman Company Limited
GPO Box 3653
Hong Kong
Tel: 852-523-1044
Fax: 852-810-5231

Yorkwo Consultancy Services
Leader Industrial Centre, Room
 311
57–59 Au Pui Wan Street
Fo Tan, Shatin, NT
Hong Kong
Tel: 852-684-1098
Fax: 852-601-6935

Banking

Barclays Bank PLC
United Centre, 11th Floor
95 Queensway
Hong Kong
Tel: 852-5-201181
Fax: 852-5-8613989

Chase Manhattan Bank NA
1 Exchange Square, 40th Floor
Hong Kong
Tel: 852-5-8414321
Fax: 852-5-8414396

Credit Suisse
3 Exchange Square, 22nd Floor
Hong Kong
Tel: 852-5-8414800
Fax: 852-5-8400020

Hong Kong & Shanghai Banking
 Corp.
1 Queen's Road C
Hong Kong
Tel: 852-5-8221111
Fax: 852-5-8101112

Manufacturers Hanover Trust Co.
Edinburgh Tower, 43rd Floor
Hong Kong
Tel: 852-5-8416888

Midland Bank PLC
2 Exchange Square, 34th Floor
Hong Kong
Tel: 852-5-8442888
Fax: 852-5-8105266

Morgan Guaranty Trust Co. of
 New York
Edinburgh Tower, 23rd Floor
Hong Kong
Tel: 852-5-8411311
Fax: 852-5-8681473

Standard Chartered Bank
The Landmark
Edinburgh Tower
Central, Hong Kong
Tel: 852-5-8422822
Fax: 852-5-8100651

Legal

Mossack Fonseca & Co.
Kowloon Centre, Room 903–5
29–43 Ashley Road, TST
Kowloon, Hong Kong
Tel: 852-3-672485
Fax: 852-3-7224308

Accounting

Peat, Marwick, Mitchell & Co.
Prince's Building
Central, Hong Kong
Publishes numerous booklets on
 banking, taxes, and investments.

Price Waterhouse
Prince's Building, 22nd Floor
Central, Hong Kong
Publishes *Doing Business in Hong
 Kong: Information Guide.*

Deloitte Ross Tohmatsu (DRT)
Wing On Centre, 26th Floor
111 Connaught Road
Central, Hong Kong
Tel: 852-545-0303
Fax: 852-541-1911
Publishes *Hong Kong: International
 Tax and Business Guide.*

Ireland

Fast Facts

Population: 3,500,000 (1990)
Capital and Largest City: Dublin, 550,000
Languages: Irish, English

Country Profile

Ireland's natural beauty is unsurpassed. It is a visual feast. Over every hilltop and around every bend is another landscape to be enjoyed. Writers, artists, and poets have celebrated this fact for centuries, but only recently has the international business traveler had the opportunity to reap Ireland's bounty as a result of attractive legislation and financial incentives.

Five-sixths of the 300 by 150 mile (approx.) island is the country of Ireland. The balance is Northern Ireland, a part of the United Kingdom.

The literacy rate is 99 percent. About 94 percent of the population is Roman Catholic.

The climate is mild, though often rainy and damp, ranging from 40°F in the winter to 60°F in the summer and contributing in large measure to the lush greenery for which Ireland is famous.

Ireland is well connected by air travel to the United States and Europe; there are frequent flights to numerous Irish cities. Dublin is only 1 hour by plane from London and is also within the London time zone, an attractive benefit when conducting business from Ireland.

Oceanic travel is available from the United States, and passenger and automobile ferries routinely traverse the Irish Sea from England.

Government.   The republic of Ireland has been a stable democratic sovereignty since its independence in 1922. Ireland is a free-market economy, with the exception of state-owned public transportation and utility companies. The right to own private property is guaranteed by the Irish constitution.

The president is elected for 7 years and is eligible for a second term. The president appoints as prime minister the party leader who wins the most seats in the Dail (house of representatives); the PM in turn nominates a cabinet that is approved by the Dail and that possesses executive power.

The senate (Seanard Eireann) and the house of representatives (Dail Eireann) make up the bicameral national parliament (Oireachtas). Although the Dail possesses the actual power, the Seanard has the ability to stall legislative proposals and to amend bills.

Legal System. The legal system comprises common and statutory law. Generally, all laws pertinent to the use of Ireland as an offshore business center are embodied in statutes.

Economy. Despite its well-publicized and continuous disputes with Northern Ireland, the Irish republic remains economically and politically stable.

Ireland is not a pure tax haven per se and is unlikely to ever join the ranks because of its participation in the Treaty of Rome, which governs relations between members of the European Community for their mutual benefit. However, the republic has similar characteristics to a tax haven in its favorable legislation, tax incentives, grants, low-interest loans, and tax exemption on nonresident company income.

Ireland is poised for strong economic growth. Membership in the EC will undoubtedly open many doors of opportunity for long-term growth. Its work force is well educated and plentiful. The country's infrastructure is excellent. And, of course, the financial incentives are in place.

Communications. An ultramodern telecommunications system delivers high-tech service around the country and allows worldwide direct dialing.

Business Profile

Banking, Money, and Foreign Exchange. The Central Bank of Ireland is responsible for supervising and licensing the country's vast banking system. The present exchange controls are expected to be abolished in 1992.

Ireland is an attractive banking and money market center with superb international relationships.

Since Ireland joined the European monetary system, the Irish pound has been quoted at approximately 10 percent less than the British pound; formerly it was pegged pound for pound.

Legal Entities. The best way to utilize Ireland as an offshore financial center is to incorporate a nonresident company. This type of company must conduct operations outside Ireland and cannot be a recipient of the numerous incentives available to qualified resident corporations that have proposed operations in the country.

Incorporation takes at least 2 weeks, sometimes longer. An off-the-shelf company can be purchased from the corporate services firm and can be put into motion overnight. The costs are modest—US $350 to $750 is reasonable. Management services, such as the use of nominee directors and nominee beneficiaries, are additional. In all cases, costs vary with the individual company performing the function.

A nonresident company is a private corporation with limited liability. Two incorporators are required, each of whom must hold a share. Nominees are used when anonymity is desired. The corporation must have a registered office in Ireland, hold an annual meeting, and file an annual return. The company may choose any name that is not "undesirable," followed by "Limited," its abbreviation "Ltd.," or "Teoranta." There is no minimum capital requirement.

Private and public resident corporations can also be organized. Incorporation procedures are very similar. There are no nationality or resident requirements.

There is no offshore bank or insurance legislation. A corporation is the principal vehicle for use by an offshore or international businessperson.

Taxation.   Nonresident companies are liable for corporation tax only on their Irish operations (if any) or other income from Ireland. Otherwise they pay no tax.

Financial and Investment Incentives.   Ireland has the welcome mat out for foreign investors. The Irish have developed a comprehensive menu of incentives and reliefs for manufacturing operations, service industries, and financial services. Here are some of the available benefits: 10 percent tax rate, cash grant aid, tax-exempt securities, Section 84 loans, leasing, urban renewal, tax depreciation, and patent income exemptions.

Contact the Ireland Industrial Development Authority for details.

Tax Treaties.   Tax treaties to circumvent double taxation exist between Ireland and Australia, Austria, Belgium, Canada, Cyprus, Denmark, Finland, France, Germany, Italy, Japan, Luxembourg, Netherlands, Norway, Pakistan, Sweden, Switzerland, the United Kingdom, the United States, and Zambia. There is also a taxation treaty with South Africa on aircraft and shipping.

Business Contacts

Information Services

Ireland Industrial Development
  Authority
Wilton Park House
Wilton Place
Dublin 2, Ireland
Tel: 353-1-686633
Telex: 93431
Fax: 353-1-603703

Maintains offices in major U.S.
  and international cities.

Dublin Chamber of Commerce
7 Clare Street
Dublin, Ireland

Accounting

Price Waterhouse
Gardner House, Wilton Place
Dublin 2, Ireland
Tel: 353-1-605199
Fax: 353-1-607638

Publishes *Ireland: A Guide for the U.S. Investor.*

Management

Spencer Company Formations
  Ltd.
Scorpio House
102 Sydney Street
Chelsea
London SW3 6NJ, United Kingdom
Tel: 44-71-352-2150/2274
Fax: 44-71-352-2260

Banking

Allied Irish Banks PLC
Bankcentre, Ballbridge
Dublin 4, Ireland

Isle of Man

Fast Facts

Population: 66,000 (1990)
Capital and Largest City: Douglas, 20,000
Language: English

Country Profile

The Isle of Man is situated in the Irish Sea between Ireland and England. This 227-square-mile island is inhabited by the Manx, a people of Celtic ancestry.

The literacy rate is 99.5 percent.

Visitors can reach the picturesque location by British Airways and Manx Airlines, which fly daily to points throughout England. Travel time to London is 1 hour.

Government.   The Isle of Man is a stable, self-governing British Crown sovereign dependency. It has never been part of the United Kingdom or the European Community.

Legal System.   The island enacts its own legislation and maintains its own court system, which basically follows the same principles of equity as the United Kingdom.

Economy.   Offshore finance and light manufacturing give the economy the greatest boost, while tourism aids the exchange earnings. Agriculture and fishing, the traditional industries, still contribute their share to the Manx system.

Communications.   Excellent communications provided by British telecommunications facilitate direct dialing worldwide.

Business Profile

Banking, Money, and Foreign Exchange. The 45 Manx banks and 48 trust companies provide a host of financial and banking services to offshore clients. Many of the larger British, Irish, European, and American banks are represented here. The monetary units are the British pound, Scottish currency, and the Isle of Man pound note.

Services available by the island's licensed financial institutions include deposit accounts in major foreign currencies, current accounts, loan and draft facilities, and foreign exchange services. Professional assistance is available in the form of incorporation services and management of corporations and trusts, providing directors, trustees, and nominee shareholders, and managing investments.

The banking and financial industry is closely governed. Licensed banks must maintain US $1,610,000 (£1 million) in share capital and maintain half of their capital in reserves. The annual bank license fee is $4025.

Deposit-taking corporations and financial advisers are also licensed. Deposit-taking companies must maintain US $805,000 (£500,000) in minimum paid-up capital.

Secrecy laws are upheld, except where criminal activities are concerned. There are no exchange controls.

Legal Entities. Manx companies can be organized in 7 to 10 days by filing the memorandum of association. The directors will then need to adopt articles of association governing the company.

The Companies Consolidation Act of 1931, as amended, distinguishes between private and public companies. Companies can be limited by shares, unlimited with shares, limited by guarantees, or hybrid—limited by guarantees with shares. Different classes of shares are permitted. Shares may be registered or bearer.

Private companies cannot sell shares to the public and are not required to file annual returns. Company names cannot include the words "Bank," "Banking," "Trust," "Building Society," "Municipal," "Chartered," "Royal," "Cooperative," "International," or "Isle of Man."

The company must be managed by at least two individuals serving as directors, plus a corporate secretary. All directors' names must appear on the company letterhead. Directors may be furnished to the corporation by a management company. The corporation must maintain a registered office on the Isle of Man.

Offshore insurance companies are chartered and licensed under the Insurance Act of 1986. Under the Exempt Insurance Companies Rule of 1981, an insurance company must have a minimum paid-up capital of £50,000 in cash. The initial license fee is £2000.

As with banks, insurance company applicants, directors, and management must satisfy government criteria and screening procedures.

Manx trusts are popular and ship registrations are common.

Taxation.   There are no capital or wealth taxes, no capital gains taxes, no death tax or estate duty, no stamp duty, no gift tax, no corporation tax, and no payroll tax.

Nonresidents are taxed only on income derived from Isle of Man sources.

Corporations managed by local directors are taxed at a standard rate of 20 percent on worldwide income. If managed from a foreign country, the corporation is considered a nonresident.

No taxes are levied on dividends and interest to shareholders of tax-exempt companies for up to 5 years.

Other taxes and other exemptions exist.

Financial and Investment Incentives.   The General Development Act of 1964 was designed to attract foreign companies and manufacturing businesses to the island. Today incentives are offered in the form of grants, exemption or reduction of income tax, low interest rates, rent reductions, and other relief.

Tax Treaties.   There is a double-taxation agreement with the United Kingdom on specific types of income and profit.

Business Contacts

Incorporation and Management

Charles Cain & Co.
36 Finch Road
Douglas, Isle of Man
Tel: 44-624-26931
Fax: 44-624-24469

Lorne House Trust Limited
Castletown, Isle of Man
Tel: 44-624-823579
Fax: 44-624-822952

Aston Corporate Management
 Limited
19 Peel Road
Douglas, Isle of Man
Tel: 44-624-626591
Fax: 44-624-625126

Overseas Company Registration
 Agents Limited
Companies House
Tower Street
P.O. Box 28
Ramsey, Isle of Man
Tel: 44-624-815544
(800) 283-4444 toll-free from USA
Fax: 44-624-815558

Island Resources
National House
Santon, Isle of Man
Tel: 44-624-824555
Fax: 44-624-823949

International Company Services
  Limited
Sovereign House
Station Road
St. Johns, Isle of Man
Tel: 44-624-801801
Fax: 44-624-801800

Abchurch Corporate Services
  Limited
Anglo International House
Bank Hill
P.O. Box 204
Douglas, Isle of Man
Tel: 44-624-662262
Fax: 44-624-662272

Isle of Man Financial Trust Ltd.
Clinches House, 5th Floor
Lord Street
Douglas, Isle of Man
Tel: 44-624-663466
Fax: 44-624-663467

Manx Corporate Services Limited
Capital House
5 Hill Street
Douglas, Isle of Man
Tel: 44-624-662727
Fax: 44-624-662332

City Trust Limited
Murdoch House
South Quay
Douglas, Isle of Man
Tel: 44-624-661881
Fax: 44-624-611423

Jordan & Sons (Isle of Man) Ltd.
24 Ridgeway Street
Douglas, Isle of Man
Tel: 44-624-624298
Fax: 44-624-626719

Aarawak Trust Co. (Isle of Man)
  Ltd.
Barclays House
Victoria Street
P.O. Box 34
Douglas, Isle of Man

CWL Management Services Ltd.
Treger House
Circular Road
Douglas, Isle of Man

Corporate Management Ltd.
Western House
Victoria Street
Douglas, Isle of Man

Jowik Corporate Trust Services
  Ltd.
11 Myrtle Street
Douglas, Isle of Man

Regent Management Services, Inc.
National House
Santon, Isle of Man

Banking

Anglo Manx Bank Limited
5 Anthol Street
Douglas, Isle of Man
Tel: 44-624-23845
Fax: 44-624-76080

Tyndall Bank International
  Limited
Tyndall House
Kensington Road
P.O. Box 62
Douglas, Isle of Man
Tel: 44-624-29201
Fax: 44-624-20200

Bell International Ltd.
Bell House
Buck's Road
Douglas, Isle of Man

Barclays Bank
Barclays House
Victoria Street
Douglas, Isle of Man

Celtic Bank Ltd.
Barclays House
Victoria Street
Douglas, Isle of Man

Mannin International Ltd.   *Accounting*
Lorne House   J. P. Collins
Castletown, Isle of Man   14 Anthol Street

William's & Glyn's Bank (Isle of   Douglas, Isle of Man
  Man) Ltd.   D. McPhee
Victory House   9 Mount Havelock
Prospect Hill   Douglas, Isle of Man
Douglas, Isle of Man
                                      Bennett Roy & Co.
                                      Viking House
                                      Nelson Street
                                      Douglas, Isle of Man

Liechtenstein

Fast Facts

Population: 29,000 (1990)
Capital and Largest City: Vaduz, 4920
Languages: German, Alemanni

Country Profile

The majestic snow-capped Alps encompassing the eastern portion of Liechtenstein produce naturally awe-inspiring views, contrasting with the idyllic low-lying valleys of colorful flowers and carpeted green hills.

This postage-stamp-size financial enclave of roughly 60 square miles is wedged between Switzerland and Austria. It has maintained its stature as a leading European tax haven since the 1920s.

The literacy rate is 100 percent. About 83 percent of the population is Roman Catholic.

The climate is typical for the Alps—snow in the winter and rain in the summer, similar to the northeast United States.

Liechtenstein's road system is well connected to the capital of Vaduz and links travelers with its Swiss and Austrian neighbors, where air connections are excellent. Rail transportation also provides a good means for getting around.

Government. Liechtenstein, a hereditary constitutional monarchy, gained complete independence on July 12, 1806, after being part of the Holy Roman Empire for nearly 100 years. The principality is headed by Prince Franz Josef II. The present constitution, dated 1921, calls for a 15-member legislature that is elected every 4 years.

Legal System.   The prince of the state and the legislature jointly pass law. Civil and criminal procedures have an Austrian influence, contract and property law a Swiss orientation, and commercial law a German base.

The principality maintains its own court system.

Economy.   Although best known as a fiscal and corporate paradise, Liechtenstein does have local industries, which have enjoyed steady growth. The major ones are textiles, metalwork, pottery, and chemicals. Exports, tourism, and (of course) postage stamps are important revenue centers.

Communications.   Excellent telecommunications afford worldwide direct dialing. The postal system is exceptional.

Business Profile

Banking, Money, and Foreign Exchange.   Three well-established banking institutions cater to residents and international business.

Liechtenstein is not a party directly or indirectly to any exchange-of-information agreements, and its secrecy laws are even greater than those of Switzerland. Bankers won't assist law enforcement officials with drug, fraud, theft, or tax investigations. They consider their rigid secrecy laws to be their most important advantage, the cornerstone of their success.

However, the three major banks have beefed up precautionary measures intended to curb money laundering. Insider trading is also under the spotlight, even though it is not a crime in Liechtenstein. For instance, when opening an account with Bank in Liechtenstein AG, the account holder is required to sign the following statement:

> Authorization in Insider Proceedings.
> The undersigned (hereinafter called the "Customer") hereby confirms that he will not carry out any transaction concerning his securities account with Bank in Liechtenstein AG which is considered as insider trading not allowed by law or other regulations in that country in which the transaction is carried out ("Insider Trading").
> If proceedings against the bank are by the authorities having jurisdiction for investigations in insider trading in the respective countries ("Authorities"), the Bank will inform the customer ("Information") immediately after receipt of a request for information.
> The Bank reserves the right to take any steps which it may deem appropriate after due consideration and the expiration of 30 days since the forwarding of the information to the Customer. In such case the Customer authorizes the Bank to reveal to the Authorities his name and details of any alleged insider trading.

This authorization shall be effective only if proceedings are initiated against the Bank because of insider trading.

(Signed by the Customer)

The Liechtensteinische Landesbank has the right to issue the Swiss franc (SF), which is the common monetary unit.

There are no restrictions on the transfer or repatriation of funds.

Legal Entities.   One immediately distinguishable feature of Liechtenstein's company law is that it permits the establishment of any type of legal entity found anywhere in the world.

A variety of corporate forms and other types of entities exist, with relatively simple procedures for incorporation or organization. The choices include the establishment (also known as the "Ansult"), the company limited by shares or association, the foundation, and the trust.

Licenses are required of banks, insurance companies, trust companies, finance firms, investment funds, and auditors. Each entity has its own characteristics.

The Establishment.   The establishment is a popular form for foreign-based holding companies. There are 40,000 in existence.

The establishment has limited liability, unlimited duration, and profit or nonprofit economic goals. No minimum number of associates (shareholders) is required but one founder is necessary. An individual or corporation may be the founder. Using a Liechtenstein resident (such as a lawyer) to incorporate provides automatic anonymity to the beneficial owner(s).

The company name must not conflict with any other name and must end with the word "Ansult," "Establishment," or "Établisment."

As in other countries, articles of incorporation must be filed. The articles should include the name of the corporation, registered office address within Liechtenstein, purpose, capital structure, board of management particulars, and auditor, plus additional information related to accounting principles, publishing notices, and liquidation procedures.

Full capitalization must be paid in to the establishment and deposited in a Liechtenstein or Swiss bank. The establishment without associates requires a minimum paid-up capital of SF 30,000 (approximately US $10,000).

Company Limited by Shares.   The limited company is organized by entering certain information into the public register, rather than by filing articles of incorporation. The entry includes the date, company name, domicile, date of the articles of association (bylaws), duration, purpose, capital stock, board members' names and addresses, and signature seal.

Formation may be either simultaneous or successive. Simultaneous formation provides that shareholders or beneficial owners be placed on public record and also serve as the founders or incorporators. They infuse their capital and issue all shares. The incorporation procedure requires the founders to sign and notarize a deed containing pertinent information that is normally disclosed in the articles of incorporation.

Successive formation calls for the founders to raise capital from the public rather than themselves. During the organization process, a representative body of the stockholders assembles for a general meeting to determine the capital structure, management, and articles of association.

The minimum paid-up capital is SF 50,000 or other currency equivalent. Bearer shares and/or registered shares are acceptable. Nonvoting shares are not allowed. Preferred shares may be issued.

One board member must be a resident. An annual audit is required.

Foundations and Trusts.   Prescribed laws govern the organization and operation of foundations and trusts. Consult a lawyer in Liechtenstein for further information and costs. (See the Business Contacts section.)

Liechtenstein trusts have attracted many foreigners, particularly Europeans. The *trust enterprise* is a private trust without the distinction of being a separate legal entity; the *figurative trust* is used for commercial reasons and has judicial personality; the *trust settlement* has a trust relationship as commonly understood in the United States.

Costs to incorporate vary from lawyer to lawyer and by type of entity desired. Overseas Company Registration Agents Limited, on the Isle of Man, is very competitive and quotes £1500 for a new Liechtenstein corporation. Management and director fees are additional. (See the worldwide service listing in Part 3.)

Taxation.   A holding company or domiciliary company that produces income from outside Liechtenstein is not liable for taxes or profits.

There is a net worth tax of .01 percent based on capital and reserves. The minimum tax is SF 1000.

Other taxes in effect are unlikely to apply to those using Liechtenstein for its tax haven merits.

Financial and Investment Incentives.   There are no special incentives.

Tax Treaties.   A double-taxation treaty exists only with Austria.

Business Contacts

Management

Bilfinanz Aktiegesellschaft
Bangarten 6
Postfach 47
Vaduz, Liechtenstein

Banking

Verwaltungs-und-Privat-Bank
 Aktiegesellschaft
Fl-9490 Vaduz
Postfach 885
Liechtenstein
Tel: 41-75-5 66 55

Liechtensteinische Landesbank
  Staatsgarantie
Fl-9490 Vaduz
Stadtle 44, Postfach 384
Liechtenstein
Tel: 41-75-6 8 11

Bank in Liechtenstein AG
Fl-9490 Vaduz
Postfach 85
Liechtenstein
Tel: 41-75-5 11 22

Legal
Dr. Peter Marxer
Fl-9490 Vaduz
Kirchstrasse 1
Liechtenstein

Dr. iur. Karlheinz Ritter
Fl-9490 Vaduz
Stadtle 36
Liechtenstein

Luxembourg

Fast Facts

Population: 375,000 (1990)
Capital and Largest City: Luxembourg City, 78,924
Languages: Letzeburgesh, French, German,
    English

Country Profile

The grand duchy of Luxembourg, with its triboundaries adjoining Belgium, France, and Germany, is equivalent in size to Rhode Island.

The literacy rate is 99 percent. The dominant religion is Roman Catholic, with small Lutheran and Jewish representations.

Luxair (national airline), Air France, British Airways, Icelandair, and Lufthansa all service the airport on the outskirts of Luxembourg City. Air travel to London, Frankfurt, and Paris is 1 hour or less.

Government. Luxembourgers, as the people are known, consider 1839 to be the year they gained independence. The country was dominated for 400 years by other European nations. Several important events leading up to the Congress of Vienna (1815) eventually brought political autonomy.

Today's parliamentary government with a constitutional monarchy is headed by Grand Duke Jean, who exercises executive power in concert with the council of government, or cabinet. The chamber of deputies is the elected legislative wing.

Legal System. The judicial branch is a legal mélange of French, Belgian, and German systems supported by local practice and legal customs. The Supreme Court is the highest house of justice.

Economy.   The country's economy is perpetuated by its growth in banking and financial services as it sheds its former reliance on iron and steel.

Communications.   Luxembourg offers excellent communications and close proximity to major European centers.

Business Profile

Banking, Money, and Foreign Exchange.   Luxembourg has rapidly evolved into a global banking center with some 130 banks, of which 100 are branches of major foreign banks. However, the rush has tapered off drastically as Luxembourg prepares to merge with the EC in 1992.

Overall, the swift expansion of the Euro-bond market in recent years is highly attributable to the substantial infusion of offshore capital. The lack of withholding tax on bond interest has spurred Luxembourg as a prominent hub of Euro-bond issues.

Luxembourg competes directly with Switzerland for portfolio management of foreign investors with a high net worth. But in comparison, the grand duchy does not provide the same quality of service.

Bank secrecy has played a valuable role in Luxembourg's success as a financial haven. However, the enthusiasm for privacy may be somewhat dampened by its participation in the EC. Luxembourg cannot match Switzerland—or even better, Liechtenstein—for secrecy. Violation of secrecy laws is only a civil offense, but money laundering is a criminal offense.

The collapse of the Luxembourg-based Bank of Credit and Commerce International (BCCI) will certainly undermine banking and secrecy not only in the grand duchy but in outposts around the world. An avalanche of secrets will tumble from this banking closet.

Unfortunately, secrecy, personal freedom, and privacy are diminishing commodities everywhere as governments reach out in the name of crime prevention.

The Luxembourg franc is the monetary unit. There are no exchange controls.

Legal Entities.   Luxembourg offers a diverse selection of legal forms, but the holding company is favored for offshore purposes. This vehicle is basically free of all taxes.

Presently, there are more than 7500 holding companies in operation. Not all share the same benefits, however. The standard holding company, as the name implies, is for holding, not operating. In other words, the company owns passive assets (stock, bonds, trademarks, patents, and so on) as opposed to actually being an operating enterprise.

The holding company designed expressly for the management of funds is particularly attractive. Today Luxembourg leads with a larger number of managed funds than any other country.

Aside from the previously mentioned advantages of Luxembourg and the tax-free nature of the standard holding company, other influencing factors include a stable government, a centralized European location, simple incorporation procedures, use of bearer shares, use of nonresident directors, low management costs, and the presence of a national stock exchange.

Taxation.   The standard holding corporation pays no taxes except a 10 percent registration tax on issued shares and a .20 percent annual capital tax on issued capital bonds.

There is no withholding tax on bank accounts. In Switzerland, by contrast, 35 percent of interest earned by nonresidents is withheld.

Financial and Investment Incentives.   Financial and investment incentives come in the form of tax concessions to attract various industries, as illustrated by the standard and fund holding companies.

Tax Treaties.   There are double-taxation agreements with Austria, Belgium, Brazil, Denmark, Finland, France, Germany, Iceland, Ireland, Italy, Korea, Morocco, Netherlands, Norway, Spain, Sweden, the United Kingdom, and the United States.

Business Contacts

Management

European Pacific Trust Co.
  (Luxembourg) SA
Forum Royal, 7th Floor
25C Boulevard Royal
L-2449 Luxembourg

Banking

Banque Générale de Luxembourg
14 Rue Aldringen
L-2951 Luxembourg
Tel: 352-4799-1
Telex: 3401 bgl lu
Fax: 352-4799-2579

BfG Luxembourg Siegesocial
17 Rue du Fosse
Boite Postale 1123
L-1011 Luxembourg

Banque de Luxembourg
80 Place de la Gare
L-1022 Luxembourg

Banque International à
  Luxembourg
2 Boulevard Royal
Luxembourg

Hoogewerf & Co.
25 Boulevard Royal
P.O. Box 878
L-2018 Luxembourg

Kredjetbank SA Luxembourgeoise
43 Boulevard Royal
L-2955 Luxembourg
Tel: 352-47971

Legal

Mr. J. Fraas
Citibank (Luxembourg)
16 Avenue Marie-Theresa
P.O. Box 1373
Luxembourg

Mossack Fonseca & Co.
43 Boulevard Joseph II
Luxembourg
Tel: 352-458193/458577
Fax: 352-458673

Malta

Fast Facts

Population: 348,000 (1990)
Capital and Largest City: Valetta, 9300
Languages: Maltese, English

Country Profile

The five Maltese islands are strategically positioned midway between Gibraltar and Suez. Italy is in close proximity to the north, and further south is North Africa.

Malta's long and colorful history dates back to the Phoenicians. Over the past 2000 years, many conquerors and cultures have influenced Maltese life.

The literacy rate is 83 percent, and the dominant religion is Roman Catholic.

The subtropical summer climate produces plenty of sunshine. Winters are mild. Year-round rainfall is only 23 inches.

Malta is comfortably accessible by air and sea. Direct flights connect 30 cities in the neighboring continents. Air travel times are: London and Frankfurt, 3 hours; Paris, 2 hours; Rome, 1 hour. Air Europe, Air Malta, British Island Airways, and Monarch provide service.

Government.   On September 21, 1964, Malta became an independent sovereignty guided by its own constitution. It remained a parliamentary democracy until 1974, when the constitution was revised and Malta became a republic within the British Commonwealth.

Legal System.   The present legal system is a patchwork of cultures resulting from a multitude of conquests over the centuries. However, company and tax laws are based on United Kingdom models.

Economy.   Malta has no agriculture or natural resources, but is the beneficiary of an ideal location. Over the years, extensive harbor facilities were built providing a Mediterranean naval base for NATO, Britain, and the United States. This produced a nice income for Malta until 1979, when naval operations were terminated.

Today, shipbuilding and repairs occupy the old British facilities. Malta's maritime services have been further enhanced by the construction of a new shipyard.

Light manufacturing of electronic components, processed foods, rubber goods, and textiles bolsters exports and stabilizes the balance of trade. New incentives are being encouraged with attractive fiscal incentives.

The Christian Democratic Party returned to office in 1987 with a mandate to open the economy and prepare the country for EC membership. Proponents for an international financial and business center envision Malta as the "Switzerland of the Mediterranean." In concert with this bold new agenda, the Malta International Business Activities Act was born.

Communications.   The communications system is excellent.

Business Profile

Banking, Money, and Foreign Exchange.   In addition to the Central Bank, Malta has three commercial banks with more than 70 branches and an investment bank that is part of the Malta Development Corporation.

With the advent of the new offshore bank legislation, branches and subsidiaries of foreign banks are being established. This trend is expected to continue. The monetary unit is the Maltese lira (Lm).

There are strict secrecy laws and no exchange controls.

Legal Entities.   Offshore companies are limited and are either trading or nontrading companies. They may be private or public. The private exempt company is for Maltese residents only.

The memorandum and articles of association are drafted and signed by a minimum of two shareholders or their local representatives. These documents contain the usual pertinent organizational information on the company. Foreign shareholders, if any, must get acceptance of the corporate documents from the Central Bank and provide character and financial references of the principals. Once approval is granted, the corporation is required to open a local account with a commercial bank for the deposit of the initial share capital. The memorandum is then filed with the Registrar of Partnerships. A certificate of incorporation will be issued if all requirements have been satisfied.

One director is necessary. There are no nationality or residency requirements. Nominees may be engaged.

All offshore entities except nontrading companies must file an annual return, which is published.

The Offshore Nontrading Company.   The nontrading company is limited to owning, managing, and administering any kind of property (real estate, ships, and the like).

The Offshore Trading Company.   The trading company may be a banking, an insurance, or a general trading entity. The offshore general trading company is not limited to ownership, management, and administration of property of any kind.

Offshore Banking Companies.   Offshore banking is divided into three categories:

Offshore overseas company—a branch of a reputable international bank that is established for offshore activities

Offshore subsidiary company—a subsidiary of a reputable international bank that is established for offshore activities

Offshore local company—a local Maltese bank that establishes a subsidiary for offshore activities

Under the Banking Act of 1970, application for a bank license is made with the Central Bank of Malta.

Offshore banks, whether overseas, subsidiary, or local, are exempt from certain requirements normally imposed, since their activities are restricted to offshore.

The minimum paid-up capital is US $1,500,000 or the foreign-currency equivalent.

Offshore Insurance Companies.   Under the Insurance Business Act of 1981, an application for insurance license is handled by the Authority and Minister of Finance. The minimum paid-up capital is US $750,000.

Offshore Trusts.   Trusts are provided for under the Offshore Trusts Act of 1988.

Flag of Convenience.   Ships and yachts may be registered and flown under the Maltese flag. The Merchant Ship Act provides for registrations by Maltese citizens or Maltese companies.

Manduca, Mercieca & Co. in Valetta quotes incorporation costs, including professional fees, starting at Lm 450 (about US $1350) for share capital of Lm 10,000 (US $30,000).

Taxation.   Nontrading companies are totally exempt from income tax, and trading companies are nearly free of income tax. Shipping companies are entirely tax-exempt.

Financial and Investment Incentives.   Malta has a package of incentives to attract more desirable industries to the progressive new haven. According to Malta Development Corporation's booklet *Malta: A Profitable Proposition*, these include

> 10-year tax holidays for new export-oriented companies; fiscal incentives, including investment and accelerated depreciation allowances for existing industry; soft loans; training grants; ready-built factories at subsidized rents; duty-free exemption on plants, machinery, and all materials; a liberal policy of work permits.

Tax Treaties.   There are double-taxation agreements with the United States, the United Kingdom, and 18 other European countries.

Business Contacts

Government

Malta International Business
  Authority
Palazzo Spinola
P.O. Box St. Julians 29
Malta
Tel: 356-319055
Fax: 356-336851

Malta Development Corporation
House of Catalunya
Marsamxetto Road
Valetta, Malta
Tel: 356-221431/223688/221523
Fax: 356-606407

Management

Malta Trust & Nominee Ltd.
Wisely House
First Floor
206 Old Bakery Street
Valetta, Malta
Tel: 356-223125/223216/243885
Telex: 1703 JENTI MW
Fax: 356-241301/247310

Fenlex Nominee Services Ltd.
198 Old Bakery Street
Valetta, Malta
Tel: 356-241232/243939/222853
Fax: 356-221893

Accounting

Manduca, Mercieca & Co.
21 Archbishop Street
Valetta, Malta
Tel: 356-220170
Fax: 356-220386

Monaco

Fast Facts

Population: 29,000 (1990)
Capital and Largest City: Monaco-Villa, 27,063
Languages: French, English, Italian, Monégasque

Country Profile

Monaco, the jet setters' capital of the world, conjures up vivid images of conspicuous consumption at its finest. The .073-square-mile (465-acre) country is in the heart of the French Riviera, where superyachts decorate the tiny harbor, Maseratis caress hairpin curves, seaside mansions perch high above the Mediterranean Sea, and rich playboys "plunge" nightly at the elegant Casino de Monte Carlo. For most people, it's a land of make-believe, its style and mood well captured by Cary Grant in *To Catch a Thief.*

The literacy rate is 99 percent, and the dominant religion is Roman Catholic.

Monaco is known for its beautiful climate.

The international airport at Nice is a 10-minute jaunt along the scenic French coast.

Government. This world-renowned principality is the second smallest country in the world. It is a stable, independent sovereignty that initially gained recognition in 1489. The government is a hereditary and constitutional monarchy led by Prince Rainier III.

Legal System. Traditionally based on Monégasque law, Monaco employs the French civil code in business practice. Monaco has close ties with France, as a result of many treaties. Some of France's regulations apply to Monaco.

Economy. Tourism is a major revenue producer for the principality. Real estate development, postage-stamp sales, and the business establishment kick into the pot. Light industry is encouraged. The "tax haven" aspects are limited, but for the right person, the specific advantages and inherent nature of Monaco can be very appealing.

During the 1800s, Prince Charles III saved the economy by introducing gambling, but today this revenue accounts for a modest 4 to 5 percent. Value-added taxes (VAT) are a principal revenue source.

Communications. Typical of Europe, Monégasque communications are top-notch.

Business Profile

Banking, Money, and Foreign Exchange. English, Swiss, and Italian banks cater to the residents, vacationers, and business interests of Monaco, but of the more than 30 banks present, French institutions are predominant. The monetary unit is the French franc (FF).

Foreign exchange transactions require approval by the postal authorities or an authorized bank.

Nonresident bank deposits are not restricted and are readily transferable in any currency.

Numbered bank accounts are nonexistent.

Legal Entities. The SAM (*société anonyme monégasque*) is limited by shares and the choice of foreigners, unless establishing a branch of a foreign corporation, in which instance, permission must be received and necessary documents filed along with audited financial statements for the previous 3 years.

Incorporation takes approximately 3 to 4 months and requires prior government approval. The requirements for organizing a SAM are as follows:

1. The corporation must be properly headquartered within the principality.
2. Two directors are necessary, one of whom must be a legal resident. Nationality of directors is irrelevant.
3. The company must be entered on the official list of companies within 15 days of incorporation.
4. Two shareholders are required.
5. Minimum capitalization is FF 500,000.
6. Shares issued in kind are restricted from trade for two years. Registered or bearer form are permitted.
7. A registered chartered accountant must be appointed as company auditor.

Incorporation costs for a SAM are approximately FF 25,000. This fee includes registration tax, stamp duty, notary fees, and publication. It's not practical to set up "shelf" companies for the purpose of reselling.

Banks, financial institutions, insurance companies, and other entities are governed by special regulations.

Taxation.   Citizens of Monaco do not pay taxes. There are no stamp duties on withholding taxes.

Foreign and local companies are responsible for 35 percent tax or net profits.

Commercial or industrial-type companies operating in Monaco pay profit tax if more than 25 percent of their income originates from non-Monégasque sources.

Companies whose incomes are derived from passive sources such as intellectual property rights, processes, and formulas pay profit taxes.

Taxes are imposed on commissions, royalties, interest, dividends, and capital gains on the disposal of assets. There are registration taxes and stamp duties on the transfer of real estate, and gift and inheritance taxes.

There are value added-taxes on a variety of products. These taxes are levied at the same rate as in France.

Financial and Investment Incentives.   Incentives for certain advanced light industries come in the form of low taxes.

Tax Treaties.   A tax treaty is in effect with France.

Business Contacts

Banking

Barclays Bank
31 Avenue de la Costa
Monte Carlo, Monaco

Compagnie Monégasque de
  Banque
Les Terrasses
2 Avenue de Monte Carlo
Monte Carlo, Monaco

Crédit Foncier de Monaco
17 Boulevard Albert 1er
P.O. Box 6
Monte Carlo, Monaco

Societé de Banque et
  d'Investissements
26 Boulevard d'Italie
Monte Carlo, Monaco

Legal

Gordon S. Blair & Co.
11 Avenue de Grande-Bretaque
MC 98003, Monaco
Tel: 33-9350-6921

Accounting

Hoogewerf & Co. SAM
2 Avenue de Monte Carlo
P.O. Box 343
MC 98006, Monaco
Tel: 33-9350-0820
Fax: 33-9325-2412

Montserrat

Fast Facts

Population: 13,000 (1990)
Capital and Largest City: Plymouth, 3000
Language: English

Country Profile

Montserrat acquired its nickname of the "Emerald Isle" from the lush green foliage of its mountainsides. The island lies in the Eastern Caribbean close to Antigua and Nevis. It was discovered by Christopher Columbus in 1493.

Montserrat is still recovering from two significant events. In 1989 Hurricane Hugo, on its rampage through the Caribbean, nearly leveled the 39-square-mile island. Only months before, an international offshore banking scandal broke wide open. Both disasters have left major cleanup tasks.

The climate is tempered by pleasant ocean breezes. Temperatures hover between 76° and 88°F.

Government.   The British dependency has a ministerial system of government and its own constitution. The governor of Montserrat represents the British monarch.

Legal System.   Montserrat's legal system is based on English common law and local statutes. The independent judicial system maintains its own courts.

Economy.   Traditionally, Montserrat's economy has been based on agriculture, light industry, and manufacturing. Tourism plays a role too. The offshore financial sector began to emerge in the late 1970s.

Passage of the International Business Companies Ordinance in 1985 drew prompt attention to the island's status as a no-tax haven with regard to international business companies (IBCs).

Montserrat's economic posture was bright. Simultaneously, the British dependency was being promoted as an offshore banking center, and the number of newly chartered banks skyrocketed in just a few short years.

Communications.   Cable & Wireless Limited provides telephone, cable, and fax services connecting Montserrat with the rest of the world.

Business Profile

Banking, Money, and Foreign Exchange. During the 1980s, the offshore sector became plagued by money-laundering problems, many of them drug-related, and financial scams.

In August 1985, the findings of the Permanent Subcommittee on Investigations of Offshore Banking were published in the U.S. Senate's report *Crime and Secrecy: The Use of Offshore Banks and Companies*. The report discussed various havens, secrecy laws, and offshore crimes, and some of the proponents fueling the trend. Specifically, it detailed the offshore banking problems in Montserrat.

In 1990, the United Kingdom published its own version of events in a document referred to as the Gallagher Report. Of 330 total banks chartered in Montserrat, one company is alleged to have organized most of the 259 bank charters that were revoked.

In light of the worldwide publicity now attached to this once-promising tax haven, there is little reason to use it for any kind of banking. It will be a long time before Montserrat is salvaged from the wreckage.

Currently, a moratorium on new bank charters is in effect. The government is restructuring its system for licensing, monitoring, and enforcing its forthcoming regulations and policies.

The monetary unit is the Eastern Caribbean (EC) dollar.

Legal Entities. The Gallagher Report makes specific recommendations for overhauling the procedures and requirements for chartering and operating an offshore bank in Montserrat.

Although the modifications place Montserrat in line with other jurisdictions, the Gallagher Report does suggest limiting offshore banking to branches or subsidiaries of recognized international banks and to applicants who possess impeccable references and financial substance. The report also makes recommendations for trust companies and insurance companies.

Under the 1985 ordinance, an IBC is limited by shares, and a minimum of one shareholder (an individual or a corporation) is required.

The registration fee is US $300, payable at the time the memorandum of association is filed. This provides a capital stock up to $50,000. No minimum capital is required.

One director is required. There are no residency or nationality requirements for directors or shareholders. The company must maintain a registered office in Montserrat.

Taxation. The tax-free status of the IBC makes it the ideal vehicle for offshore business.

Financial and Investment Incentives.   Tax holidays of 10 to 15 years are granted to businesses that are "approved enterprises" and that manufacture approved products.

Hotel construction and operations are encouraged through capital expenditure allowances. A 5-year tax exemption is extended under certain conditions.

Tax Treaties.   There are double-taxation agreements with Denmark, Japan, Norway, Sweden, Switzerland, and the United Kingdom.

Business Contacts

Banking

Barclays Bank International Ltd.
P.O. Box 131
Plymouth, Montserrat

Royal Bank of Canada
Parliament Street
P.O. Box 222
Plymouth, Montserrat

Canadian Credit Bank Ltd.
P.O. Box 207
Plymouth, Montserrat

Legal

Kenneth Allen, Solicitor
Chambers
Plymouth, Montserrat

Nauru

Fast Facts

Population: 9053 (1990)
Capital and Largest City: Yaren
Languages: Nauruan, English

Country Profile

Nauru is the smallest country in the world, with a single national resource: phosphate.

The island nation is 8 square miles of visually unappealing terrain. Giant columns of phosphate jut from the center and create an eerie silhouette at sunset.

The people have one of the highest per capita incomes in the world as a result of their government's desire to share the wealth with the 4000-plus Nauruans. Each year, every man, woman, and child receives nearly $30,000 in royalties from the production and export of phosphates.

This dwindling commodity is mined from the island and is expected to be depleted by the year 2000. In anticipation of this predictable outcome, the government has taken measures to secure the future of the Nauruan race.

The government has established five trusts of which all Nauruans are beneficiaries. If these trusts were liquidated today, every Nauruan would be a millionaire. Meanwhile, the trusts have invested wisely, owning and operating prime real estate in Australia and in Guam, Hawaii, and other Pacific islands.

Nauruans are managerial people, choosing to delegate work to imported labor. Another 4000-plus residents from other Pacific islands are permitted to live and work in Nauru. There are also European and Chinese workers. Nauruans have grown accustomed to all modern conveniences, including automobiles, TVs, VCRs, and microwaves.

There is 100 percent literacy. The dominant religions are Protestant (58 percent) and Roman Catholic (24 percent).

The typical monsoonal climate is hot, 76° to 93°F, with humidity running 70 to 80 percent.

The Nauru people are a mixture of Melanesian, Micronesian, and Polynesian. Whenever the population drops below 1500, which has occurred only a few times, they consider themselves to be on the extinction list. The government desires to perpetuate their existence; that is why so much emphasis is placed on their financial and physical wellbeing.

Unlike many islands, Nauru does not have a tourist industry and for several good reasons. It's not a place that most tourists would pay to visit. Outsiders are uninvited, and getting onto the island is nearly impossible, requiring special written permission from the government. At last report, Air Nauru was still on strike, as it has been for years.

Government. Nauru has had a parliamentary system of government with its own constitution since 1968.

Economy. In a determined effort to diversify out of its monolithic phosphate industry, Nauru has enacted tax haven legislation to transform the country into a Pacific offshore financial paradise. The government has also entered into a variety of enterprises and investments.

Even though the apparatus is in place, Nauruan leaders have done little to promote the island as a tax haven. Apparently, they are relying on their investments to meet the country's economic needs.

Communications. Communications are hampered by poor connections and transmission errors in faxing. Operator assistance is usually required.

Communication is further complicated by the fact that only two people on the island handle offshore arrangements. And they are not always accessible, sometimes vacationing for months.

Business Profile

Banking, Money, and Foreign Exchange.   The Bank of Nauru is the only bank aside from offshore entities. The monetary unit is the Australian dollar, which is freely convertible.

Although Nauru has been touted as an "up and coming" tax haven and "emerging" offshore bank center, its legislation was enacted 20 years ago. From all apparent indications, Nauru is unlikely to be the next go-go tax haven in the near future.

Legal Entities.   Nauru has plenty of attractive legislation, but what's written and what's practiced are two different things.

There is specific legislation for corporations, banks, trusts, and insurance companies. Both holding and trading corporations are recognized.

In order to organize any entity in Nauru, a principal must work through a solicitor (attorney) or another professional who has been designated as having "solicitor status."

A consortium of 10 corporations handles all matters of incorporation, management, and issuances of licenses for all Nauruan entities. This group, known as the Nauru Group of Corporations, includes the Nauru Agency Corporation, Nauru Trustee Corporation, Nauru Secretaries Incorporated, Nauru Nominee Corporation, Buadu Corporation, Initial Holding Corporation, Central Pacific Agency Corporation, and three others.

The Nauru Agency Corporation is the principal company, headed by attorney M. N. Kushu and his assistant. It is exclusively empowered by the government to perform its functions and deal directly with the Registrar of Companies.

The single biggest difficulty in doing business with Nauru is finding a professional who knows anything about local laws and customs. The customs part is of particular importance, since interpretation of statutes is at the discretion of Nauruan leaders. Their attitude to outsiders is also of paramount importance to anyone who hopes to maintain smooth operations.

Recently, the New Zealand Serious Frauds Office claimed that bogus banks are operating from Nauru. Apparently, the banks are being used for money laundering of drug and crime proceeds. Director Charles Sturt of the New Zealand office asserts that although Nauru has banking laws, they have never been imposed. Let the buyer beware!

Tax Haven Encyclopedia, edited by Barry Spitz, contains portions of the various acts and forms used in organizing entities in Nauru. The publisher of this directory may be found in Part 3.

In sum, many other tax havens have much more to offer than Nauru.

Taxation. Nauru is a no-tax haven.

Financial and Investment Incentives. No special incentives are offered.

Tax Treaties. Nauru has no tax treaties.

Business Contacts

Incorporation and Management
Nauru Agency Corporation
P.O. Box 300
Nauru, Central Pacific

Central Pacific Agency
  Corporation
P.O. Box 302
Nauru, Central Pacific

Banking
Bank of Nauru
P.O. Box 289
Nauru, Central Pacific

Netherlands

Fast Facts
Population: 14,900,000 (1990)
Capital and Largest City: Amsterdam, 680,000
Language: Dutch

Country Profile

The Netherlands, also known as Holland, occupies the low, flat, land between Belgium and Germany along the North Sea.

The literacy rate is 99 percent. About 36 percent of the population is Roman Catholic; 19 percent is Dutch Reformed.

The weather is generally cool. The long winters are damp and cold. The most pleasant time of the year is between June and September, but seldom do temperatures exceed 75°F.

International airlines service Schipol Airport near Amsterdam regularly.

Government. The constitutional monarchy is comprised of the Crown, the states general (parliament), and the courts. Amsterdam is the capital, but the government and parliament are domiciled in The Hague.

Legal System. The legal system is based on civil and penal law.

Economy. The Netherlands is an industrial country that has gained recognition as a tax haven. The economy is based on private enterprise, although the government significantly influences the economy through its social programs and regulations.

Banking and insurance account for half of the national income.

The industrial sector is dominated by chemical, electronics, food processing, metalworking, and oil refining.

Communications. As is true throughout Europe, communications are excellent.

Business Profile

Banking, Money, and Foreign Exchange. The Netherlands Bank is the country's central bank, with responsibility for issuing currency and controlling credit. The National Investment Bank contributes to the credit system through long-term loans.

The monetary unit is the Dutch guilder (Dfl), known for being one of the world's strongest currencies.

Dutch banking is recognized worldwide for its outstanding reputation and sophistication. Many large international commercial banks maintain branches in the Netherlands.

Bank secrecy is not a hallmark of this tax haven and the identities of account holders must be disclosed. Numbered accounts are unavailable.

Legal Entities. The two types of corporations are both limited by shares and taxed identically.

The NV (*naamloze Vennootschap*) is permitted to have bearer or registered shares and can be either a private or public company.

The BV (*besloten Vennootschap met beperkte Aansprakelijkheid*) permits only registered shares, which have restrictions on their transferability. This type of company can only be privately owned.

The NV must be incorporated by at least two people, and the BV by a minimum of one person. Nominee shareholders may be engaged, and a board of directors is optional.

The articles of association are prepared by a notary and forwarded to the Ministry of Justice. If there are no objections to the articles, they are returned to the notary, who then issues the deed of formation.

The minimum paid-up capital for the NV is Dfl 100,000. The minimum for the BV is Dfl 40,000.

Taxation.   The Netherlands has a complex tax system and tax rates are generally high. Obviously, there are certain advantages, or the country wouldn't have attained its reputation as a tax haven.

Groups of companies are generally favored by their ability under certain circumstances to consolidate for taxation purposes and by preferential treatment on profits and capital gains.

Financial and Investment Incentives.   There are attractive incentives designed to lure new manufacturing by advancing cash grants. Purchased or improved industrial buildings are eligible for accelerated depreciation and investment allowances. Double taxation is avoided on income from interest and royalties, and there's a lower tax on export income and other incentives.

Tax Treaties.   There are several dozen tax treaties in effect with many countries.

Business Contacts

Banking

Rabobank Nederland
Croeselaan 18
3521 CB Utrecht
Netherlands
Telex: 40200

ABN Bank
32 Vijzelstraat
Amsterdam, Netherlands
Tel: (31) 20-29-3249
(31) 20-29-4090
(31) 20-29-3222

Bank Mees & Hope NV
548 Herengracht
P.O. Box 293
1000 AG Amsterdam, Netherlands

KmG Klynveldkraayenhof & Co.
Prinses Irenestraat 59
1077 WV Amsterdam, Netherlands

Nederlands Middenstandsbank NV
Eduard van Beinumstraat 2
P.O. Box 1800
1077 XT Amsterdam, Netherlands

Nederlandsche Credietbank NV
Heregracht 458
P.O. Box 941
1017 CA Amsterdam, Netherlands

Legal

Derks & Partners
P.O. Box 9230
3506 Ge Utrecht
Netherlands

Netherlands Antilles

Fast Facts
Population: 189,000 (1990)
Capital and Largest City: Willemstad (Curaçao)
Languages: Dutch, English, Spanish, Papiamento

Country Profile

The Netherlands Antilles are autonomous domains of the kingdom of the Netherlands. The Antilles are comprised of two groups: The Leeward Islands group includes Curaçao and Bonaire, and the Windward Islands group includes St. Maarten, St. Eustatius, and Saba.

The two groups are separated by 500 miles of Caribbean sea. The two Leeward Islands are situated 30 miles north of Venezuela, and the three Windward Islands are in the northern portion of the Caribbean chain of islands 100 miles east of Puerto Rico.

The literacy rate is 95 percent and the dominant religion is Roman Catholic.

Until the late 1980s, Aruba was part of the Leeward group, but has since seceded from the Netherlands Antilles. It remains a self-governing entity of the Netherlands. In 1996, Aruba will tentatively break away from the Netherlands and move toward complete independence.

Government. The Netherlands Antilles are a constitutional and parliamentary form of government. The governor represents the Royal Crown.

Legal System. The civil law system parallels that of the Netherlands.

Economy. The economy is largely based on oil refining, transhipment, tourism, and offshore financial services.

Communications. Communications are excellent.

Business Profile

Banking, Money, and Foreign Exchange. The banking structure is well established. The Central Bank was started 165 years ago.

Offshore banking has grown over the past few decades, but the qualifications and requirements are sufficiently strict to limit all but established bankers from going into business.

The monetary unit is the Netherlands Antilles guilder (NAf).

Generally, if funds or assets are moved into the Antilles by nonresidents, exchange controls are not imposed. This is not always the case, however. Residents must work through a bank licensed to handle foreign exchange.

There are plenty of offshore funds resting in the Antilles.

Legal Entities. The corporation is the premiere offshore vehicle, known in the Netherlands Antilles as *naamloze Vennootschap,* or NV for short.

The NV is incorporated by one person, usually a nominee who is furnished by a local trust company.

A deed containing the articles of incorporation is drafted in Dutch, notarized, submitted to the Minister of Justice for approval, and then published in the *Official Gazette.* This process takes approximately 2 weeks. The corporation is then a legal entity. After incorporation, shares are transferred to the beneficial owners.

The minimum paid-up capital is NAf 10,000 (US $5600). The minimum capital tax is NAf 250. Incorporations performed by professionals like Bakhuis, Curiel & Partners charge NAf 2700.

The shareholders appoint at least one managing director (an individual or corporation). If the managing agent is the sole director, that party must be a resident or corporation of the Netherlands Antilles. Certain companies are required to file financial statements annually with the Commercial Register.

Offshore banks are required to have a minimum paid-up capital of NAf 1 million. Only principals of banks already chartered in a country with strict bank regulations need apply.

Today more than 30,000 corporations enjoy the benefits of the Antilles.

Taxation. For many years, the Netherlands Antilles was a popular place to form holding companies as conduits for investing in U.S. real estate. Nonresident U.S. and other aliens were then able to capture the many tax benefits that the Antilles had to offer. Unfortunately, this attractive formula ended when the treaty between the Netherlands Antilles and the United States was terminated in 1980. Barbados is now an alternative.

Aruba's departure from the Antilles, and its subsequent legislative actions in favor of no-tax companies, is severely hurting its former ally in the offshore game. Aruba is developing into a very promising offshore center.

The Netherlands Antilles still has attractive features. Holding companies pay a low 2.4 to 3 percent tax on net income. Companies receiving royalties, dividends, and capital gains pay no tax on their incomes and profits.

There are other tax ramifications, but they are beyond the scope of this book.

Financial and Investment Incentives. Income tax exemptions may be granted for 10 to 11 years on corporate profits of industrial operations that will significantly contribute to the country's economic progress.

Other incentives are extended to specific industries.

Tax Treaties. There is no longer a double-taxation agreement with the United States or the United Kingdom. Treaties exist with Denmark, Japan, Norway, Netherlands, and Surinam. An unsigned, unenforced treaty exists with France.

Business Contacts

Management

Holland Intertrust (Antilles) NV
De Ruyterkade 58a
P.O. Box 837
Willemstad, Curaçao
Netherlands Antilles

Banking

Maduro & Curiel's Bank NV
Plaza Jojo Correa 2–4
Willemstad, Curaçao
Tel: 599-9-611100

Curaçao International Trust Co.
  NV
Handelskade No. 8
P.O. Box 812
Willemstad, Curaçao
Netherlands Antilles

First Curaçao International Bank
  NV
Breedestraat (0) 16
P.O. Box 299
Willemstad, Curaçao
Netherlands Antilles

Algemene Bank Nederland NV
Pietermaai 17
Willemstad, Curaçao
Tel: 599-9-611488

Banco di Caribe NV
Schottegatwey Oost 205
Willemstad, Curaçao
Tel: 599-9-616588

Banco Industrial de Venezuela CA
Heerenstraat 19
Willemstad, Curaçao
Tel: 599-9-611621

Accounting

Bakhuis, Curiel & Partners
Touche Ross & Co.
Scharlooweg 41
Willemstad, Curaçao
Netherlands Antilles
Tel: 599-9-614288/614535
Fax: 599-9-613626
Mailing address:
P.O. Box 809
Willemstad, Curaçao
Netherlands Antilles

Nevis

Fast Facts

Population: 49,000 (1990)
Capital and Largest City: Basseterre (St. Kitts),
     19,000
Language: English

Country Profile

In 1493 Christopher Columbus discovered this tranquil oasis due west
of Antigua in the Lesser Antilles of the Caribbean. Nevis is well pre-
served. Although some development is in progress, it has remained un-
spoiled.

The literacy rate is 90 percent, and the dominant religion is Anglican.

From the United States, fly via Antigua, St. Kitts, or St. Maarten. From
Britain, fly via Antigua. From Holland or France, fly via St. Maarten.

Government.   Nevis was a British Crown colony from 1628 to 1983,
when it gained its independence and formed the Federation of St. Kitts
and Nevis, a member of the British Commonwealth. Today Nevis is a
very politically stable democracy. The twin islands have a parliamentary
system of government.

Legal System.   The legal system is based on English common law.

Economy.   Agriculture, tourism, manufacturing, trading, and financial
services support a steady economy.

Communications.   The island's digital telecommunications system, in
use since 1980, employs fiber-optic cable for outstanding transmissions.
Services include international direct dialing, fax, telex, telegraph, data,
IDAS, and 800 international numbers. Cellular phoning, paging, and
voicemail are also available.

Business Profile

Banking, Money, and Foreign Exchange.   Nevis has a strong banking
system with several major international banks. The monetary unit is the
Eastern Caribbean (EC) dollar.

The Confidentiality Relationship Act of 1985 protects bank customers from disclosure of financial information to foreign investigators and regulators. The penalty for violation of this act is prison.

There are no currency exchange controls.

Legal Entities. In 1984 Nevis introduced the Business Corporation Ordinance with the intent to stimulate offshore business. The island has been very successful in its efforts, attracting more than 4000 new companies.

The offshore corporation, with its exempt, limited-liability status, offers many benefits for those seeking flexibility, versatility, secrecy, minimal regulations, no taxes, and low costs.

Nevis is giving stiff competition to some of the other, more desirable tax havens. However, it's still a sleeper. Many corporations that fled Panama redomiciled in the Caribbean. Nevis picked up a fair share of business, since it welcomed and permitted foreign companies to resume operations there. Benefits similar to those offered in Panama attracted many Panamanian corporate owners and managers.

Here are some distinct advantages of a Nevis corporation, as pointed out by Morning Star Holdings Limited:

1. No filing of annual corporate financial returns is required.
2. Shareholders and management may be of any nationality.
3. Beneficial owners, officers, and directors may reside anywhere.
4. Registered or bearer shares may be issued.
5. Par-value shares may be denominated in any currency.
6. A managing director may be retained to run the company.
7. A corporation or individual may serve as the corporate secretary.
8. A corporation may serve as director.
9. No shareholder meeting is required if there is unanimous shareholder consent.
10. Shareholders and directors may issue proxies in writing or by telex.
11. The principal office of the corporation, along with company records, may be located anywhere.
12. Articles of incorporation may be amended.
13. Companies may consolidate or merge with other foreign or Nevis corporations.
14. Foreign corporations are invited to redomicile in Nevis.

Incorporation costs are nominal. Nevis is one of the least expensive tax havens for establishing a company.

Morning Star Holdings Limited provides complete incorporation services. The charges are US $780 to file articles of incorporation and $450 for annual renewal. The incorporation procedure can be finalized within 48 hours.

The suggested articles of incorporation grant the corporation maximum latitude under the liberal Business Corporation Ordinance. Morning Star Holdings Limited will prepare the articles for clients. The following is an example:

ARTICLES OF INCORPORATION

1. The name of the corporation shall be

_____

2. The registered office of the corporation shall be Memorial Square, P.O. Box 556, Charlestown, Nevis. The corporation's registered agent at this address shall be Morning Star Holdings Limited.

3. The aggregate number of shares that the corporation is authorized to issue is One Thousand (1000) registered and/or bearer shares without par value.

The procedural provisions respecting bearer shares shall be set forth in the bylaws of the corporation.

The holder of a stock certificate issued in the name of the owner may cause such certificate to be exchanged for another certificate to bearer for a like number of shares, and the holder of a certificate issued to bearer may cause such certificate to be exchanged for another certificate in his name for a like number of shares.

4. The corporation shall have as a principal purpose the right to engage in any lawful act or activity for which corporations may now or hereafter be organized under the Nevis Business Corporation Ordinance 1984.

5. The corporation shall have every power which a corporation now or hereafter organized under the Nevis Business Corporation Ordinance 1984 may have.

The name and address of each incorporator and subscriber of these Articles is:

Name	Address	No. of Shares Subscribed
Incorporator furnished by Morning Star Holdings	P.O. Box 556 Charlestown, Nevis	One

In witness whereof, I have executed this instrument on this _____ day of _____ , 19 _____ .

Taxation. There are no income, dividend, or distribution taxes on income earned outside Nevis.

Financial and Investment Incentives. Special incentives are provided under the Business Corporation Ordinance of 1984.

Tax Treaties. There are double-taxation agreements with Denmark, New Zealand, Norway, Sweden, Switzerland, and the United Kingdom.

Business Contacts

Incorporation and Management

Morning Star Holdings Limited
Memorial Square
P.O. Box 556
Charlestown, Nevis, WI
Tel: (809) 469-1817
Fax: (809) 469-1794

Nevis Services Limited
Suite 2000, 555 US Highway 1
  South
Iselin, NJ 08830 USA
New York City tie line:
Tel: (212) 575-0818
Fax: (212) 575-0812

Banking

Nevis Cooperative Banking Co.
  Ltd.
P.O. Box 60
Charlestown, Nevis, WI
Tel: (809) 469-5277
Fax: (809) 469-1493

Panama

Fast Facts
Population: 2,322,000 (1990) *Capital and Largest City:* Panama City, 600,000 *Languages:* Spanish, English

Country Profile

The republic of Panama is strategically located in Central America between the Pacific Ocean and the Caribbean Sea. Its role as an international passage make it a vital interest to world powers, particularly the United States. For years Panama has been the financial hub of Central and South America and an international banking center.

The literacy rate is 90 percent, and the dominant religion is Roman Catholic.

Panama's relations with the United States and U.S. vested interests in the region, coupled with a highly developed banking system and economic strength, have traditionally given stability to this former military dictatorship.

In recent years, that stability, as well as international relations and confidence, has been compromised by the presence of drug runners and arms smugglers flying shipments via Panama and by the emergence of massive money-laundering operations. Today the door has opened for the outside world to step in and have a voice in Panama's affairs.

The trial of former leader Noriega, following the U.S. invasion of Panama in 1991, leaves this tax haven in a precarious position and promises to alter Panama's future—positively or negatively, depending on whose views are heard. Based on the outcome of these events, changes are inevitable.

Panama City is a financial capital and well connected to the rest of the world through communications, transportation, and banking.

Government.   Panama's constitution allows for a republican form of government. Elections are held every 5 years. The president is head of the republic. The government is divided into three branches: executive, legislative, and judicial.

Legal System.   The legal system of civil and commercial codes is based on civil law.

Economy.   Panama is to Central and South America what Hong Kong is to Asia. The prosperous economy stems from the country's stability, ideal location, bank secrecy, laissez-faire attitude toward business, superior reputation as a bank and financial center, simplicity of corporate organization, confidentiality of principals, and prominence in shipping. These points, though shaken in recent years, remain the cornerstones of Panama's tax haven franchise.

Communications.   Panama has state-of-the-art communications.

Business Profile

Banking, Money, and Foreign Exchange.   The most important banks in the world have branches or subsidiaries in Panama City. The monetary unit is the balboa, but the U.S. dollar is widely used along with Panamanian coins.

Panama is renowned as a global banking center, offering maximum secrecy to perpetuate its growth and popularity. Although Panama has been employed more than once for hiding or laundering funds in the past, its legitimate banking trade is impressive and stands on its own.

Unfortunately, many new stipulations and directives are coming from foreign influences and powers such as the United States. Panamanian bankers have not taken the attack on their system lightly. Most have resisted change. When legal changes have been imposed, often they are ignored. To what extent Panama and its bankers will succumb to the pressure is yet unknown. People who desire legitimate privacy in their business transactions and personal lives can only hope that Panama will be allowed to return to its own ways of conducting business and banking, without outside interference.

There are no exchange restrictions.

Violations of strict bank secrecy are punishable by fines and jail sentences. Numbered accounts are permissible.

Legal Entities.   The Panama corporation has been a very popular tax haven tool. This legal entity is still a great vehicle for those who desire privacy in their business dealings. Negative publicity may have damaged Panama's public image, but the reality of the corporation has not changed.

As corporations fled Panama by the thousands after the U.S. invasion, many reincorporated in the Bahamas, British Virgin Islands, and Nevis. Some went elsewhere. These companies may never return. Even so, Panama has unique advantages that will continue to attract new business.

Corporations are commonly purchased "off the shelf." Generally, the corporate names will have little meaning to the purchaser, but this instant vehicle is particularly convenient for those in a rush.

A newly organized corporation takes about 10 days to set up. The process is simple. A lawyer usually incorporates the company, providing the necessary three directors and officers, each of whom subscribes to one share. The articles of incorporation are drafted and notarized and submitted for recording, along with the appropriate fees.

The attorney will provide the purchaser with an official-looking document that contains the original articles in Spanish and a certified English translation.

A fully executed general power of attorney is provided with a blank line where the person's name should be typed. This individual can do virtually anything on behalf of the company. The power of attorney is the instrument commonly used by principals to exercise their powers, thereby giving them maximum privacy.

Bearer shares are issued rather than being registered in someone's name. The shares represented by the certificates provided by the attorney have voting powers. Transfer of ownership is easy: Just hand the stock certificate to the next person.

The maximum tax for up to US $10,000 of registered capital is $50. The tax goes up according to the amount of capital stock desired. Attorney's fees, agent's fees, and other costs are not reflected in these figures.

At the moment, Panama corporations are very reasonable. In 1990, they were being marketed for US $1000 to $2000. Presently, the going price is well under $1000.

Management Services Overseas, Inc. has an exceptional deal. It will incorporate one company for US $500 or five companies for $1250. A shelf company can be purchased for $350. (See the Business Contacts section.)

Panama is not a base for offshore banks. Banking is strictly regulated. The last of the pirate and small-time bankers were run out of town 20 years ago. There are better offshore locales for establishing an in-house or merchant bank.

Taxation. There are no taxes on income generated from outside Panama.

Financial and Investment Incentives. Under the Investment Incentives Act of 1970 and its 1986 revisions, certain incentives have been established to attract American companies, particularly in manufacturing.

Tax Treaties. Presently, only a double-taxation agreement on shipping income is in effect with the United States.

Business Contacts

Incorporation

Management Services Overseas, Inc.
P.O. Box 6-5879
El Dorado
Panama 6A, Panama
Tel: (507) 27-2658
Fax: (507) 33-3459

Management

First Incorporating Business (Swiss management)
P.O. Box 550142
Paitilla, Panama
Tel: (507) 69-1677
Fax: (507) 69-1037

PanAmerican Management Services SA
P.O. Box 7402
Panama 5, Panama

Boliva International
Apartado 4508
Panama 5, Panama

Interglobe Consultants, Inc.
P.O. Box 6-1714
El Dorado
Panama City, Panama

Lamar, Westford & Assoc.
P.O. Box 6-5879
El Dorado
Panama 6A, Panama
Tel: (507) 27-2658
Fax: (507) 33-3459

Banking

Banco Nacional da Panama
P.O. Box 5220
Panama 5, Panama

Caja de Ahorros
P.O. Box 1740
Panama 1, Panama

Swiss Bank Corp. (Overseas) SA
P.O. Box 3370
Panama 4, Panama

Legal

Mossack Fonseca & Co.
Arango-Orillac Building
P.O. Box 8320
Panama 7, Panama
Tel: (507) 63-8899
Fax: (507) 63-9218

Francis & Francis
Eastern Building, 12th Floor
Frederico Boyd Avenue
P.O. Box 8807N 7283
Panama 5, Panama
Tel: (507) 63-8555

Edis Esquiral Gonzalez
Building 13
2W Floor, Office 9
Via España
Panama City, Panama

Hutchinson y Asociados
P.O. Box 1290
Panama 9A, Panama
Tel: (507) 27-5156

Morgan y Morgan
Bancosur Building
53rd Street
P.O. Box 1824
Panama City, Panama

Pardini & Assoc.
P.O. Box 9654
Panama 4, Panama

St. Vincent

Fast Facts

Population: 108,000 (1990)
Capital and Largest City: Kingstown, 18,378
Languages: English, French patois

Country Profile

St. Vincent in the Windward Islands lies 100 miles west of Barbados, another Caribbean paradise for vacationer and investor alike. This Columbus discovery dates back to 1498.

The literacy rate is 85 percent. The dominant religion is Anglican, with Methodist and Roman Catholic representations.

To reach this mountainous, 11-mile-long island, Americans should make flight connections through Barbados or St. Lucia.

Government. Formerly a British Crown colony, St. Vincent gained its independence on October 26, 1979. The governor-general of the island represents the sovereign, Queen Elizabeth II. The prime minister, who has executive power, is elected by the 13-member unicameral legislature. St. Vincent is a politically and socially stable democracy.

Legal System.   The legal system is based on English common law.

Economy.   Food processing and exporting fuel the economy. There is also light industry. The modest tourist trade is attributed to inadequate accommodations. The offshore trade supports the local business community.

Communications.   There are modern communications to the outside world and dependable postal service.

Business Profile

Banking, Money, and Foreign Exchange.   Major international banks include Barclays Bank International, Bank of Nova Scotia, Canadian Imperial Bank of Commerce, and Royal Bank of Canada. The National Commercial Bank of St. Vincent is the government bank.

The monetary unit is the Eastern Caribbean (EC) dollar.

No currency exchange controls exist with regard to offshore companies and trusts.

Legal Entities.   The present International Companies Act was adopted in 1976, making the Business Companies Ordinance of 1966 obsolete.

An offshore company with limited liability can be incorporated promptly by filing the memorandum of association and articles of association with the St. Vincent Trust Authority.

Companies not doing business locally are considered "international" and are not subject to the usual 45 percent tax rate.

Three directors are required for incorporation, but only one is necessary to manage the company's affairs.

The company name must end with "Limited." There is no minimum capital requirement.

Nominee subscribers are acceptable, providing anonymity to the beneficial owners.

There is offshore bank legislation. The minimum capital required for a bank is EC $500,000. The minimum reserve requirement is EC $1,000,000.

Aston Corporate Management Limited, based in the Isle of Man, can assist with the organization of a St. Vincent bank. (See the International Investor Directory in Part 3.)

Taxation.   The international company pays no taxes on income originating outside St. Vincent, but is required to pay the nominal company registration fees.

Financial and Investment Incentives.   St. Vincent's offshore legislation for banks, corporations, insurance companies, shipping companies, superannuation funds, and trusts provides its own incentives. In addition, the Pioneer Industries Ordinance of 1952 gives exporters outside CARICOM countries a 15-year tax holiday. The Hotel Aid Ordinance of 1969 encourages hotel and resort projects.

Tax Treaties.   There are 60 double-taxation agreements with other countries.

Singapore

Fast Facts

Population: 2,700,000 (1990)
Capital and Largest City: Singapore, 2,600,000
Languages: Malay, Chinese (Mandarin), Tamil, English

Country Profile

Singapore lies directly south of Thailand in southeast Asia. Over the past 25 years, a strategic location and attractive legislation have transformed Singapore into an important industrial center and home to Asian dollars.

The literacy rate is 86 percent. The Islamic, Christian, Buddhist, Taoist, and Hindu religions are represented.

Major airlines conveniently connect Singapore to other Asian business centers within a few hours' time.

Government.   This parliamentary democracy was once a British Crown colony. In 1965, Singapore gained independence from the federation of Malaya.

The government is comprised of the executive, legislative, and judicial branches. The ceremonial president is elected by an 81-member unicameral parliament. The prime minister and cabinet retain executive power.

Economy.   Several factors account for the continued growth of this healthy economy since Singapore's independence in 1965.

The country is ideally located for shipping, warehousing, and trading. High technology and manufacturing have capitalized on Singapore's industrious work force and enticing British-style tax legislation.

Multinational companies are encouraged to establish southeast Asian headquarters in Singapore. Real estate costs are considerably less than in Hong Kong or Tokyo, and Singapore (unlike Hong Kong) offers continued political stability. It is an increasingly popular base for management of offshore funds.

Government officials are not anxious to promote their country as purely a tax haven, even though corporations do not pay tax on income earned outside Singapore. The government wishes to interest companies with significant operations to relocate or establish a base in Singapore.

Communications. There are excellent worldwide communication services.

Business Profile

Banking, Money, and Foreign Exchange. Singapore is capital to Asian dollars coming from neighboring Asian countries such as Hong Kong and Japan. The Middle East has also moved capital into Asia because of unrest at home. Singapore's own development contributes significantly.

Singapore is the leading banking center in Asia, with nearly 200 foreign financial institutions. The Singapore dollar is quoted against the floating market.

Nonresidents, foreign corporations included, can earn and accumulate interest-free income from approved Singapore banks. Interest rates are high! Numbered bank accounts can be opened.

There are no exchange controls.

Legal Entities. A private limited company can be formed for US $2000 to $3000, including professional fees.

The company name must first be reserved for 2 months prior to filing the memorandum of association and articles of association with the Registrar of Companies. Two shareholders are required to incorporate, one of whom must be a resident. There must also be a resident company secretary.

Transfer of shares in a private company is restricted.

Offshore and merchant banking legislation is in effect, but reserved for highly qualified foreign bank applicants.

Taxation. Income derived from outside Singapore goes untaxed. There are no taxes on dividends or disbursements of profits and no withholding taxes on interest paid on foreign income deposits.

No taxes are levied on capital gains or income on profits derived from services outside Singapore. There is no withholding tax on passive income by foreign or domestic shareholders in a Singapore corporation.

Financial and Investment Incentives.   Singapore has wide-ranging incentives and tax holidays for foreign industries to explore.

Tax Treaties.   There are double-taxation treaties with Australia, Bangladesh, Belgium, Canada, China, Denmark, Finland, France, Germany, India, Israel, Italy, Japan, Malaysia, Netherlands, New Zealand, Norway, Philippines, South Korea, Sri Lanka, Sweden, Switzerland, Taiwan, Thailand, and the United Kingdom.

Business Contacts

Banking

Bank of New Zealand
31-05 OCBC Centre
65 Chulia Street
Singapore 0104, Singapore
Tel: 65-915744

Switzerland

```
                    Fast Facts
Population: 6,600,000 (1989)
Capital: Bern, 136,000
Largest City: Zurich, 347,000 (1988)
Languages: French, German, Italian, Romansch
```

Country Profile

Nestled high in the Alps, Switzerland is centrally located in Europe with its borders shared by France, Germany, Austria, Liechtenstein, and Italy.

The literacy rate is 99.5 percent. The population is almost equally divided between Protestant and Roman Catholic.

The rail and public transportation systems are excellent. Scheduled airlines service Geneva and Zurich daily.

Government.   The Swiss federal government has three branches: executive, legislative, and judicial. The 26 cantons (states) are administrative subdivisions with independent powers.

Switzerland is a very stable country and politically neutral. At the present time, Switzerland is attempting to join the European Community, which will abolish its present position of neutrality.

Legal System.   The legal system is based on civil law and commercial law.

Economy.   Switzerland's healthy economy is supported by banking, financial services, manufacturing, foreign trade, and tourism.

Communications.   Swiss communications are excellent.

Business Profile

Banking, Money, and Foreign Exchange.   Switzerland's neutrality during otherwise turbulent times in this century, coupled with its highly confidential banking practices, fostered this Alpine center of precision-made watches and fine chocolates as the ideal cache for frightened money around the world. The monetary unit is the Swiss franc (SFr).

Switzerland polished its image for decades into a golden shine as the eminent international banking center. The Swiss banking community expanded operations into foreign countries. Gradually, Swiss autonomy became threatened by the pressure of other governments who wanted to share Switzerland's secrets. In recent history, the Swiss banking image has been tarnished by negative publicity surrounding banking cases in which secrecy was compromised at the expense of the account holder.

The U.S. Securities and Exchange Commission has exerted enough influence on the Swiss to compel them to pass laws against insider trading. Money laundering has also been denounced as illegal, and preventive laws have been imposed at the behest of the U.S. government. Tax avoidance is not a crime, but there is a test to determine if a transaction is a construction to circumvent taxes. Tax avoidance and evasion are measured by the economic purpose of a transaction.

Even with these exceptions, Swiss bank secrecy is regarded as superior to that of most countries. If an activity isn't considered a crime in Switzerland, the Swiss will not cooperate with foreign authorities seeking to gain access to confidential bank information. The penalty for breaking bank secrecy is 6 months in jail or a fine of SFr 50,000 (approximately US $33,000).

Now in its golden years, and boasting hundreds of billions of Swiss franc deposits from around the world, Swiss banking has elevated its posture and is less reliant on its former position as the premiere bank haven for secrecy. Although secrecy is still paramount, deposed leaders and criminal figures beware. Swiss banks do accept small depositors, but they are rapidly emerging as the bankers to the world's rich.

Private banking is a Swiss banker's preference, availing the affluent of the best services that Swiss banking offers. Typically, a minimum of SFr

1 million and up is required to manage a client's funds, but a limited-service account may be managed with a minimum SFr 100,000.

Times have changed and so has Swiss banking.

Numbered bank accounts are available. They do not afford total secrecy, but rather limit the number to only a couple of people who know the true identity of the account holder.

There are no exchange controls.

Legal Entities.   The Aktiegesellschaft (AG) is the most common company entity organized under the Laws of Obligation. It is a stock company that issues shares with nominal value, either registered or bearer.

The incorporators draft the articles of incorporation, much as in the United States. A unique difference, however, is the way the company is capitalized. The next step is to establish a bank account and deposit at least the minimum paid-up capital required by law; the bank then issues a certificate as proof. This official evidence is provided to the notary at the meeting of the incorporators, at which time the articles of incorporation and incorporation minutes are signed by the organizers and witnessed.

The incorporators may be nominees, to provide anonymity to the beneficial owners, and may either be individuals or corporations.

Incorporation takes approximately 2 weeks, once the notary has completed the final task of registering the deed with the Registrar of Commerce.

The directors in the AG are elected at an annual shareholder meeting. Directors must also be stockholders, even if they hold only one share. Directors and incorporators may be the same persons of any nationality.

Incorporation costs for the minimum capitalization of SFr 50,000 is SFr 1500. Additional costs associated with incorporation include a notary fee, professional fees, and, depending on the location of incorporation, the applicable canton fee. There is also a 3 percent stamp duty on the capital stock at the time of incorporation.

Taxation.   Switzerland has taxes, but they are modest compared with those of high-tax countries like the United States and United Kingdom.

An operating company within Switzerland can expect to pay 3.63 to 9.8 percent worldwide income tax. Holding companies receive favorable tax treatment.

Domiciliary companies function as offshore companies and pay the same taxes as operating companies. There are also control taxes. In the case of domiciliary companies, these can sometimes be negotiated.

Companies and banks are obligated to retain the 35 percent withholding tax on interest and dividends.

Financial and Investment Incentives. Depending on the individual canton's economic situation and needs, a company or investor may be able to negotiate for financial and investment incentives.

Tax Treaties. Switzerland has numerous double-taxation agreements with other countries, including the United States and the United Kingdom.

Business Contacts

Incorporation and Management

M. Weibel
Confidesa AG
Baarerstrasse 36
CH-6300 Zug, Switzerland
Tel: 41-12-213288
Telex: 86 4913 CONF CH
Fax: 41-12-221049

DeBerig SA
P.O. Box 116
1211 Geneva 17, Switzerland

Uptrend Treuhand
  Managementberatung Trading
Schauenbergstrasse 12
8046 Zurich, Switzerland
Tel: 41-13-711110
Fax: 41-13-711211

Management

Arthur R. Moussalli, Managing Director
Business Advisory Services SA
7 Rue Muzy
1207 Geneva, Switzerland
Tel: 41-22-030540
Fax: 41-22-7860644

Trade Administration Services AG
P.O. Box 4818
Baarerstrasse 23
CH-6304 Zug 4, Switzerland

Banking

Bank Institute Zurich
P.O. Box 5138
CH-8022 Zurich, Switzerland

Bank vonErnst & Cie AG
63–65 Marktgasse
3001 Berne, Switzerland

H. Sturzenegger & Cie
St. Jakobsstrasse 46
4002 Basel, Switzerland

Swiss Bank Corp.
1 Aeschenvorstadt
CH-4002 Basel, Switzerland

Ueberseebank AG
P.O. Box 8024
Limmatqual 12 Zurich, Switzerland

Trust Services

Hoogewerf Trust Co. SA
P.O. Box 347
CH-1211 Geneva 3, Switzerland
Tel: 41-22-218393
Fax: 41-22-216407

Legal

Mossack Fonseca & Co.
40 Rue du Stand
P.O. Box 138
CH-1211 Geneva 25, Switzerland
Tel: 41-22-290222
Fax: 41-22-290135

Turks and Caicos

Fast Facts

Population: 9531 (1990)
Capital and Largest City: Grand Turk, 3200
Language: English

Country Profile

The Turks and Caicos islands lie at the base of the Bahamas chain, directly north of Haiti and the Dominican Republic.

Anticipate 2-hour air travel time from Miami. Atlantic Gulf Airlines and British Caribbean Airways arrive and depart regularly.

Government.   The Turks and Caicos are another stable, self-governing British Crown colony and are content with their present system.

Legal System.   There is a good legal system based on English common law.

Economy.   A major economic thrust is tourism. Exports of seafood and a few agricultural products also contribute. The offshore sector does a brisk business and has steadily increased since the passage of the New Company Act in 1982.

Communications.   There are excellent communications around the clock and around the world.

Business Profile

Banking, Money, and Foreign Exchange.   Several international banks operate in the Turks and Caicos. The monetary unit is the US dollar.

There are no longer any exchange controls. Foreigners are permitted to maintain bank accounts in US dollars.

Legal Entities.   Two types of companies may be organized. The ordinary company is principally for doing business within the islands; the exempt company is specifically for offshore activities.

The exempt company has certain advantages over the ordinary version: Members, directors, and officers do not have to be identified in the statutory register; the company may purchase or own its own shares, with or without par value; capital may be in any currency; no business license is required; and placing "Ltd." at the end of the name isn't mandatory.

The memorandum of association contains the company name, details of the capital stock, registered office, objects or purpose of the company and whether the company is ordinary or exempt.

There is no minimum authorized capital. Shares are generally issued according to the amount required. The par value may be fixed at any amount.

Only one shareholder is required for registered stock. Bearer shares may also be issued. A director and a secretary are also necessary. One person may hold both positions and be the sole stockholder.

The memorandum and articles of association are prepared for filing by a professional who can also provide nominee officers and directors and shareholders as needed, handle the company's annual requirements, and provide the registered office. Incorporation time is 2 to 3 days.

The government fee for incorporating an exempt company is $325. The annual fee is $300. To this must be added the cost of engaging the legal, management, or accounting firm.

Bank and insurance licenses have been issued in the past, but no bank licenses have been granted since 1985, when the colony was hit by a banking scandal. Until new legislation is drafted, the Turks and Caicos may be closed to all but branches or subsidiaries of reputable international banks.

Taxation.   There are no capital gains, corporation, dividend, estate, gift, income, inheritance, property, sales, or succession taxes.

Financial and Investment Incentives.   Hotel and resort projects are invited by the Encouragement of Development Ordinance of 1972, which provides guarantees against approved developments.

Tax Treaties.   There are no tax treaties to avoid double taxation.

Business Contacts

Government

Superintendent of Offshore
  Finance Centre
Finance Department
Grand Turk, BWI
Tel: (809) 946-2937/2935
Fax: (809) 946-2557

Registrar of Companies
Grand Turk, BWI
Tel: (809) 946-2550/2002

Management

Caribbean Management Services
  Limited
P.O. Box 127
Town Centre Mall
Providenciales
Turks and Caicos, BWI
Tel: (809) 946-4732/4733
Fax: (809) 946-4734

Grand Turk International Trust
  Co.
P.O. Box 61
Grand Turk, BWI
Tel: (809) 946-2047

Morris Cottingham Assoc. Ltd.
Hibiscus Square
P.O. Box 156
Grand Turk, BWI
Tel: (809) 946-2504
Fax: (809) 946-2503

International Company Service
  (T&C) Limited
Oceanic House
Duke Street
P.O. Box 107
Grand Turk, BWI
Tel: (809) 946-2828
Fax: (809) 946-2825

Banking
Barclays Bank International Ltd.
P.O. Box 61
Cockburn Town
Grand Turk, BWI

Legal
Misick and Stanbrook
MacLaw House
Duke Street
P.O. Box 103
Grand Turk, BWI
Tel: (809) 946-2476/2171/2172
Fax: (809) 946-2173

Northcote & Co.
P.O. Box 164
Grand Turk, BWI

Coriat & Co.
Sabre House
P.O. Box 171
Grand Turk, BWI
Tel: (809) 946-2621

Savoy & Co.
P.O. Box 157
Harbor House, Queen Street
Grand Turk, BWI
Tel: (809) 946-2601

Vanuatu

Fast Facts

Population: 150,000
Capital and Largest City: Port Vila, 15,100
Languages: Melanesian, French, English

Country Profile

Vanuatu, formerly the New Hebrides, is an archipelago stretching across the South Pacific 1400 miles northeast of Australia. This 5700-square-mile chain, a former condominium of the United Kingdom and France, is part of the larger group of islands forming Melanesia.

The literacy rate is less than 20 percent. The dominant religion is Presbyterian, with small Anglican and Roman Catholic representations.

This tropical, fiscal paradise is so lush that the fenceposts sprout vegetation. The wet cyclone season is January through April. The dry season is May through November.

Government. Vanuatu became an independent republic with its own constitution on July 20, 1980, and has since remained politically stable. This parliamentary democracy is headed by an elected president. The government is divided into three branches: executive, legislative, and judicial.

Legal System. Commercial law is based on English common law. Regulations were influenced by the British prior to independence. Today, both British- and French-type companies are incorporated, but only the British type has any usefulness offshore.

Economy. Agriculture is the principal economic force. The major products are copra, cocoa, coffee, cattle, and timber. Other industries include saw milling, tourism, and financial services. The chief exports are copra, beef, cocoa, and timber.

The gross domestic product (GDP) is US $84 million. Gross per capita income is a marginal $580.

Communications. Port Vila is the financial center and capital where modern communications service the demands of the offshore financial sector.

Business Profile

Banking, Money, and Foreign Exchange. Commercial banking services are available from ANZ Bank (Vanuatu) Limited and several other international banks in Port Vila.

The government promotes Vanuatu as a financial center, encouraging offshore corporate, bank, insurance, and trust formations.

The monetary unit is the Vatu (Vt).

There are no exchange control regulations. Currencies are freely traded and can be transferred anywhere without permission or restriction.

Legal Entities. Companies can be incorporated for a wide variety of purposes. Typical legal entities are holding companies, trading companies, shipping companies, agency and distribution companies, management services companies, and contracting companies.

Insurance and reinsurance companies, captive insurance companies, international banks, and finance companies require special licenses to conduct business.

Foreign companies can also register to do business.

Offshore Companies.   Companies are defined as local or exempt and public or private. Local companies carry on business within Vanuatu and are of no interest to offshore operations.

The exempt company is the ideal vehicle for offshore activity. No audits are required. Returns and documents are not public record. There is no disclosure of beneficial owners. The company cannot make a public offering. Secrecy is guaranteed under Section 381 of the Companies Act, which carries penalties if violated.

The private company restricts transfer of shares and limits the number of shareholders to 50. A minimum of one director and two shareholders is needed. Nominee shareholders are optional.

A maximum capital stock of Vt 50,000,000 (US $417,000) or any currency equivalent may be authorized, with a minimum fee of Vt 40,000. The fee is higher if the capital is greater, but the maximum fee is Vt 250,000.

Professional accounting and incorporation services are available through several local accounting firms or branches of international accounting companies, including Coopers & Lybrand, Price Waterhouse, Peat Marwick, Moore Stephens & Co., and Moores & Rowland. All these concerns are familiar with local practices.

Incorporation is a simple process that is handled by the local management or accounting firm. The applicant is asked to complete an application to assist the local professional in completing the memorandum and articles of incorporation in accordance with the applicant's wishes. In some cases, a deed of indemnity may be required protecting the professional under certain circumstances while engaged by the applicant or corporation.

Offshore Banks.   Vanuatu licenses two types of banks: local and exempt. The local bank is permitted to transact business within Vanuatu and the exempt bank can conduct business only outside of Vanuatu.

Offshore banks and finance companies utilize the exempt company for incorporation purposes and simultaneously apply for the appropriate license. These banks do not have to meet any reserve or equity ratio criteria or Central Bank requirements.

An exempt company wishing to operate as a finance company must first apply for a financial institution license. This permits taking deposits and lending funds. Essentially it can function as a merchant bank. The license fee is US $2500.

A bank license grants the same powers of a financial institution but also allows deposits to be withdrawn by check. This license permits the word "Bank" within the company name. The license fee is US $2500.

Either type of financial institution may perform functions other than banking, as authorized in the memorandum and articles of incorporation.

The following is the government's official guideline for the licensing of exempt banks:

A. Where promoted or owned by recognized international banks or financial institutions, the paid-up capital may by negotiation be a nominal figure.

B. Where owned by individuals or groups of individuals or by them through private companies, we shall be guided by the following criteria. However, every application will be judged on its own merits and further information may be required:

    (1) Where the activities of the bank will be of an in-house nature, and monies will not be solicited from the general public, we normally would look for:

        i. A minimum capital or combination of capital and subordinated loan capital comprising $150,000, paid up upon incorporation and before commencement of operations.

        ii. Evidence of suitable experience in the day-to-day management of the bank which should be provided at the time of application.

        iii. An element of responsible local Vanuatu involvement in the company's operations. This would normally be in the form of Directorship(s) held by representatives of the Vanuatu trust companies.

        iv. Independent written evidence of the good character and bona fides of the beneficial owners of the bank, which should be provided at the time of application.

        v. Some evidence that at least one of the beneficial owners is a man or woman of some financial substance.

        vi. A written undertaking confirming the in-house nature of the bank and its activities, which should be provided at the time of application.

    (2) Where the activities of the bank are such that it may wish to solicit funds from the general public whether withdrawable by cheque or not, then, in order to protect the public, the good name of Vanuatu, and the Finance Centre, the criteria in B(1) i. to v. above would normally be strictly applied, with such other more stringent requirements as may be appropriate to the case.

Insurance Companies. Vanuatu has distinct advantages for insurance companies. They include minimal formation and maintenance requirements, maximum latitude, and reasonable qualification requirements of the beneficial owners and management. The insurance license is US $835 per annum.

Professional firms in Vanuatu are very helpful and will provide valuable information on their country at request.

Peat Marwick publishes a helpful booklet entitled *Vanuatu: The Tax Haven of the Pacific* and Pacific International Trust Company Limited publishes *Port Vila, Vanuatu: The Pacific's Premier Financial Centre*. Both firms provide extensive services to offshore business. (See the Business Contacts section.)

Taxation.   There are no income or capital gains taxes.

Financial and Investment Incentives.   No incentives are provided other than those inherent in Vanuatu's tax haven policies.

Tax Treaties.   Vanuatu has no tax treaties with other countries.

Business Contacts

Management

Pacific International Trust
  Company Limited
P.O. Box 45
Port Vila, Vanuatu
Southwest Pacific
Tel: 678-2957
Fax: 678-3405

KMPG Peat Marwick
P.O. Box 212
Port Vila, Vanuatu
Southwest Pacific
Tel: 678-2091
Fax: 678-3665

Investor's Trust Limited
G.P.O. Box 211
Port Vila, Vanuatu
Southwest Pacific
Tel: 678-2198
Fax: 678-3799

Banking

ANZ Bank (Vanuatu) Limited
P.O. Box 123
Port Vila, Vanuatu
Southwest Pacific

Barclays Bank
P.O. Box 123
Port Vila, Vanuatu
Southwest Pacific

Melanesia International Trust Co.
  Ltd.
Rue Pasteur
P.O. Box 213
Port Vila, Vanuatu
Southwest Pacific

Legal

Geoff Gee & Assoc.
P.O. Box 782
Port Vila, Vanuatu
Southwest Pacific

Wayne J. McKeague & Assoc.
P.O. Box 140
Port Vila, Vanuatu
Southwest Pacific

Western Samoa

```
Fast Facts

Population: 167,000 (1990)
Capital and Largest City: Apia, 33,400
Languages: Samoan, English
```

Country Profile

Western Samoa is a group of Polynesian islands clustered in the middle of the South Pacific northeast of Australia and further northeast of Fiji.

The literacy rate is 90 percent. The dominant religion is Congregationalist, with significant Roman Catholic and Methodist representations.

International air service from Faleolo International Aerodome is provided by Polynesian Airlines, Air Pacific, Air New Zealand, South Pacific Island Airways, and Hawaiian Airlines. Polynesian Airlines also services local stops.

Government.   Western Samoa is a parliamentary government with a constitution that provides for a head of state, a prime minister and a cabinet of ministers. Parliament is represented by two major parties, both of which support offshore financial activities.

The United States gained control of Eastern Samoa, now known as American Samoa, in a treaty signed in 1899. In 1914, New Zealand gained control of Western Samoa, which was held by Germany. Total independence was achieved in 1962.

Legal System.   English and Commonwealth common and statutory law prevails.

Economy.   Agriculture is the principal industry, producing half of the gross domestic product (GDP) and 90 percent of export earnings.

Five acts passed in 1987 form the basis of Western Samoa's offshore legislature, making this independent sovereignty one of the newest tax havens.

Communications.   The country has a well-developed infrastructure and excellent communications that allow 24-hour direct dialing to all parts of the world.

Business Profile

Banking, Money, and Foreign Exchange. Bank of Western Samoa
bills itself as "bankers to the nation" and provides international and domestic banking facilities with 15 branches and agencies. Central Bank of
Samoa regulates banks, credit policies, and currency issues. The monetary unit is the Tala, which is pegged to a basketful of six currencies.

There are no currency exchange controls, restrictions, or regulations
that affect the offshore sector.

Strict secrecy laws and penalties are imposed on financial, banking,
and insurance companies. All documents filed with the Registrar of
Companies are confidential.

Legal Entities. Western Samoa is progressive and is promoting itself as
a competitive offshore base.

International Companies. The International Companies Act of 1987,
as revised in 1989, is the governing legislation. Incorporating an international company is a simple and fast procedure performed by a local
trustee company.

The completed application, including the memorandum and articles
of incorporation and the incorporation fee, is filed with the Registrar of
International and Foreign Companies. Incorporation time is 1 or 2
days.

No minimum capital is required. Par or no par value may be stated.
Shares may be quoted in any currency. Bearer warrants may be issued or
exchanged for fully paid-up shares. A minimum of one shareholder is
required, and a nominee may be used.

A minimum of one director is necessary. There is no residency requirement, and a director may be a corporation. A trustee company can
provide one of its offices to act as director. Director meetings may be
held anywhere.

The company secretary must be a resident, and can be provided by
the trustee company. The company must have a registered office in
Western Samoa.

A private company does not require an audit. A company that wishes
to solicit the public must have an auditor and a registered prospector.

Foreign companies may register to do business in Western Samoa or
reincorporate.

The application fee is US $400 for an international company, $250
for a redomiciled company, and $400 for a foreign company.

Offshore Banks. The Offshore Banking Act of 1987 governs the issuance of a bank license to a company that is registered under the International Companies Act of 1987.

An application is filed with the Registrar of International and Foreign

Companies and is passed along to the Ministry of Finance, which then determines the suitability of the applicants. This screening process is common in tax havens when a bank license is sought. The procedure includes verifying the financial standing of the beneficial owners and proposed management through financial statements and bank references as well as professional references.

There are three classes of licenses:

1. *Class A license for banking within Western Samoa.* The minimum capitalization is US $10 million. The application fee is $5000, and the license fee is $10,000. Annual renewal is $15,000.

2. *Class B license restricting banking to offshore.* The Class B bank cannot accept deposits less than US $100,000. The cost of the bank license depends on how many currencies it is authorized to handle. The minimum paid-up capital is $2,000,000. For one currency only, the application fee is $2500. The license fee is $2000 and annual renewal is $4500. Fees would be greater if the bank deals in more than one currency.

3. *Class B license restricting location, currency, and depositors.* This license permits only offshore business in a specified currency or currencies with specific persons. Deposits cannot be solicited from the public. The minimum capitalization is US $250,000. The application fee is $1000 and the license fee $2000. Annual renewal is $3000.

Offshore banks are exempt from currency and exchange controls. There are no reserve ratios or other requirements normally imposed by the Central Bank.

Insurance Companies. Insurance companies are provided for under the International Insurance Act of 1988. The application procedure is handled by the Registrar of International Insurance. Evidence of financial standing and stock ownership may be requested.

There are four types of insurance business:

1. *General insurance.* Minimum capitalization is US $1 million. The application fee is $1000 and the license fee is $1500. Annual renewal is $2500.

2. *Long-term business.* Minimum capitalization is US $500,000. The application fee is $1000 and the license fee is $1500. Annual renewal is $2500.

3. *Reinsurance.* Minimum capitalization is US $200,000. The application fee is $500 and the license fee is $1000. Annual renewal is $1500.

4. *Captive insurance.* Minimum capitalization is US $100,000. The application fee is $500 and the license fee is $1000. Annual renewal is $1500.

Taxation.   Companies or licensees under any of the international offshore acts do not pay taxes.

Financial and Investment Incentives.   There are no incentives beyond the inherent tax haven benefits.

Tax Treaties.   There are no tax treaties.

Business Contacts
Banking

Bank of Western Samoa
Beach Road
P.O. Box L-1855
Apia, Western Samoa
Tel: 685-22-422
Fax: 685-22-595

Pacific Commercial Bank
P.O. Box 1860
Apia, Western Samoa
Tel: 685-20-000
Fax: 685-22-848

Central Bank of Samoa
Registrar of International and
  Foreign Companies
P.O. Private Bag
Apia, Western Samoa
Tel: 685-24-071
Telex: 200SX 24100

Trust Services

Western Samoa International
  Trust Company Limited
Ioane Viliamu Building, Level 1
Falealili Street
P.O. Box 3271
Apia, Western Samoa
Tel: 685-24-550
Telex: SAMTRUST 2958 SX
Fax: 685-21-837

Maintains associated offices in
  Hong Kong, Singapore, Sydney,
  Melbourne, Cook Islands, and
  Vanuatu.

European Pacific Trust Company
  (Western Samoa) Limited
P.O. Box 2029
Apia, Western Samoa
Tel: 685-21-758
Telex: 685-265 FIRSTPAC SX
Fax: 685-21-407

Maintains associated offices in
  Hong Kong, Australia, New
  Zealand, and Cook Islands.

Legal

Drake & Company
P.O. Box 757
Apia, Western Samoa
Tel: 685-24-280
Fax: 685-24-370

Apa & Enari
P.O. Box 1192
Apia, Western Samoa
Tel: 685-22-234

Epati, Stevenson & Nelson
P.O. Box 210
Apia, Western Samoa
Tel: 685-21-751
Telex: 685-247 COCENTR SX
Fax: 685-24-166

H. T. Retzlaff
P.O. Box 1863
Apia, Western Samoa
Tel: 685-23-325
Telex: 685-266 SX
Fax: 685-23-038

Va'ai & Co.
P.O. Private Bag
Apia, Western, Samoa
Tel: 685-20-545
Telex: 685-202 UNITEDCO SX

Kamu & Peteru
P.O. Box 2949
Apia, Western Samoa
Tel: 685-20-799

Kruse, Vaai & Barlow
P.O. Box 2029
Apia, Western Samoa
Tel: 685-21-758
Telex: 685-265 FIRSTPAC SX
Fax: 685-21-407

Sapolu & Company
P.O. Box 4027
Apia, Western Samoa
Tel: 685-21-778

Accounting

Coopers & Lybrand
P.O. Box 4463
Apia, Western Samoa
Tel: 685-24-336
Telex: 685-201 COLYB SX
Fax: 685-21-316

Pala Lima
P.O. Box 173
Apia, Western Samoa
Tel: 685-21-953

Price Waterhouse & Company
P.O. Box 1599
Apia, Western Samoa
Tel: 685-20-321
Telex: 685 PWWF SX
Fax: 685-23-722

Herota F. M. Luteru
P.O. Box 1411
Apia, Western Samoa
Tel: 685-22-965

Marginal and Incidental Tax Havens

This whirlwind tour of marginal and incidental tax havens reviews 13 jurisdictions that are less important for one reason or another: lack of sophistication, insufficient corporate and tax legislation, remote location, poor communications, or inadequate infrastructure for servicing international business. Although there are exceptions, only in special situations might a marginal or incidental tax haven be of use. Because of their potential, they do merit brief description here.

Andorra

This tiny principality, a highly independent sovereignty, is situated in the eastern Pyrenees between France and Spain. Since foreigners are not permitted to start businesses, incorporation is an impractical, though not impossible, idea. The SC (*societate de responsibilitat limitada*) is the private limited company.

Communications via France or Spain are excellent. There are no direct taxes and no tax treaties or exchange-of-information agreements with other countries. There are no exchange controls. The monetary units are the Spanish peseta and French franc. Strict bank secrecy is enforced and punishable by law. Numbered accounts are offered.

Contact:

Anthony Courtney, LLB, Chief Executive, CONSULT SL, Carrer Dr. Nequi No. 7, 3 er A, Andorra la Vella, Andorra; Tel: 33628 29190, Telex: 391 CONSULT, Fax: 33628 29783

Bahrain

This Persian Gulf sheikdom emerged from the 1970s as *the* Arab tax haven and money capital. There are no income or capital gains taxes, no foreign exchange controls, and no double-taxation agreements. Legislation was enacted permitting foreign-owned exempt companies. Unfortunately, political stability and investor confidence have been eroded in recent years, causing flight of capital to other major business and offshore centers such as New York City, London, and Cyprus.

Belize

This Central American parliamentary democracy is developing into an international offshore center. Formerly British Honduras, the republic of Belize has recently enacted attractive legislation. It's doing everything possible to encourage offshore business and investment by competing hard with other Caribbean tax havens.

The new International Business Companies Act of 1990, coupled with tax holidays, offers a major incentive. There is no double-taxation agreement with the United States, but there is an exchange-of-information agreement in certain tax cases. Belize has a ways to go before it will be recognized as a major tax haven, even though it has many of the legislative and incentive signs in place.

Contacts:

Pannell Kerr Forster, Chartered Accountants, Regent House, 35 Regent Street, P.O. Box 280, Belize City, Belize, Central America

Belize Corporate Services Limited, 60 Market Square, Belize City, Belize, Central America; Tel: (5012) 30274, Fax: (5012) 77018

Campione

Campione d'Italia ("Sample of Italy") is an Italian enclave situated in southern Switzerland along Lake Lugano. It's a speck of a tax haven comparable in size to Monaco. It possesses some distinctively unique features, however. Although officially Italian, Campione is entirely engulfed by Switzerland and is considered its back door. Residency in the enclave brings with it many of the benefits of Swiss residency, including Swiss auto registration, driver's license, and banking, postal, and telephone services. Even the mailing address is the Swiss postal code CH-6911. The nearby Swiss financial center of Lugano is only minutes away by car. Travel to and from Campione, Switzerland, and Italy is unrestricted. There are virtually no taxes imposed on non-Swiss and non-Italian residents.

Campione is ideal as an international business headquarters. A private limited-liability company known as the SRL (*societa responsibilita limitada*) can be formed. Although official organization takes 2 months, the company may operate as an SRL "under formation" in the meantime. Shareholders have complete anonymity, foreigners can own stock, and the minimum paid-up capital is approximately US $1000. There is no tax liability if the company avoids doing business with Italy.

Other types of companies to consider forming include the SAS (*societa accomandeta semplice*), a private unlimited-liability company; the AG, or Swiss Aktiengesellschaft, a joint stock company; or the establishment, a Liechtenstein Anstalt. Each of these corporate entities has its advantages and tax consequences. There are no tax treaties. Disclosure of tax information under the Swiss-U.S. income tax treaty is highly unlikely.

Cyprus

The sunny island of Cyprus is situated in the eastern Mediterranean Sea. Cyprus is attaining a reputation as a premiere offshore banking center as it attracts petro dollars from Arab oil-exporting countries and away from Bahrain, the former Arab money capital. Its location is particularly conducive for business and financial activities between the Arab world and western Europe.

Presently, the 5500 registered offshore companies pay a modest income tax of 4.25 percent on their profits. There are 19 tax treaties in effect with various countries for the avoidance of double taxation. Nonresidents and exclusively nonresident-owned corporations are exempt from exchange controls. The open economy is propelled by an expanding export-oriented industry and hearty tourist and service sector.

Contacts:

Central Bank of Cyprus, P.O. Box 5529, Nicosia, Cyprus; Fax: 357-2-472012

Metaxas, Loizides, Syrimis, Touche, Ross, Accountants, Stassinos Building, 2 Ayias Elenis Street, P.O. Box 1121, Nicosia, Cyprus

Grenada

The "Island of Spice" is now more commonly remembered as the target of a surprise U.S. invasion to rid communist infiltration in 1983. Grenada has been a "pure" tax haven since 1986, when personal and corporate income taxes were eliminated. Meanwhile, the local economy is struggling, In the past 2 years this Caribbean island has blossomed into an offshore bank haven of sorts—sorts that have triggered a wave of financial fraud. Of the 118 offshore banks currently chartered in Grenada, 31 are operated from a 7-by-10-foot law office in St. George. Some 52 banks actually have no banking license, but are only incorporated companies with the word "Bank" in their names. License enough, or so buyers are led to believe!

Coincidentally, many of the 220 offshore banks that had their licenses revoked during the Montserrat scandal decided to set up shop in this sleepy paradise. The key international marketer of these "banks" is the same Los Angeles-based company that marketed a couple of hundred Montserrat banks for $29,500 each. Grenada is just the continuation of a long and familiar pattern. Although Grenada may be an easy place to start an offshore bank now, the repercussions that are sure to come will cause plenty of grief and expense to legitimate bankers. Grenada isn't a true offshore bank center, but a temporary loophole.

Contact:

Grenada Industrial Development Corporation, Frequente Industrial Park, St. George's, Grenada, WI

Liberia

This English-speaking North African country, though an economically and politically unstable tax haven, is favored for ship registrations. There are no exchange controls. A tax treaty is in full force with the United States exempting shipping and aircraft income from double taxation. The Port of Monrovia is a free trade zone.

Contact:

Liberian Corporation Services, Inc., 551 Fifth Avenue, New York, NY 10176; Tel: (212) 286-0070

Madeira

This Atlantic Ocean tax haven is situated off the northwest African coast and enjoys complete autonomy from Portugal, while still being a part of the European Community (EC). Madeira is free from foreign exchange restrictions. All types of offshore corporate operations are welcome. Through Portugal, there are double taxation agreements with Austria, Belgium, Brazil, Denmark, Finland, France, Germany, Italy, Norway, Spain, Switzerland, and the United Kingdom. Nonresidents may use or maintain accounts in any currency, but the local monetary unit is the Portuguese escudo.

There are financial and tax incentives to attract foreign development and investment in Madeira. Communications are excellent. Companies are easy and inexpensive to establish. Full secrecy, autonomy, and confidentiality are assured. Strict bank secrecy is enforced. There is a free trade zone, and a deep water harbor is under construction. This is a particularly attractive tax haven for European and African trading companies.

Contact:

Madeira Management Companhia Limitada, Rua das Murcas No. 68, P.O. Box 7, 9000 Funchal, Madeira, Portugal; Tel. 351-91-20666, Fax: 351-91-27144

Malaysia

The island of Labuan in Malaysia is one of the newest offshore financial centers and a convenient hub to the rapidly expanding Asia Pacific region. Malaysia is strategically located in the same time zone as Singapore and Hong Kong.

The legal system is based on English common law and is suitable for the establishment of trusts.

Shareholders and management face minimal regulations, while confidentiality is guaranteed. The offshore activities that are encouraged are banking, trust and fund management, insurance, and investment holdings. There are minimal taxes. Malaysia maintains political stability, and under its constitutional monarchy, is a democratic system of government.

Contact:

Director, Industrial Promotion Division, Malaysian Industrial Development Authority (MIDA), Wisma Damansara, Jolan Semantan, 50720 Kuala Lumpur, Malaysia; Fax: 03-255-0697

Palau

A little-known Micronesian tax haven, Palau offers the potential for establishing an offshore bank, though none presently exists. Under the joint venture corporation, it's possible to incorporate "comparatively quickly"—or in Palau island time, 6 to 12 months. There is a secrecy act. Onshore banks include Bank of Hawaii, Palau Branch; Bank of Guam,

Palau Branch; Bank of Palau, a local bank; and Palau Development Bank, the government bank.

Incorporation and related costs total US $6625, broken down as follows:

Drafting articles and bylaws	$1500
Securing corporate charter	125
Preparing application for foreign investment business license	850
Hearings before Palau Foreign Investment Board	1750
Consultation or conference with client	750
Miscellaneous	1000
Application fees	200
Photocopying documents	450

Forthcoming offshore bank legislation is in progress, but when it will actually be enacted and enforced remains to be seen.

Contact:

John S. Tarkong, Attorney-at-Law, P.O. Box 728, Koror, Palau 96940; Tel: 618, Fax: 1314

Seychelles

A beautiful, tropical zero-tax haven in the Indian Ocean lined with scantily clad sunbathers, the Seychelles enacted exempt-company legislation to encourage offshore business, particularly corporations and family trusts. Incorporation costs and time are reasonable. The monetary unit is the rupee. There are no exchange controls. Six major banks are located on the islands, and foreign banks are encouraged to establish offshore banking units. Double-taxation agreements exist with various countries.

Contacts:

Seychelles Corporate Services AG, Limmatquai 52, 8001 Zurich, Switzerland

Seychelles Trust Company Ltd., Victoria, Seychelles

Minister of Finance, Central Bank Building, Independence Avenue, P.O. Box 313, Victoria, Seychelles; Tel: 248-21790, Fax: 248-22265

Sri Lanka

Located about 30 miles off the southern tip of India, Sri Lanka is considered part of the Far East. Tentatively, this island country is enacting legislation to convert into a tax haven to capture offshore business from the huge populations in the region. For the present, resident companies are taxed at the rate of 50 percent on income. Bank confidentiality is highly regarded. In recent years there has been political unrest. The government does grant investment guarantees. Investment protection agreements are in force with the United States and a number of other countries.

Contact:

Ministry of Finance and Planning, Galle Face Secretariat, 1st Floor, Room 120, Colombo 1, Sri Lanka; Cable: SEC FIN, Telex: 21409 FINMIN CE

Truk

Truk is another Micronesian "tax haven" like Palau. There is no information presently available. The contact for Palau may be helpful.

PART 3

Contacts and Resources

International Investor Directory

Banks Issuing Offshore Debit Credit Cards

TSB Bank Channel Islands
Limited
8 David Place
P.O. Box 597
St. Helier, Jersey, JE4 8XW
Channel Islands
Tel: 44-534-27306
Fax: 44-534-23058
Issues a debit VISA card.

Finsbury Bank and Trust Company
Transnational House
West Bay Road
P.O. Box 1592
Grand Cayman, BWI
Tel: (809) 947-4011
Issues a gold debit MasterCard.

Offshore Bank Management Companies

Aston Corporate Management
Limited
19 Peel Road
Douglas, Isle of Man
Tel: 44-624-626591
Fax: 44-624-625126

International Finance Marketing,
Inc.
2050 Mansfield, Suite 602
Montreal, QC, Canada
Tel: (514) 842-9120
Fax: (514) 842-5722
Mailing Address:
P.O. Box 831, Station A
Montreal, QC, Canada H3C 2V5

Worldwide Corporate Service Companies

These companies provide complete corporate services in numerous countries for new incorporations, banks, insurance companies, trusts, shelf companies, and management.

Abchurch Corporate Services
  Limited
Anglo-International House
Bank Hill
P.O. Box 204
Douglas, Isle of Man
Tel: 44-624-662262
Fax: 44-624-662272

Ansbacher International Trust
  Group
Cayman Islands:
Ansbacher Limited
P.O. Box 887
Grand Cayman, BWI
Tel: (809) 949-4653
Fax: (809) 949-7946

Channel Islands:
Ansbacher (CI) Limited
La Plaiderie
P.O. Box 79
St. Peter Port, Guernsey
Channel Islands
Tel: 44-481-26421
Fax: 44-481-26526

Gibraltar:
Ansbacher (Gibraltar) Limited
P.O. Box 515
Gibraltar
Tel: 350-74846
Fax: 350-76672

Monaco:
Ansbacher (Monaco) SAM
4 Boulevard des Moulins
Monte Carlo, Monaco
Tel: 33-93-509686
Fax: 33-93-305344

Aston Corporate Management
  Ltd.
19 Peel Road
Douglas, Isle of Man
Tel: 44-624-626591
Fax: 44-624-625126

Bahamas International Trust
  Company Limited
P.O. Box N-7768
Nassau, Bahamas
Tel: (809) 322-1161
Fax: (809) 326-5020

BIL Securities
70 King William Street
London EC4N 7HR, United
  Kingdom

Cayman International Trust
  Company Limited
P.O. Box 500
Grand Cayman, BWI
Tel: (809) 949-4277
Fax: (809) 949-8293

Falcon Business Service Limited
Falcon House
24 North John Street
Liverpool L2 9RP, United
  Kingdom
Tel: 44-51-236-3443 (24 hours)
Fax: 44-51-255-1050

ICS Trust Company, Inc.
British Virgin Islands:
Columbus Centre Building
Road Town, Tortola, BVI
Tel: (809) 494-3215
Fax: (809) 494-3216

Hong Kong:
Tower III
918 China Hong Kong City
Tsimshatsui
Kowloon, Hong Kong
Tel: 852-736-9000
Fax: 852-735-7800

Toronto:
Suite 300
124 Eglinton Avenue West
Toronto, ONT, Canada M4R 2GB
Tel: (416) 440-4000
Fax: (416) 487-4724

International Company Services
  (T&C) Limited
Oceanic House
Duke Street
P.O. Box 107
Grand Turk, BWI
Tel: (809) 946-2828
Fax: (809) 946-2825

Gibraltar:
International Company Services
  (Gibraltar) Limited
15A Tuckey's Lane
Gibraltar
Tel: 350-76173
Fax: 350-70158

Hong Kong:
Sovereign Trust International
Room 902
55 Connaught Road
Central, Hong Kong
Tel: 852-850-4422
Fax: 852-850-5311

Isle of Man:
International Company Services
  Limited
Sovereign House
Station Road
St. Johns, Isle of Man
Tel: 44-624-801801
Fax: 44-624-801800

London:
International Company Services
  (UK) Limited
Standbrook House
2-5 Old Bond Street
London W1X 3TB, United Kingdom
Tel: 44-71-493-4244
Fax: 44-71-491-0605

International Trust Company
  (BVI) Limited
P.O. Box 659
Road Town, Tortola, BVI
Tel: (809) 494-3215/2368
Fax: (809) 494-3216

Island Resources
National House
Santon, Isle of Man
Tel: 44-624-824555
Fax: 44-624-823949

Jordan & Sons Ltd.
Jordan House
Brunswick Place
London N1 6EE, United Kingdom
Tel: 44-71-253-3030
Fax: 44-71-251-0825

Mossack Fonseca & Co., Attorneys-
  at-Law
Bahamas:
Bitco Building, 3rd Floor
P.O. Box N-8188
Nassau, Bahamas
Tel: (809) 322-7601
Fax: (809) 322-5807

British Virgin Islands:
Skelton Building
Main Street
P.O. Box 3136
Road Town, Tortola, BVI
Tel: (809) 49-44841

Channel Islands:
P.O. Box 168
St. Helier, Jersey JE4 8RZ
Channel Islands
Tel: 44-534-42800
Fax: 44-534-42054

Geneva:
40 Rue du Stand
P.O. Box 138
CH-1211 Geneva 25, Switzerland
Tel: 41-22-290 222
Fax: 41-22-290 135

Hong Kong:
Kowloon Centre, Room 903-5
29-43 Ashley Road, TST
Kowloon, Hong Kong
Tel: 852-3-672485
Fax: 852-3-7224308

Luxembourg:
43 Boulevard Joseph II
Luxembourg
Tel: 352-458193/458577
Fax: 352-458673

Panama:
Arango-Orillac Building
P.O. Box 8320
Panama 7, Panama
Tel: (507) 63-8899/64-2322
Fax: (507) 63-9218/63-7327

Overseas Company Registration
  Agents Limited
Isle of Man:
Companies House
Tower Street
P.O. Box 28
Ramsey, Isle of Man
Tel: 44-624-81544
Fax: 44-624-815558

London:
72 New Bond Street
London W1Y 9DD, United
  Kingdom
Tel: 44-71-355-1096
Fax: 44-71-495-3017

Foreign Sales Corporation Representatives

The following management companies can assist with incorporation of foreign sales corporations (FSCs), their management, invoicing, and collections. Many of these companies can also perform valuable corporate services in their own countries. They may be contacted by calling FSC U.S. representatives through:

Overseas Press and Consultants
9 Old Farm Lane
Hartsdale, NY 10530
Tel: (914) 946-4089

Barbados:
  Allyne & Allyne
  Pannell, Ker & Forster

Cayman Islands:
  International Management Services

Channel Islands:
  FSC Corporate Management Limited (Guernsey)
  Spicer and Pegler (Guernsey)
  Trident Trust Company Ltd. (Jersey)
  Brown Shipley Trust Company (Jersey)

Isle of Man:
  International Trust Group Limited (Ramsey)
  Mannin International (Ballasala)

Manxtrust Financial Ltd.

Charles Cain & Company (Douglas)

Monaco:

Hoofewerf and Company SA

European Business Consultants

Netherlands Antilles:

Corporate Trust (Curaçao)

Netherlands Antilles Corporate Trust (Aruba)

United Kingdom:

Rowland & Debono Ltd. (London)

U.S. Virgin Islands and Guam:

Trident Trust Company (VI) Ltd.

Worldwide Office Services

Belgium:
Contact Business Center SA/NV
9–21 Rue Capouillet
1060 Bruxelles, Belgium
Tel: 32-2-536 86 86 (20 1)
Fax: 32-2-536 86 00

Canada:
Canada Business Centers, Ltd.
6600 Trans Canada Highway
Pointe Claire, QC, Canada H9R
 4S2
Tel: (514) 697-9600

France:
Arenas Partners
Nice Premier 455
Promenade des Anglais
06200 Nice, France
Tel: 33-93-18-15-20
Fax: 33-93-18-15-21

Spain:
Executive Business Center
Casanova, 59–61, entlo. 4.a.
08011 Barcelona, Spain
Tel: 34-93-451 19 80
Fax: 34-93-451 13 27

Switzerland:
Business Advisory Services SA
7 Rue Muzy
1207 Geneva, Switzerland
Tel: 41-22-36 05 40
Fax: 41-22-86 06 44

Confidesa
Fekistrasse 24
CH-8004 Zurich, Switzerland
Tel: 41-1-242 92 73
Maintains other offices in Zug and
 Luzerne.

International Office Services AG
(A Worldwide Business Centres
 Network)
Rennweg 32
CH-8001 Zurich, Switzerland
Tel: 41-1-214 61 11
Fax: 41-1-214 62 03

United Kingdom:
The Business Quarter
80 Ebury Street, Belgravia
London SW1W 9QD, United
 Kingdom
Tel: 44-71-730-9222
Fax: 44-71-730-2477

United States:
HQ Network Systems
120 Montgomery Street, Suite
  1040
San Francisco, CA 94104
Tel: (800) 227-3004 toll free
Fax: (415) 781-8034
Maintains other offices in Canada
  and the United Kingdom.

Worldwide:
Worldwide Business Centres
575 Madison Avenue
New York, NY 10022
Tel: (212) 605-0224
Fax: (212) 308-9834
Maintains 70 offices in Europe,
  Asia, and the United States.

Accounting Firms

DRT International publishes the *International Tax and Business Guide* series.

British Virgin Islands:
Deloitte & Touche
P.O. Box 362
Road Town, Tortola, BVI
Tel: (809) 494-2868
Fax: (809) 494-6247

Japan:
DRT International
MS Shibauru Building
4-13-23 Shibauru
Minato-ku, Tokyo 108, Japan
Tel: 81-3-457-1691
Fax: 81-3-457-1698

United Kingdom:
DRT International
Hill House
1 Little New Street
London EC 4A 3TR, United
  Kingdom
Tel: 44-71-936-3000
Fax: 44-71-583-8517

United States:
DRT International
1633 Broadway
New York, NY 10019-6754
Tel: (212) 489-1600
Fax: (212) 245-0839

KPMG Peat Marwick publishes the *Investment in . . .* series and maintains offices in the principal cities of the following countries:

Africa

Bophuthatswana	Malawi	South Africa
Botswana	Mauritius	Swaziland
Ciskei	Morocco	Transkei
Gambia	Namibia	Tunisia
Ivory Coast	Nigeria	Zaire
Kenya	Seychelles	Zambia
Lesotho	Sierra Leone	Zimbabwe

Australasia

Australia	Guam	Solomon Islands
Cook Islands	New Caledonia	Vanuatu
Fiji	New Zealand	
French Polynesia	Papua New Guinea	

Caribbean

Antigua	Cayman Islands	Puerto Rico
Aruba	Dominican Republic	St. Lucia
Bahamas	Haiti	Trinidad and Tobago
Barbados	Jamaica	U.S. Virgin Islands
British Virgin Islands	Netherlands Antilles	

Central America

Costa Rica	Guatemala	Panama
El Salvador	Honduras	

Europe

Austria	Greece	Norway
Belgium	Iceland	Portugal
Channel Islands	Ireland	Spain
Cyprus	Isle of Man	Sweden
Denmark	Italy	Switzerland
Finland	Liechtenstein	Turkey
France	Luxembourg	United Kingdom
Germany	Malta	
Gibraltar	Netherlands	

Far East

Brunei	Japan	Philippines
China	Korea (Republic of)	Singapore
Hong Kong	Macau	Sri Lanka
India	Malaysia	Taiwan
Indonesia	Pakistan	Thailand

Middle East

Bahrain	Kuwait	Saudi Arabia
Egypt	Lebanon	Sudan
Iran	Oman	United Arab Emirates
Jordan	Qatar	Yemen Arab Republic

North America

Bermuda	Mexico	United States
Canada		

South America

Argentina	Colombia	Surinam
Bolivia	Ecuador	Uruguay
Brazil	Paraguay	Venezuela
Chile	Peru	

International Resources

International Publications

Periodicals

Asiaweek, a newsweekly published by:

Asiaweek
71 F Toppan Building
22 Westlake Road
Quarry Bay, Hong Kong

The Bahamas Financial Digest, a monthly magazine published by:

The Bahamas Financial Digest
P.O. Box N-4271
Nassau, Bahamas

The Banker, a monthly magazine published by:

Financial Times Business Information Ltd.
Bracken House
10 Cannon Street
London EC40 4BY, United Kingdom

Business Latin America, published weekly by:

Business International Corporation
215 Park Avenue South
New York, NY 10003
Tel: (212) 750-6300

Caribbean Basin Initiative, 1989 Guideboook, published by:

U.S. Department of Commerce
International Trade Administration
U.S. and Foreign Commercial Service
CBI Center, Room H-3203
Washington, DC 20230
Tel: (202) 377-0703

Caribbean Business, published weekly by:

Caribbean Business
1700 Fernandez Juncos Avenue, Stop 25
San Juan, PR 00909
Tel: (809) 728-3000

Caribbean Dateline, published monthly by:

Caribbean Dateline
P.O. Box 23276
Washington, DC 20026
Tel: (Roanoke, VA) (703) 569-9011

Caribbean Travel and Life, published monthly by:
Caribbean Travel and Life
8403 Colesville Road, Suite 830
Silver Springs, MD 20910
Tel: (301) 588-2300

CBI Bulletin, published by:
CBI Business Bulletin
U.S. Department of Commerce
Room H-3203
Washington, DC 20230

China Daily (English translation of a Chinese newspaper), published by:
China Daily
15 Mercer Street, Suite 401
New York, NY 10013

The Economist, published weekly by:
The Economist Newspaper Ltd.
10 Rockefeller Plaza
New York, NY 10020
Tel: (212) 541-5730

Euromoney, a monthly magazine published by:
Business International Press (USA)
205 E. 42nd Street
New York, NY 10017

Far Eastern Economic Review, a weekly magazine published by:
Far Eastern Economic Review
G.P.O. Box 160
Hong Kong

Financial Times (London financial newspaper), published daily by:
FT Publications
14 E. 60th Street
New York, NY 10022
Tel: (212) 752-4500

Focus on Finance and Industry in The Isle of Man, a monthly magazine published by:
FOCUS
a26 Ridgeway Street
Douglas, Isle of Man

Fund Management International, published by:
Fund Management International
IBC Limited
Bath House, 56 Holborn Viaduct
London EC1A 2EX, United Kingdom

Guam Business News, a monthly magazine published by:
Guam Business News
P.O. Box 3191
Agana, Guam 96910

Hang Seng Economic Monthly (economic report on Hong Kong, Singapore, South Korea, and Taiwan), published by:
Hang Seng Bank Ltd.
Economic Research Department
G.P.O. Box 2985
Hong Kong

The International: A Worldwide Guide to Personal Finance, published monthly and free subscription offered by:
Financial Times
International Boundary House
91 Charterhouse Street
London EC1M 6HR, United Kingdom

International Herald Tribune (international Paris newspaper), published daily by:
IHT
850 Third Avenue
New York, NY 10022
Tel: (800) 882-2884

Offshore Financial Review, published monthly by:
Offshore Financial Review
Greystoke Place and Fetter Lane
London EC4A 1ND, United Kingdom

Offshore Investment, a monthly magazine published by:
The Journal of the Offshore Institute
P.O. Box 66
Douglas, Isle of Man

Pakistan Pictorial, a monthly magazine published by:
Pakistan Pictorial
P.O. Box 1102
Islamabad, Pakistan

The Voice, a local biweekly newspaper published by:
The Voice
Odessa Building
Dailing Road
P.O. Box 104
Castries, St. Lucia, WI

Directories

The Caribbean Business Directory, published annually by:
Caribbean Tunprint Directory Services
Box 350, Dept. D.C.
West Falmouth, MA 02574
Tel: (617) 540-5378

Countries of the World, published annually by:
Gale Research, Inc.
835 Penobscot Building
Detroit, MI 48226-4094

Directory of American Firms Operating in Foreign Countries, published by:
World Trade Academy Press
50 E. 42nd Street, Suite 509
New York, NY 10017
Tel: (212) 697-4999

Practical International Tax Planning, by Marshall J. Langer, published by:
Practising Law Institute
810 Seventh Avenue
New York, NY 10019

Tax Havens of the World, published quarterly by:
Matthew Bender & Co., Inc.
1275 Broadway
Albany, NY 12204
Tel: (212) 967-7707 (NYC)
(415) 446-7100 (Oakland, CA)

Tax Havens Encyclopedia, published annually by:
Butterworth & Co. (Publishers) Ltd.
88 Kingsway
London WC2B 6AB, United Kingdom
Distributed by Butterworth Legal Publishers—St. Paul, MN; Seattle, WA; Boston, MA; and Austin, TX

Newsletters

Business International, published
weekly by:
Business International SA
12–14 Chemin Rieu
1208 Geneva, Switzerland

Business Opportunities Digest, published monthly by:
Business Opportunities Digest
301 Plymouth Drive NE
Dalton, GA 30721-9983

Business Panama, published
monthly by:
Politech, Inc.
Apartado 6-6502
El Dorado
Panama 6A, Panama

Costa Rica Report, published
monthly by:
Jobec Communications
P.O. Box 6283
1000 San José, Costa Rica

The Costa Rican Beacon, published
monthly by:
The Costa Rican Beacon
Apartado 5399
1000 San José, Costa Rica

Import/Export Business, published
monthly by:
Treico International Services
93 Willets Drive
Syosset, NY 11791

Indonesia—News & Views, pub-
lished monthly by:
Information Division
Embassy of Indonesia
2020 Massachusetts Avenue NW
Washington, DC 20036

International Money Line, published
weekly by:
International Money Line
25 Broad Street
New York, NY 10004

International Tax Report, published
monthly by:
International Tax Report
P.O. Box 65
Ben Franklin Station
Washington, DC 20044

International Tax Report, published
monthly by:
Stonehart Publications Ltd.
57–61 Mortimer Street
London W1N 7TD, United
Kingdom

Internationale Newshaus, published
by:
Internationale Newshaus
Sucursal H de Correos
Apartado Postal 14
Colonia la Laja
Acapulco Gro, Mexico

Lloyd's Mexican Economic Report,
published monthly by:
Lloyd's Mexican Economic Report
Mariano Otaro 1915
Guadalajara, Jalisco, Mexico

Mexletter, published monthly by:
Mexletter
Apartado Postal 10-711
Mexico DF, 11000 Mexico

Private Islands Unlimited, published monthly by:
Private Islands Unlimited
P.O. Box 22775
Ft. Lauderdale, FL 33335

Select Information Exchange
2315 Broadway
New York, NY 10024
Write for a free investment publications catalog. Receive 20 trial subscriptions (1 to 5 issues) of your choice of investment publications in the SIE program for only $11.95.

Tax Haven Reporter, published monthly by:
Tax Haven Reporter
P.O. Box SS-6781
Nassau, Bahamas
Tel: (809) 327-7359

The Washington Pacific Report (newsletter on the Pacific Rim), published bimonthly by:
Washington Pacific Publications, Inc.
P.O. Box 2918
Washington, DC 20013

Information Booklets

Deloitte Haskins & Sells
Distribution Department
1114 Avenue of the Americas
New York, NY 10036
(212) 790-0500

This international accounting firm publishes the informative booklets *Taxation of U.S. Citizens Abroad* and *Taxation of Foreign Nationals by the United States.* It also publishes a series of information booklets titled *International Tax and Business* by country. Presently, booklets for the following countries are available:

Argentina	India	Saudi Arabia
Australia	Ireland	Singapore
Belgium	Italy	South Africa
Brazil	Japan	Spain
Canada	Korea	Sri Lanka
China	Malaysia	Switzerland
Colombia	Mexico	Taiwan
Costa Rica	Netherlands	United Kingdom
Ecuador	New Zealand	United States
France	Panama	Uruguay
Germany	Peru	Venezuela
Guatemala	Philippines	
Hong Kong	Puerto Rico	

Books

Building Wealth, by Adam
  Starchild, published by:
AMACOM Division
American Management Associa-
  tion
135 West 50th Street
New York, NY 10020

Everyman's Guide to Tax Havens, by
  Adam Starchild, published by:
Paladin Press
P.O. Box 1307
Boulder, CO 80306

Offshore Haven Banks, Trusts,
  and Companies: *The Business of
  Crime in the Euromarket,* by Rich-
  ard H. Blum, published by:
Praeger Publications
Division of Greenwood Press
1 Madison Avenue
New York, NY 10010

Secret Money, by Ingo Walter, pub-
  lished by:
Lexington Books
D. C. Heath & Co.
125 Spring Street
Lexington, MA 02173

Swiss Bank Accounts, by Michael Ar-
  thur Jones, published by:
TAB Books, Inc.
Liberty Hall Press/McGraw-Hill
Blue Ridge Summit, PA 17294-
  0214

Tax Havens, by Adam Starchild,
  published by:
Arlington House
Crown Publishers
1 Park Avenue
New York, NY 10016

Tax Havens of the World, by
  Thomas P. Azzara, published by:
Tax Haven Reporter
P.O. Box SS-6781
Nassau, Bahamas
Tel: (809) 327-7359

Tax Havens for Corporations, by
  Adam Starchild, published by:
Gulf Publishing Co.
P.O. Box 2608
Houston, TX 77252

Products and Services for the International-Minded

Passport Services

Global Money Consultants (GMC)
26 Kleomenous Street
Athens, Greece
Tel: 30-1-7243820
Fax: 30-1-7219080

Markets books and provides services of interest to offshore investors.

Sage & Company
16 Connaught Street, Suite 129
London, W2 2A6, United
  Kingdom
Tel: 44-71-723-3773
Fax: 44-71-724-5766

Antisurveillance and Privacy Equipment

CSC Communication Control
160 Midland Avenue
Port Chester, NY 10573
Tel: (914) 934-8100

Maintains offices in New York City, Beverly Hills, Washington DC, Miami, Houston, Montreal, London, and Paris. Call for information.

Publishers

Business International
The Economist Intelligence Unit
Business International Corp.
90 New Montgomery Street, Suite 1020
San Francisco, CA 94105

Publishes international financial and business information.

Croner Publications, Inc.
International Publishers
211-03 Jamaica Avenue
Queens Village, NY 11428
Tel: (718) 464-0866/465-6171

Request a catalog of interesting directories of the world.

Eden Press
11623 Slater "E"
P. O. Box 8410
Fountain Valley, CA 92728

Offers a catalog of unusual books and hard-to-find information; many offshore books.

R&H Publishers
P.O. Box 3587, Georgetown Station
Washington, DC 20007
Tel: (703) 524-4226 (Arlington, VA)

Publishes directories and newsletters on banking, import-export, finance, and other subjects.

Scope Books, Ltd.
62 Murray Road
Horndean, Hants PO8 9JL, United Kingdom

Publishes books of interest to offshore investors.

Caribbean Basin Initiative (CBI)

The Caribbean Basin Initiative is a program developed to stimulate economic growth in Central America and the Caribbean. The CBI is extended between the United States and 28 CBI-designated recipient nations.

The CBI provides for investment incentives for eligible countries with the intent to diversify their economies into nontraditional areas and to expand export sales. Of course, the United States is automatically a principal supplier and importer. This program contributes to economic growth, political stability, and regional security.

The U.S. Department of Commerce's annual booklet *Caribbean Basin Initiative* outlines the benefits of the CBI and how to use it. To receive a copy, contact: U.S. Department of Commerce, International Trade Administration, U.S. and Foreign Commercial Service, CBI Center, Room H-3203, Washington, DC 20230; Tel: (202) 377-0703.

To quote this booklet directly:

The major elements of the program are:

1. Duty-free entry to the United States for 12 years beginning January 1, 1984, for a wide range of products manufactured in CBI countries, as an incentive for investment and expanded export production.
2. Increased U.S. economic assistance to the region to aid private sector development, by financing essential imports and by establishing development banks, chambers of commerce, skills training programs, industrial free zones, and other essential infrastructure. Aid to the region more than tripled from 1981 to 1986.

3. Caribbean Basin country self-help efforts to improve the local business environment and support efforts by investors and exporters.

4. A deduction on U.S. taxes for companies that hold business conventions in qualifying Caribbean Basin countries, to increase tourism.

5. A wide range of U.S. government, state government, and private-sector promotion programs, including trade and investment financing, business development missions, technical assistance programs, and a U.S. government special-access program for textiles and apparel.

6. Support from other trading partners and multinational development institutions, such as the Inter-American Development Bank and World Bank. For example, Canada has implemented CARIBCAN, a package of trade development and economic assistance measures for countries in the Caribbean Basin, including duty-free entry for products to Canadian markets.

The countries eligible for CBI benefits include

Antigua and Barbuda	Haiti
Aruba	Honduras
Bahamas	Jamaica
Barbados	Montserrat
Belize	Netherlands Antilles
British Virgin Islands	Panama
Costa Rica	Puerto Rico
Dominica	St. Kitts-Nevis
Dominican Republic	St. Lucia
El Salvador	St. Vincent and the Grenadines
Grenada	Trinidad and Tobago
Guatemala	U.S. Virgin Islands
Guyana	

Tax Information Exchange Agreements (TIEA)

CBI countries have the option of signing a TIEA. The agreement allows the IRS and any other tax authority to obtain information related to taxes with a CBI country, and vice versa. The goal is to assure tax authorities in both countries that they will get adequate assistance to secure information that otherwise might be impossible to obtain in order to enforce their own tax laws. For instance, an American taxpayer who is also a stockholder in a Grenada corporation is subject to the long arm of U.S. tax authorities because of an existing TIEA between the United States and this Caribbean island.

A CBI country that enters into a TIEA can benefit from foreign sales corporations (FSCs) that incorporate and headquarter their offices in the country. This means more businesses within the country which promotes greater import-export trade. A U.S. exporter that established an FSC subsidiary in a CBI/TIEA country gains significant tax advantages.

Appendix B
Long Distance and International Calling Codes

Country	Dialing Code from the United States
Anguilla	1-809
Antigua and Barbuda	1-809
Aruba	011-297-8
Austria	011-43
Bahamas	1-809
Barbados	1-809
Bermuda	1-809
British Virgin Islands	1-809
Cayman Islands	1-809
Channel Islands	
Guernsey	011-44-481
Jersey	011-44-534
Cook Islands	011-682
Costa Rica	011-506
Gibraltar	011-350
Hong Kong	011-852
Ireland	011-353
Isle of Man	011-44-624

Country	Dialing Code from the United States
Liechtenstein	011-41-75
Luxembourg	011-352
Malta	011-356
Monaco	011-33-93
Montserrat	1-809
Nauru	011-674
Netherlands	011-31
Netherlands Antilles	011-599
Nevis	1-809
Panama	011-507
St. Vincent	1-809
Singapore	011-65
Switzerland	011-41
Turks and Caicos	1-809
Vanuatu	011-678
Western Samoa	011-685

Appendix C
International Currencies

Country	Currency
Anguilla	Eastern Caribbean dollar
Antigua and Barbuda	Eastern Caribbean dollar
Aruba	Aruban florin
Austria	Shilling
Bahamas	Bahamian dollar
Barbados	Barbadian dollar
Bermuda	Bermuda dollar
British Virgin Islands	US dollar
Cayman Islands	Cayman Islands dollar
Channel Islands	Pound sterling
Guernsey	Guernsey pound
Jersey	Jersey pound
Cook Islands	New Zealand dollar
Costa Rica	Colon
Gibraltar	Gibraltar pound
Hong Kong	Hong Kong dollar
Ireland	Irish pound (punt)
Isle of Man	Isle of Man pound
Liechtenstein	Swiss franc
Luxembourg	Luxembourg franc

Country	Currency
Malta	Maltese lira
Monaco	French franc
Montserrat	Eastern Caribbean dollar
Nauru	Australian dollar
Netherlands	Dutch guilder
Netherlands Antilles	Netherlands Antilles guilder
Nevis	Eastern Caribbean dollar
Panama	US dollar, Panamanian balboa
St. Vincent	Eastern Caribbean dollar
Singapore	Singapore dollar
Switzerland	Swiss franc
Turks and Caicos	US dollar
Vanuatu	Australian dollar
Western Samoa	Tala

Appendix D

Overseas Private Investment Corporation (OPIC)

The Overseas Private Investment Corporation is a U.S. government agency that provides two valuable programs to assist and protect American investors and in return promote economic growth in designated countries. The programs are:

- Financing investment projects through direct loans and/or loan guarantees
- Insuring investment projects against a broad range of political risks

Other programs include investment missions and opportunity bank and investor information services. OPIC is self-sustaining and has its own substantial economic resources. In addition, guaranty and insurance obligations are backed by the full faith and credit of the U.S. government.

OPIC can provide valuable information and assistance to U.S. investors in the following countries. For further information contact: Public Affairs Officer, OPIC, 1615 M Street NW, Washington, DC 20527; Tel: (202) 457-7011.

Anguilla	Bahrain
Antigua and Barbuda	Bangladesh
Argentina	Barbados
Aruba	Belize
Bahamas	Benin

Bolivia
Botswana
Brazil
Burkina Faso
Burundi
Cameroon
Cape Verde
Central African Republic
Chad
Colombia
Congo
Cook Islands
Costa Rica
Côte d'Ivoire
Cyprus
Djibouti
Dominica
Dominican Republic
Ecuador
Egypt
El Salvador
Equatorial Guinea
Fiji
French Guiana
Gabon
Gambia
Ghana
Greece
Grenada
Guatemala
Guinea
Guinea-Bissau
Guyana
Haiti
Honduras
Hungary
India
Indonesia

Ireland
Israel
Jamaica
Jordan
Kenya
Korea
Kuwait
Lebanon
Lesotho
Liberia
Madagascar
Malawi
Malaysia
Mali
Malta
Marshall Islands
Mauritania
Mauritius
Micronesia
Morocco
Mozambique
Nepal
Netherlands Antilles
Niger
Nigeria
Northern Ireland
Oman
Pakistan
Panama
Papua New Guinea
Philippines
Poland
Portugal
Qatar
Rwanda
St. Kitts-Nevis
St. Lucia
St. Vincent and the Grenadines

São Tomé and Príncipe
Saudi Arabia
Senegal
Sierra Leone
Singapore
Somalia
Sri Lanka
Sudan
Swaziland
Syria
Taiwan
Tanzania
Thailand

Togo
Tonga
Trinidad and Tobago
Tunisia
Turkey
Uganda
Uruguay
Western Samoa
Yemen Arab Republic
Yugoslavia
Zaire
Zambia

Appendix **E**
Time Zones

Country	Time in Relation to Eastern Standard Time (EST)
Anguilla	1 hour ahead
Antigua and Barbuda	1 hour ahead
Aruba	EST
Austria	6 hours ahead
Bahamas	EST
Barbados	1 hour ahead
Bermuda	1 hour ahead
British Virgin Islands	1 hour ahead
Cayman Islands	EST
Channel Islands	5 hours ahead
Cook Islands	16½ hours ahead
Costa Rica	1 hour behind
Gibraltar	6 hours ahead
Hong Kong	13 hours ahead
Ireland	5 hours ahead
Isle of Man	5 hours ahead
Liechtenstein	6 hours ahead
Luxembourg	5 hours ahead
Malta	6 hours ahead
Monaco	6 hours ahead
Montserrat	1 hour ahead
Nauru	16½ hours ahead

Country	Time in Relation to Eastern Standard Time (EST)
Netherlands	6 hours ahead
Netherlands Antilles	1 hour ahead
Nevis	EST
Panama	EST
St. Vincent	EST
Singapore	13 hours ahead
Switzerland	6 hours ahead
Turks and Caicos	EST
Vanuatu	16 hours ahead
Western Samoa	16 hours ahead

Index